Disability and the Superher

ALSO OF INTEREST
AND FROM MCFARLAND

The Image of Disability: Essays on Media Representations
(edited by JL Schatz and Amber E. George, 2018)

Disability and the Superhero

Essays on Ableism and Representation in Comic Media

Edited by AMBER E. GEORGE

McFarland & Company, Inc., Publishers

Jefferson, North Carolina

This book has undergone peer review.

ISBN (print) 978-1-4766-8097-2
ISBN (ebook) 978-1-4766-4908-5

Library of Congress and British Library
Cataloguing data are available

Library of Congress Control Number 2023006967

Front cover images © NoraVector/Piotr Urakau/Shutterstock

Printed in the United States of America

*McFarland & Company, Inc., Publishers
Box 611, Jefferson, North Carolina 28640
www.mcfarlandpub.com*

Table of Contents

Preface

AMBER E. GEORGE

I grew up with an older sibling who loved comic books. Eventually, that love transitioned into loving graphic novels and superhero films. Our home was struck by what everyone dubbed a "once in a lifetime flood," which destroyed his treasured comic collection. I watched as he mourned the mounds of pulp hauled out of the flooded house. I had never seen my brother so devastated, so disturbed. I soon realized the immense impact that comics can have on their fanbase. My brother moved on to have a successful career as a comic book editor and author, but those agonizing mental images will be with me for a lifetime.

Since then, I have met several people with disabilities who love comics. Many people, however, are upset by the comic industry's insistence on reproducing ableist imagery and narratives. These reactions compelled me to investigate disability more thoroughly in comics to identify areas of ableism that demand critical analysis. The essays in this book are the product of exploring these realms. Essays that demonstrate how far the comic industry needs to go before positive representations of disability in comics become the norm. My overriding aim is that the insights contained in this book will benefit fans and creators alike, particularly those with disabilities.

Introduction

Making Sense of Superheroes and Their Social Identities

AMBER E. GEORGE

There is no shortage of books, college classes, or academic critiques that explore how cultural productions such as television, advertisements, social media, and literature shape the social construction of identities based on gender, race, and sexuality. These critiques stem from a long history of cultural investigation that has helped rethink how identity shapes discourse. This collection, *Disability and the Superhero: Essays on Ableism and Representation in Comic Media,* adds to this cultural history by assessing how ableism manifests in the artistic elements of film, television, and graphic comics under the guise of superhero narratives. The facts are that inaccurate representations of disability or disability-related experiences in the media can lead to misinformation, stigma, and exclusion. Disability is defined as a bodily condition that makes performing everyday activities difficult and that, combined with social barriers, may prevent equitable participation in society. Ableism is a system of oppression that supports discrimination, prejudice, and bias against persons with disabilities or people perceived as having disabilities. Ableism supports the notion that disability identity makes one inferior, leaving one open to inequity, abuse, and hardship. The contributors use critical disability studies, media studies, cultural studies, and other interdisciplinary fields to explore ableism within popular storylines and characters from franchises such as DC Comics, Marvel, *Sesame Street*, and more.

Comic narratives are extremely valuable artifacts for understanding culture and social identity. They are continually rehashed, rebooted, and re-released by different writers, artists, and editors who often change storylines to fit the social climate of the day. Comics undergo a reconditioning process known as "retroactive continuity" or "retcon." When a storyline or character is "retconned," any aspect may have been changed to correct errors or social ills, no matter how benevolent or benign. This retcon nature of comic narratives makes studying the constructions of disability and superheroes exciting because creators often erase or gloss over various components of disability for exciting effects. This lends itself to questions such as, are the changes benevolent to the disability community and other social identity groups such as those based on race, sexuality, and gender? Do they cast disability differences in empowering ways? Do they take into consideration the current call for equitable representation and inclusion?

Thus, retcon as a process has the potential to be powerful for social justice causes. Consider the retcon case of Barbara Gordon, [aka] Batgirl, in the comic *The Killing Joke* (1966). In one iteration of her character, she is a pawn in Batman and the Joker's disputes. The Joker causes immediate physical paralysis by shooting Gordon, then undresses and photographs her during a sexual assault. The Joker then finds Commissioner Gordon (Barbara's father), kidnaps him, undresses him, and forces him to look at the naked photographs of his daughter during her sexual assault. During the first few iterations of the storyline, Gordon lives what appears to be pitiful existence due to her disability.

Furthermore, the Joker mocks Gordon's status as a librarian with a disability by stating, "Frankly, she won't be walking off the shelves in that state of repair … in fact, the idea of her walking anywhere seems increasingly remote, but then, that's always a problem with softbacks" (Moore and Bolland 2008, 14). Storylines that involve this level of violence, sexism, and ableism are widely popular in DC Comics. Why is it that the creator of this storyline, Alan Moore, felt Batgirl had to be disabled, abused, and disempowered to advantage men superheroes while devaluing women?

These perspectives reinforce the notion that becoming visibly disabled means a loss of power, privilege, and positionality which conjoins with the already prevalent idea that being a woman means being subject to abuse. In a later retcon of this storyline, Batgirl is portrayed as empowered, giving credence to the notion that characters can and must change. By breaking continuity among storylines, contributors invite the reader to think more inclusively about superhero-ness, disability, race, and gender.

Not all retconned superhero characters portray positive representations of disability experience. When superheroes are recreated, sometimes minimal consideration is given to dismantling ableist stereotypes, prejudices, and hegemony. Consider Reed Richard, aka Mr. Fantastic, who Marvel retconned to have autism. At first glance, disability scholars and activists may be ecstatic that Marvel decided to illustrate disability identity in cultural form. However, as fan conversations on Reddit and

Twitter show, Mr. Fantastic's portrayal of autism is fraught with exaggeration and inaccuracy. To avoid spreading ableist preconceptions about what it means to be "high-functioning" and neurodivergent, creating a character without a serious examination of a disability as complex as autism must be done with care.

When studying superhero narratives within the academy, the field has gained increased importance in recent years as superhero movies, games, and television shows dominate the global cultural landscape. A superhero is anyone with remarkable "super" abilities that are unnatural to ordinary humans. However, a person with superpowers is not always a hero; heroism comes from one's actions. Within comic studies, there is often a tendency to use a deep analysis of a specific superhero, or a range of narratives, to explore how different aspects of cultural, political, and social life are represented via the medium. For instance, Noah Berlatsky (2015), and Carolyn Cocca (2014) have critiqued *Wonder Woman* and other female characters to explore the changing debates about gender and feminism. Adilifu Nama's *Super Black: American Pop Culture and Black Superheroes* (2011), offers an in-depth examination of superheroes of color including Luke Cage, Blade, Storm, and Black Panther—tell us about racial anxieties. While Scott Smith and José Alaniz (2019) use superhero narratives to theorize disability of lesser known characters such as Echo, Omega the Unknown, and Silver Scorpion,

Disability and the Superhero: Essays on Ableism and Representation in Comic Media explores both the well-known and lesser known influential comic characters and beyond such as Iron Man, Daredevil, Dr. Strange, Thor, Nick Fury, Jessica Jones, War Machine, Wonder Woman and Dr. Poisden, the Joker, Bucky Barnes, Punisher, Rocket and Groot, Luke Cage, Captain America, Super Grover from *Sesame Street,* and more. This collection goes beyond simple character sketches to reveal insightful analyses of entire series, films, and shows such as *Arrowverse* and *The Ables.* Several authors in this collection use Alainz's (2014; 2019) analyses as a starting point for contributing to superhero and disability studies. This collection defines both the successes and areas for improvement within the superhero genre, with the ultimate goal of challenging ableism.

This collection exposes the ableism present in film and print that may go unrecognized by everyday audience members. These misunderstandings, assumptions, and biases about disability identity must be dispelled within popular cultural artifacts. For instance, some of Stan Lee's most iconic characters follow a formula in which they are given psychological and physical disabilities (perceived as flaws) to make the superhero genre more realistic and dramatic. Using disability identity and experience in such a way is disempowering and unrealistic. These superheroes with disabilities also function as a negation, or counterbalance to the able-bodied/ able-minded characters that are elevated as the norm. Contributors in this collection deconstruct the myths of weakness, pitifulness, and helplessness that confine people with disabilities in the media and in real life.

The first few essays in the book investigate how disability relates to heroism. In some cases, heroism has come to mean disparaging disability entirely. Villains appear explicitly disabled through physical conditions and impairments. In other instances, heroism is overcoming one's limitations to fight for what is morally right. While superheroes can inflict us with a sense of awe, wonder, and inspiration, most people with disabilities do not revel in being an inspiration just simply for being themselves As defined by Joseph Shapiro, a "supercrip" is an "inspirational disabled person … glorified … and lavishly lauded in the press and on television" (1993, 16). The supercrip feels enormous pressure to overcompensate for their "otherness" or lack created by the perception of disability. In either case, disability is shrouded in negative representations that affect how individuals perceive the difference between good and evil. These essays critique the ideology of supercrip heroism, exposing how the tropes superhero narratives often rely upon are saturated with ableism. This starting point will help readers gain familiarity with superheroes as a genre and disability studies as a discipline. By the end of this section, readers will be well-versed in several disability studies and superhero applications. They can then delve into the intersectional analysis and alternatives presented in this book's second and third sections.

The collection begins with "Hyper-Normative Heroes, Othered Villains: Differential Disability Narratives in the Marvel Cinematic Universe," written by Kelly A. Kane. This essay examines the differential treatment of disability narratives among the protagonists and antagonists in the plethora of Marvel films and television shows. Specifically, it explores disability narratives such as José Alaniz's "superpowered supercrip" in the context of protagonists Bucky Barnes and Phil Coulson within the Marvel Cinematic Universe. It also discusses the impact of the "supercrip" and "kill or cure" narratives on perceptions of individuals with disabilities. Furthermore, recommendations for using positive portrayals in recent comics such as *Hawkeye* and *Alpha Flight* are a model for future films, given that these narratives provide a potential path forward for better representations in Marvel media.

The next essay, "Living in the Mutant Underground: Marvel's *The Gifted*" by Sue Scheibler, investigates the Fox TV series *The Gifted* through the lens of both disability and media studies. The combined theorizing from these disciplines exposes the complicated ways media texts use literary and visual props to represent disabilities. Thus, how the X-Men are socially constructed reinforces the ableist notion that disability amounts to deviance and needs policing. The various interpersonal conflicts offer a constructivist argument about disability and are still grounded in fundamentally ableist assumptions.

Following this comes "Isolation, Overcoming, and the Filmic Stare in the Marvel Cinematic Universe's *Iron Man* Films," by Grace McCarthy, which explores Tony Stark's character arc in his three standalone films with the Marvel Cinematic Universe. Stark overcomes a playboy lifestyle and matures into the role of superhero. However, the narrative of "overcoming" also extends somewhat problematically to Stark's acquired physical disability and post-traumatic stress disorder (PTSD). Using Rosemarie Garland-Thomson's sociological "stare theory" and discourses of social privilege theories, McCarthy argues that the combination of the filmic stare and the principles outlined by Martin Norden in his *Cinema of Isolation* reveal an ableist undercurrent in the representation of Stark's disabilities.

This volume goes on to explore superheroes in terms of their intersectional identities. As such, contributors examine how disability intersects with sexism, heteronormativity, speciesism, and racism. Several essays critique the ableist ideologies mentioned earlier by using fan-created superhero art and fiction. This analytical approach allows readers to comprehend comic studies in tandem with the fans who internalize superhero messages. This can help readers understand how ableist metaphors of heroism have been scripted onto other identities outside of disability itself. For those who are not fully aware of disability studies, these essays will pique their interest and perhaps bridge their knowledge by deploying scholars from other disciplines with whom they may already be familiar. Simultaneously, it will prove why it is necessary to investigate disability alongside gender, species, race, and sexuality. The use of superheroes and fan fiction in this section also enables these essays to be immediately relatable to readers interested more explicitly in superheroes because they are fans themselves.

Courtney Stanton provides an in-depth analysis of the four shows housed within Arrowverse in her essay, "Tech as Ableist Tool: Understanding the Role of Disability in the *Arrowverse* Series." By exploring the shows that include *Arrow* and its spin-off *The Flash*, and *Supergirl*, along with its newest addition, *Legends of Tomorrow*, Stanton demonstrates how race, age, sexuality, spirituality, and gender are visible while disabled identity remains conspicuously absent. This essay serves as a call to action to be more inclusive in their limited representations of disability. Using various examples—ranging from "cure" technologies to instances when comic legacies are forgotten, and characters' disabilities are erased—this analysis critiques how the Arrowverse treats disability as an antithesis to technology. Ultimately, the creators must reevaluate their portrayal of disability given the shows' growing popularity, bolstered significantly by exclusive licensing deals with Netflix, as well as the CW's expanding domain over DC-based television. Such changes are necessary.

The next essay written by Shanti Srinivas, "Cultural Appropriation and Ableism: Dr. Strange's Strange Concoction," explores the intersectionality of ableism with racial, cultural appropriation in the film, *Dr. Strange* (2016). Through a character analysis of Dr. Strange, readers learn how ingrained the film is with classist, ableist, racist, and sexist themes. This essay highlights the negative impact such intertwined oppressions can have on people with disabilities. Readers form lasting impressions of how to read the film in ways that do not disempower those it aims to represent.

The issue of physical ability is perhaps most overtly foregrounded in superhero narratives. The focus on characters with superpowers serves as a binary opposition to what one might assume is the weakness of ordinary humans. While movies and comics about superheroes predominantly focus on men heroes, they also include several heroines, including perhaps the most famous one, Wonder Woman. In "Of Sexism and Ableism: *Wonder Woman's* (Ab)Use of Disability," Tatiana Prorokova-Konrad explores how two women superheroes Wonder Woman (Gal Gadot) and Dr. Poison (Elena Anaya), provide narrative strategies for combating sexism and ableism. Prorokova-Konrad demonstrates how fans have critiqued using binaries to denote a character's strength and weakness, masculine and feminine, and disability and ability through the weapons of sexism and ableism.

Given the nature of superhero narratives—the centrality of war and violence that can cause a physical and mental disability—it is almost inevitable that disability becomes an inescapable part of superhero culture. Mental health conditions as a disability often get ignored in mainstream media, especially in superhero culture discourse. However, in "Assimilating Queer/Disabled Subjects in Marvel Superhero Fanfiction," Divya Garg investigates how fan art can highlight the often hidden or ignored trauma narratives in mainstream literary canons. Since mental health conditions are mainly invisible, fan art makes the effects of war and violence on superheroes visible. The analysis of *Avengers* fan art by Garg provides psychological depth into characters to visibly address issues related to disability and its intersection with race, nationality, gender, and sexuality.

The final few essays in the collection address alternatives to the ableist metaphors used in many superhero narratives. The contributors of these essays suggest that alternative representations require attentive engagement with superheroes to forge anti-ableist perceptions. Consumers should remain mindful that not all representations are perfect, and striving for perfection causes one to disparage disability as incomplete in the first place—these authors highlight empowering portrayals and readings of disability.

Young adult literature and programming in the twenty-first century have increasingly portrayed characters with disabilities to challenge negative perceptions and educate young people about disability issues within American culture. Indeed, since 2004 the American Library Association has offered the Schneider Family Book Award to "an author or illustrator for a book that embodies an artistic expression of the disability experience for child and adolescent audiences." Books such as *Marcelo in the Real World* (2009), *Five Flavors of Dumb* (2010), and *Paperboy* (2013) were thoroughly scoured by academics, taught in high school classrooms, and enjoyed by young readers alike. Similarly, comic studies increasingly use the lens of disability studies to interrogate superheroes such as Batgirl/Oracle, Professor X, and Daredevil for their impact upon popular perceptions of disability.

"Enabling New Perspectives of (Super)Power and Disability in Jeremy Scott's *The Ables*" is written by Robin E. Field and Christopher Boucher and explores Jeremy Scott's young adult novel *The Ables* (2015) as uniquely bringing together both disability and superpowers in protagonist Phillip Sallinger, a blind twelve-year-old with telekinetic abilities. Scott's vastly popular novel (a #1 Barnes & Noble bestseller and a #1 "Amazon Hot New Release") places readers in Phillip's first-person perspective, a viewpoint that unmasks ableist assumptions and questions the limitations placed upon people with disabilities. Scott portrays Phillip and his friends, all of whom have different disabilities, as better able to fight the villainous Finch than the non-disabled superheroes who doubt the boys' abilities to protect themselves, let alone the larger community. Ableism is identified and challenged in the novel, from the discriminatory situations experienced by Phillip and his friends to the very language they use to communicate with each other.

Scholarly work on superheroes reflects their complex relationship to disability and ableism, reinforcing the myth of the perfect body and representing a distinct break from socially defined norms. What, then, of the loveable, furry superhero, Super Grover, from the long-running children's television show *Sesame Street*? Daisy L. Breneman's essay, "It is I, Super Grover, Here to Challenge Ableism!" explores the roots of social justice and disability within the *Sesame Street* character Super Grover. While he occupies the liminal space of a superhero with no apparent superpowers, the message he sends for disability empowerment is noteworthy. In his bumbling efforts to save the day, this essay explores how Super Grover challenges ableism and offers a more inclusive and just way of ordering the social and physical worlds. Super Grover teaches to embrace failure and question definitions of success when bodies and minds do not operate according to problematic expectations; laugh and care. He shatters categories with courage and humor and empowers us to challenge social constructions of our bodies and abilities. Super Grover, who often needs assistance as he strives to provide it, teaches us powerful lessons about reciprocity and the fluidity of being the giver/receiver of help. When examined through an ethics of care, Super Grover reveals that caring for and with others is a fruitful path toward peace and justice. Challenging our individualistic notions of (in)dependence, Super Grover reinforces connectedness. He exists in deep and inherent relation to his diverse, and sometimes disorderly, community. Super Grover offers meaningful ways to challenge categories, interrogate power, embrace possibility, cultivate resilience, and find superhero-ness in our very ordinariness in relationships with others.

Jester characters often use their non-normative cognition or disruptive physicality to offer social commentary through comedy. Jesters are also often depicted as having disabilities. Through their comedic routines, jesters often engage in exaggerated performances of disability that transcend their implied impairment. The last essay, written by Sean Thomas Milligan, "The Joker: Disrupting Perceptions of Disability in *Batman* Comic Books," explores one of the most famous comic book jesters of all time—the Joker from the *Batman* mythos. The Joker forces others such as his henchmen to dress up as clowns, apply makeup, flash a forced grin, and bleach their skin, resulting in an ambiguous, yet undetectable "disability" for himself and others. The analysis of projecting his own "disabled" likeness onto others creates a transformative space to reassess how ableism manifests in the process of labeling. By presenting the Joker's narrative for inspection, one hopes that readers can learn from and move beyond the negativity associated with the disability label.

By concluding this book with popular reconfigurations of superheroes, readers can close feeling optimistic about moving forward with more socially progressive characters that present storylines free from ableism. Similar to how good and evil must battle it out, empowering representations of disability and heroism may not be achieved easily, but the struggle must continue. Ultimately, concluding the book in this fashion encourages readers to include in their critical dialogues about media, superheroes, and comic studies with a serious consideration of identity politics.

References

Berlatsky, Noah. 2015. *Wonder Woman: Bondage and Feminism in the Marston / Peter Comics 1941–1948*. New Brunswick, NJ: Rutgers University Press.

Cocca, Carolyn. 2014. "Negotiating the Third Wave of Feminism in Wonder Woman." *PS: Political Science & Politics 47* (1): 98–103. doi: 10.1017/S1049096513001662.

George, Amber, E. 2012. "Disney's Little 'Freak' Show of Animals in the Environment: A Dis-Ability Pedagogical Perspective." In *Earth, Animal, and Disability Liberation: The Rise of the Eco-Ability Movement,* edited by Anthony J. Nocella, Judy Bentley, and Janet Duncan. New York: Peter Lang.

Moore, Alan, and Bill Bolland. 2008. *The Killing Joke: The Deluxe Edition.* DC Comics.

Nama, Adilifu. 2011. *Super Black: American Pop Culture and Black Superheroes.* Austin, TX: University of Texas Press.

Shapiro, Joseph. 1993. *No Pity: People with Disabilities Forging a New Civil Rights Movement.* New York: Times Books.

Hyper-Normative Heroes, Othered Villains

*Differential Disability Narratives
in the Marvel Cinematic Universe*

KELLY A. KANE

Given the escapist nature of superhero stories, notable for being unconstrained by realist concerns and widely regarded as "low-brow" or inane, many writers and fans of the genre argue that such stories need not be held to strict standards of cultural justice (Gavaler 2015, 76). However, the Marvel Cinematic Universe (MCU) is a sprawling franchise that includes over 20 films (e.g., *Iron Man* 2008) and over ten television series (e.g., *Daredevil* 2015), that exist all within the same narrative framework. This makes the MCU arguably the most important benchmark of American popular culture in the last decade and, therefore, cannot escape cultural scrutiny. This franchise has brought widespread awareness of and appreciation for superhero stories even among audiences who might not have traditionally engaged with such media in the past. For instance, its entry *Avengers: Endgame* (2019) currently ranks as the highest grossing film ever released (Tartaglione 2019). The MCU's wide reach helps it set many cultural trends and allows audiences to enter the world of superheroes (McMillan 2019). Although these films and shows are part of a broader superhero canon, they set trends followed by other superhero franchises (e.g., the DC Cinematic Universe, named for the Marvel Cinematic Universe). They also define the very comic books they adapt, such as Baby Groot becoming part of the "Guardians of the Galaxy" comic canon only after appearing in the MCU movie *Guardians of the Galaxy* in 2014 (Duggan, Kuder, and Svorcina 2017). These stories' role as a cultural benchmark then invites interrogation and further examination related to disability identity and ableism.

One of the lures of superhero stories is their straightforward and familiar appeal, which also contributes to their problematic portrayals of characters and cultural artifacts. Social psychologists David Pizarro and Roy Baumeister (2013) assert that superhero stories are a form of "moral pornography" because "much like the appeal of the exaggerated, caricatured sexuality found in pornography, superhero comics offer the appeal of an exaggerated and caricatured morality that satisfies a natural human inclination toward moralization […] built to satisfy our moralistic urges but ultimately unrealistic and, in the end, potentially misleading" (20). This analysis characterizes superhero stories as appealing because they remove the complexities of moral decision-making, portraying the triumph of clearly marked moral agents over clearly marked immoral ones.

According to this framework, superhero stories are morally pornographic because they focus on simple, satisfying endings and high success rates (Pizarro and Baumeister 2013, 22). Just as pornography features the most enjoyable aspects of sexuality with an unrealistically nonexistent risk of sexual rejection, superhero stories depict moral struggles with a shallow risk of failure and unambiguous answers about the moral course of action. Therefore, superhero stories must demarcate heroes and villains to signal for the reader who the moral and immoral agents will be. Ergo, some of the most popular Marvel comics characters include Loki, a self-described "agent of chaos" (Lee 1962, 1) and Magneto, leader of the "Brotherhood of Evil Mutants" (Lee and Kirby 1963, 8). Pizarro and Baumeister (2013) point out that in the early stages of most literary forms, "the villain could be seen twirling his mustache, cackling, and rubbing his hands together[....] Later, such overtly wicked characters were dismissed from serious literature as not being sufficiently realistic. But their perennial popularity in comic books indicates the appeal of moral clarity" (24–25). If superhero stories at least partially derive their appeal through portraying simplified moral conflicts, then by necessity, they rely upon these overt signals of villainy. Many surface-level markers have lost their popularity in superhero stories. For instance, in the film version, Magneto leads a "Brotherhood of Mutants" without mentioning evil (*X-Men: Last Stand* 2006), and MCU's Loki claims to be motivated by justice rather than destruction (*Thor* 2011). However, one especially troubling visual symbol has persisted: that of disability marking a character's immorality.

Understanding how disability so often functions as a visual symbol of a fictional character's alleged virtue (or lack thereof) is illustrative of the evolutionary psychology of moral judgment. Contrary to popular belief, natural selection prioritizes trusting and helping close others (de Waal 2008). There is even a "truth bias" wherein individuals are inclined to believe all assertions unless given reason to disbelieve those assertions (Vrij and Baxter 1999, 27). However, natural selection did not favor absolute trust in all conspecifics; humans have always had to decide who to trust and who to avoid. Therefore, Pizarro and Baumeister (2013) argue, moral judgment is inherently pleasurable for the same reason that sexual intercourse is inherently pleasurable: it increases the odds of survival for both groups and individuals. Given that "individuals so easily arrive at conclusions about the dispositions of others (and are motivated to do so) with only minimal information," deciding who to trust conveys intrinsic pleasure to the judging individual, and superhero stories provide the same simplified pleasure (Pizarro and Baumeister 2013, 27).

As disability scholars David Mitchell and Sharon Snyder discuss in their analysis *Narrative Prosthesis: Disability and the Dependencies of Discourse* (2000), disability is perceived as an external marker of one's moral status dating back to Aristotle's writings, and perhaps even earlier (57). This specific human bias, also known as the "what is beautiful is good" effect, automatically leads to assuming that physically attractive individuals are more moral than those who are less physically attractive (Dion, Berscheid, and Walster 1972, 285). Within many Western cultures, standards of masculine beauty emphasize smooth skin, large muscles, broad shoulders, short but thick hair, and narrow waists (Murnen and Karazsia 2017). The MCU overwhelmingly portrays masculine superheroes as conforming to these beauty standards. For instance, Punisher presents with enormous musculature and smooth skin (*Punisher* 2017). Meanwhile Punisher's nemesis Jigsaw demonstrates characteristics that are less traditionally masculine (e.g., he self-describes as "pretty") and less traditionally beautiful (e.g., he incurs facial scarring) by Western standards. This physical marker of "goodness" makes moral judgment straightforwardly pleasurable while also reinforcing cultural stereotypes. The linkage between the physical and moral qualities of a person, which includes perceiving physical disability as "ugly," persists throughout these narratives.

One can even witness such contrasts manifest within a single MCU character. During *Captain America: The First Avenger* (2011), Bucky Barnes is a heroic sidekick to the protagonist Captain America. In this film, Bucky's appearance adheres closely to Western ideals of masculinity, including short hair, smooth skin, and a non-disabled body. However, when Bucky reappears as the antagonist in the sequel *Captain America: The Winter Soldier* (2014), his appearance has moved away from these traditional ideals: he now has shoulder-length hair, bodily scarring, and an apparent prosthetic arm. The third film *Captain America: Civil War* (2016), then hybridizes Bucky's appearance with moderate-length hair and a de-emphasized prosthesis, reflecting his morally ambiguous role. Thus,

the apparent signal of normative American masculinity becomes synony-
mous with the literal goodness of Bucky's character. Thus, the physicality
of the man character's body represents a manifestation of their virtuous-
ness or sinfulness.

Although past investigations of disability have definitively refuted
the assumption that the physical body is a reflection of morality, superhero stories nevertheless demonstrate bias against the moral character of
disabled individuals. One reason for this persistent ableism derives from
implicit biases in the system of moral judgment. It also stems from humanity's insistence on framing all differences into binary oppositions or either/
or distinctions. Evolutionary psychologists David Buss and Douglas Ken-
drick (1998) posit that humans have evolved to judge one another rapidly
based on appearance. This judgment system can be prone to error to the
extent that it perceives evidence of untrustworthiness where none exists.
Specifically, human perception results from many "good enough" mechanisms that lead to mistakes and accurate judgments but usually priori-
tize avoiding the more serious class of errors. This principle then biases
humans toward mistrust for any individuals whose outward appearance
potentially signals unfamiliarity or disease. Still, it does help to explain
why humans often make snap judgments to avoid individuals perceived as
physically unusual, including those with non-normative physicality or gait
(e.g., individuals with wheelchairs, visible scarring, or mobility impairments). Humans not only can but should overcome this impulse to avoid
disabled individuals, just as we usually overcome the impulse to copulate
with every physically attractive person we encounter.

Nevertheless, it can be easy to fall prey to the temptation to justify
these impulses through individual and systemic ableism, both of which
exclude disabled individuals from public spaces. An unfortunate manifestation in some superhero stories is that it may be easier to mark villains with mustaches or black hats and also a disability. Creators must find
other ways to create drama aside from leaning on ableist tropes for character development. Using the disabled body as a container for ableist perspectives about disability experience is disempowering. The MCU makes
heavy use of these types of metaphors when it portrays disability, along
with other representations including race, gender, and sexual identities.

In his book *Death, Disability, and the Superhero: The Silver Age and
Beyond*, disability scholar José Alaniz (2014) traces the history of the
major superhero comics lines, and notes that Marvel, more so than its
competitors such as DC and Dark Horse, has frequent representation of
disabled heroes among its headliners. Alaniz (2014) notes that DC presents the occasional hero with a disability such as the Doom Patrol. However, Marvel also has a wide plethora of characters with disabilities,

including A-list heroes such as Daredevil, Iron Man, and Professor X. One possible explanation for this discrepancy is the influence that Greek mythology had on informing the DC universe's Norse mythology, which informs Marvel to a similar degree. The Greek pantheon values physical perfection and features primarily non-disabled and beautiful gods, with the arguable exception of Hephaestus. By contrast, the Norse pantheon includes amputees such as Tyr, visually impaired deities such as Odin and Hodr, and selectively mute trickster Loki. Ancient Greek philosophy emphasized that "what is beautiful is good." In contrast, ancient Norse philosophy was far more likely to regard disability as a signifier of sacrifice and honor earned through surviving injury (Mitchell and Snyder 2000, 42–43). To a large extent, Marvel narratives have also embraced disability as ubiquitous, while at the same time sadly treating it as metaphorical rather than literal.

Mitchell and Snyder (2000) problematize the "symbolic manipulation of bodily exteriors" that literature often employs when portraying disability (59). Treating disability as a metaphor removes its potential to localize fictional characters within a disability culture and community. To localize disability within the individual avoids troubling the social order that creates disability by privileging certain experiences over others. Disability as a metaphor rather than a social identity affirms the existing social order and offers no challenge to harmful stereotypes. This treatment of disability is, in its own way, as comfortingly unrealistic and immediately gratifying as pornography.

Even in relatively positive representations such as *Thor* (2011) and *Avengers* (2012), depicting one-eyed characters (Odin and Nick Fury, respectively) is more discerning because of their lack of connection to worldly cares, and failure to address ableism as a literary device. Nick Fury's missing eye does not change his distance weapons or piloting software (e.g., *Captain Marvel*). Instead, disability appears along metaphorical lines like when Fury comments on the death of a friend by saying, "I just lost my one good eye" (*Avengers*). Then another ableist quip comes when Fury gloats over a defeated villain by saying, "If you want to stay ahead of me, Mr. Secretary, you need to keep both eyes open" (*Captain America: The Winter Soldier*). One character in *Avengers* even questions the lack of accessibility in Fury's multi-monitor computer console. This would have been the perfect segue into discussing unaddressed accessibility barriers, but instead Fury's assistant simply answers that he must turn his head more often to compensate. The franchise thereby emphasizes that Fury's missing eye is *only* a metaphor for his keen discernment ability, rather than a truly integrated part of his character or even an accurate portrayal of that disability.

This theme recurs in *Captain America: Civil War* when superhero War Machine experiences a permanent spinal injury while fighting for his best friend, Iron Man. Later on, rival superhero Hawkeye blames Iron Man for the fight when he declares, "You gotta watch your back with this guy. There's a chance he's gonna break it." The film then equips War Machine with a fantastical prosthesis that essentially nullifies his disabled experience by giving him the same range of motion as his non-disabled teammates, entirely without side effects or the need for maintenance. The MCU films present disability as a metaphor for inner morality and characterization. War Machine has few experiences of being a disabled man through his spinal injury. However, War Machine appears emotionally "impaired" by the damage his friendship with Iron Man caused to his social standing. Nick Fury's partial blindness recurs not as a visual difference but as a metaphor for his secret "sight" because he has concealed his blind left eye with an eye patch.

These and other MCU portrayals use disability, not as an identity or a social category but rather as a physical manifestation of qualities or phenomena that otherwise would remain abstract. *Avengers* does not find fault with Fury having to use an inaccessible computer console. Instead, the narrative flippantly dismisses this feature of his workspace. *Captain America: Civil War* offers no discussion of War Machine's intersectional identities (e.g., how disability intersects with his identities as a black man and a veteran). Instead, creators employ the trope of "hiding" his disability as quickly as possible through the prosthetic (Alaniz 2014). The MCU offers no critique of ableism or inaccessibility, and instead disability identity is localized as a problem with the body and the individual.

Other metaphorical uses of disability abound. *Thor: Ragnarok* (2017) uses Thor's partial blindness to analogize him to his deceased father Odin, and in the process, fails to examine how losing an eye could affect his fighting style, balance, or even emotional adjustment. *Iron Man* does not discuss Tony Stark's cardiac injury in the context of identity or access, but rather as "proof that Tony Stark has a heart." As these examples suggest, the social context of the disability is subsumed to its use as a literary device. In the most egregious cases of disability being only a metaphor, disability itself becomes a marker of moral judgment from higher powers, whether explicitly or implicitly. Several of these metaphors directly connect disability to morality through differentiating the outcomes for characters with disabilities. For instance, some heroes who experience "cures" for their disability can be rendered once again non-disabled, and villains can develop permanent disabilities before being killed off. Nowhere is this dichotomy more explicit than in the *Captain America* film series.

In *Captain America: The First Avenger,* wise mentor Abraham Erskine tells future hero Steve Rogers that he will undergo an incredible transformation, describing it thusly: "The serum amplifies everything that is inside, so good becomes great; bad becomes worse." At the time, Rogers had been barred from the Army because of asthma, arthritis, partial deafness, and other chronic illnesses. However, Erskine's magical serum erases these disabilities, and the film makes explicit that this change comes about because Rogers is a virtuous man worthy of becoming Captain America. According to Erskine, this occurs because Rogers is "not a great soldier, but a good man." When the megalomaniacal Johann Schmidt is treated with the same serum, he incurs a disability where none previously existed. The transformation renders him the physically deformed Red Skull, absent a nose and most of the skin on his face. With the line "bad becomes worse" played over an image of Schmidt transforming, the film clarifies that this change has occurred because of the serum's ability to echo one's moral character in one's physical form. Thus, *Captain America: The First Avenger* juxtaposes Captain America's and Red Skull's morality by casting Captain America's hypernormative physicality as proof of his moral superiority and Red Skull's non-normative appearance as proof of his moral bankruptcy. The manifestations of "bad" and "good" are located within the body itself and reflected in physical appearance.

A similar case occurs in the MCU series *Jessica Jones* (2015). Both protagonist Jessica Jones and antagonist Alisa Jones are dosed with phantasmagorical chemicals after their minivan crashes. Jessica Jones, the altruistic private detective, emerges unscarred and normatively attractive, with smooth skin and flowing hair. Alisa Jones, the impulsive and often enraged serial killer, incurs extensive facial scarring from the same accident. She also loses her hair, thus rendering her appearance less normatively feminine. Captain America and Red Skull have approximately the same superpowers, set apart only by the protagonist's normative beauty and the antagonist's lack thereof. Alisa eventually dies while Jessica lives.

The same dichotomy persists throughout the MCU. In *Captain America: The Winter Soldier,* both hero Falcon and villain Crossbones narrowly escape the same collapsing building. In the sequel *Captain America: Civil War,* Falcon is as normatively beautiful as ever, whereas Crossbones receives excessive scars. Reinforcing the stereotype of disabled individuals as seeking self-destruction, Crossbones self-immolates within minutes of appearing onscreen following his injury (Alaniz 2014, 98). Both protagonist Daredevil and the unnamed antagonists of Madame Gao's empire become blind after chemical exposure; Daredevil retains an unscarred appearance while the evil minions have visible facial scarring (*Daredevil* 2015). Daredevil survives the show while several of the evil minions are killed. Thus, the MCU implicitly invites the viewer to judge individuals based on their appearances and assume that less normatively beautiful individuals are less moral and less deserving of life.

Even when the MCU portrays heroic characters as disabled, it often does not fully embrace disability experience. Many disabled MCU heroes fall into the curious space that Mitchell and Snyder (2000) describe wherein a protagonist's disability is simply stated to exist, and then has an inexplicable lack of impact on the individual's life any time it is not convenient for purposes of characterization or literary device (56). Sami Schalk (2016) defines this phenomenon in the MCU and related portrayals as the "superpowered supercrip," a character from speculative fiction whose superpowers operate in direct contrast with the individual's disability, thereby acting to remove the influence of disability on the character's personal narrative (74). The superpowered supercrip is a subset of the stereotype of disabled individuals as "overcoming" disability through hard work and willpower, which ultimately denies the experiences of disabled individuals by suggesting that they must change their own bodies and minds rather than ask that environments accommodate them as they currently are (Schalk 2016, 81). In the case of the superpowered supercrip, the disability experience is acknowledged but then denied through the use of speculative powers that give the ostensibly disabled character the lived experience of a non-disabled person.

Daredevil is perhaps the most notable superpowered supercrip in the MCU. The heroic Matt Murdock becomes blind as a child when exposed to harmful chemicals. He trains himself to use his other senses to compensate for his lack of sight to the point where he is more skilled at spatial navigation than most sighted individuals when he becomes Daredevil (Smith 1998). Alaniz (2014) points out that Daredevil exists in a strange state of being whereby he functionally acts as a sighted person throughout his comic appearances, and yet also champions blind individuals through co-opting his prostheses—dark glasses and a collapsible cane—as the tools of his superheroism (69). Daredevil's portrayal varies greatly from one comic series and screen adaptation to another, with some relatively nuanced depictions of access and ability status (*Daredevil* 2003) and some deeply problematic depictions of negative stereotypes that blind individuals fake disability to gain unneeded benefits (*Elektra* 2005) or misinformation indicating that blind individuals can "feel" colors (Smith, 3).

However, the lived experience of Daredevil in the MCU is not that of a blind person. The *Daredevil* (2015) television show largely fails to engage with ableism, simply hand-waving the protagonist's navigation of environments with poor accessibility (e.g., the New York City subway) through suggesting that his "radar sense" acts the same as sight. The show often overcompensates for Daredevil's disability by simply adding a new super-power to his repertoire any time blindness would otherwise change his lived experience, until eventually he can play pool unassisted, read hand-writing through running his fingers over a surface, and use distance weap-ons against his opponents. Thus, Daredevil's superpowers mitigate his lived experience to be like that of a non-disabled person. This dulling of his disability sets an unrealistic precedence that localizes disability within his body rather than calling upon society to change. As Alaniz (2014) argues, introducing disability into a narrative transgresses hypernorma-tive societal definitions of embodiment. This transgression represents a "problem" that must be "resolved," often at the expense of the individual character (135).

Perhaps the most excruciatingly self-aware moment in the show occurs in the episode "Nelson v. Murdock," when Daredevil's best friend Foggy Nelson finds out about the character's superpowers. Angry at the deception Daredevil has been perpetrating, Foggy angrily demands, "How many fingers am I holding up?" and Daredevil correctly answers "One." It is, of course, Foggy's middle finger. The *Daredevil* series portrays its pro-tagonist (among other deceptions) pretending to be unable to navigate, luring a love interest into helping him, and mimicking helplessness when law enforcement confronts him amid illegal activities. It thereby plays into the deeply ableist fear of disabled individuals secretly "faking" to gain undeserved advantages (Alaniz 2014, 140). *Daredevil* portrays its protago-nist's superpowers as the product of his specialized training and strength of character, extensively flashing back to a younger Matt Murdock learn-ing to use his powers with the help of mentor Stick. It also falls into the ste-reotype of blind individuals as possessing compensatory advantages that mean they do not need disability-accessible environments or prostheses, such as changes to the infamously inaccessible New York subway system (Patel 2019).

These portrayals are specifically problematic in that, like all supercrip narratives, they suggest that disability can be "overcome" through will-power alone. As Schalk (2016) suggests, these narratives imply low expec-tations for people with disabilities. The assumption is that any person with a disability who marries, takes care of a family, or earns money is extraor-dinary, and that those who achieved their goals did so through willpower alone rather than breaking societal barriers (74). Like the system justifica-tion inherent in the "what is beautiful is good" bias, this type of narrative comfortably assures ableist society that the problem lies not in the many barriers standing between disabled individuals and full participation in society, but within people with disabilities themselves. These narratives present a single blind individual able to play pool as implicit proof that all blind individuals can play pool with enough effort, rather than calling for adaptations to pool tables that would make pool playing equitable for visually impaired users to enjoy. However, even in the absence of compensatory superpowers, Marvel heroes will often "overcome" disabilities through self-discipline alone, thereby falling into the glorified supercrip trope.

Schalk's (2016) analysis describes the glorified supercrip narrative as depicting an individual with a disability engaged in extraordinary feats such as climbing Mount Everest or winning a Nobel Prize. These narratives focus on the individual's personal characteristics, such as determination and willpower, that helped ensure personal success. These portrayals often make mawkish appeals to common humanity that implicitly cast most individuals with disabilities as "other" through holding up a single individual who has achieved extraordinary feats of mental or physical prowess (Schalk 2016, 77). The glorified supercrip narrative implicitly casts disability as a personal failure through suggesting that any athlete with a disability who cared enough would be able to bypass ableism and win a chess tournament or the Paralympics. In doing so, it frequently overlooks other privileges afforded to individuals with disabilities—who are usually wealthy, white, and men—that can account for their success as much as the "willpower" to "overcome" their disabled status.

This glorified supercrip narrative drives much of the plot of Season 2 of the television series *Iron Fist*. In the episode "The Dragon Dies at Dawn," protagonist Danny "Iron Fist" Rand breaks his leg during a fight; subsequent episodes portray medical professionals such as doctors and physical therapists assuring Iron Fist that the injury is permanent. However, Iron Fist refuses physical therapy and drug therapy alike, insisting that he can train himself to regain all his extraordinary skill at martial arts through meditation and effortful exertion of will. The subsequent narrative arc focuses on Iron Fist's willpower, dwelling on scenes where he pushes through exhaustion to continue training and ignores pain to accomplish his goals. It thus localizes the success of this training (Iron Fist does regain the ability to fight with swords and with his fists) within the individual himself. This glorified supercrip narrative neglects much of the same intersectionality that all such narratives do. It fails to recognize that Iron Fist, an extremely wealthy white man with a full-time romantic partner willing and able to act as caretaker, has privileges that most individuals with disabilities lack. For instance, 29 percent of disabled Americans lived in poverty according to the 2014 census (Denavas-Walt and Proctor 2015). *Iron Fist* does not acknowledge that the protagonist's "overcoming" relies on his ability to avoid working or doing anything other than training for several hours a day, failing to examine how his intersecting privileges contribute to his experience of disability.

Furthermore, these glorified supercrip narratives derogate the very systems and prostheses that help real individuals with disabilities navigate life. Supercrips, including those in the MCU, frequently reject therapy and systemic forms of assistance. Too often, the MCU portrays this rejection as a signifier of personal strength. Not only does *Iron Fist* describe Danny as heroic and self-disciplined for refusing physical therapy, but *Daredevil* specifically contrasts Daredevil's ability to fight ninjas with other blind characters' use of canes and assistants in a way that implies Daredevil is the only one with the alleged strength of character not to need prostheses. While *Punisher* contains a sympathetic mental health professional who has a disability and not a supercrip, it also portrays the character as unable to help his clients in any meaningful way. In *Agents of SHIELD* (2013), psychologist Andrew Garner is a murderous supervillain who uses his therapy appointments as an opportunity to manipulate his clients into doing evil. Consistently, the MCU presents mental health services as useless at best and sinister at worst.

Perhaps the most egregious motif of valuing individual willpower over the support of others comes in Marvel's consistently negative portrayal of support groups. *Jessica Jones, Punisher, Luke Cage*, and *Iron Fist* have minor recurring roles for support groups, all of which are portrayed as unethical and ineffective. Jessica Jones attends a group meeting for survivors of mind control only long enough to mock its members as pathetic before setting out on her own, allegedly more heroic, path of violent revenge. Despite her series-long struggle with trauma, Jones rejects all forms of treatment and states, "screw therapy" and later, "it's called whiskey" when asked if she could benefit from professional assistance ("AKA It's Called Whiskey"). Jones instead demonstrates an attitude that therapy is an indulgence and a form of weakness; she crudely rejects the suggestion that she join the support group, stating "Like I'd waste my time circle jerking with a bunch of whiners" ("AKA 99 Friends"). The specific assertion that group therapy is a "circle jerk," or a form of meaningless self-indulgence, is repeated by two other characters during the series, reinforcing the show's contempt for the support of others ("AKA The Kumbaya Circle Jerk"; later changed to "AKA I've Got the Blues"). Jones has used violence to defeat the supervillain who harmed her by the end of the season but has made no meaningful effort to seek healing for her trauma and alcoholism. Instead, she regards both conditions as hopelessly unfixable, an assumption the show itself does not directly contradict. This attitude persists through the related MCU shows such as *Punisher, Luke Cage,* and *Iron Fist*, which all depict support group leaders using their groups to engage in unethical or illegal behavior.

Social psychologist Mikhail Lyubansky (2013) argues that this consistent portrayal of mental health professionals as incompetent serves a specific purpose within superhero stories: justifying the heroes' violent revenge against villains (182). After all, if mental health assistance is a valid alternative to murder or physical assault for individuals with dissociative identity disorder (Mary Walker, *Iron Fist*), violent expressions of post-traumatic stress disorder (Lewis Wilson, *Punisher*), or unspecified mental disabilities (Alisa Jones, *Jessica Jones*), then the entire profession of superhero vigilantism is rendered invalid. Lyubansky suggests that mental health professionals must be portrayed as "immoral and corrupt" or else "emasculated and ridiculed for being unable to do their job" for superhero stories to function (181). The alternative would be to acknowledge the potential for restorative justice and humanize the villains of such stories to the point where the entire process of having a man in a cape beat strangers unconscious for acts of petty theft becomes morally questionable. Therefore, the superheroes cannot possibly rely upon the assistance of trained professionals but must "overcome" disability alone, or else the entire narrative of simple moral judgment comes under threat.

Whether they feature superpowered supercrips or glorified supercrips, these supercrip narratives are consistently only available to the superheroes in Marvel adaptations. Disabled supervillains, even within the same works, often receive very different treatment. A hero with a disability usually has the disability removed or nullified, but villains with disabilities are vilified as embittered outsiders who seek to destroy the non-disabled world. This is a specific stereotype that Alaniz (2014) describes as a villain "possessed of traits straight out of the ableist's worst nightmare: malformed, malevolent, mighty" (57). In *Iron Man 3* (2013), villain Aldrich Killian also uses a cane due to an unspecified mobility-related disability in his first appearance. Still, he develops a "cure" for all disabilities, a chemical known as Extremis. Killian describes himself as embittered and jealous toward Iron Man because of his perceived physical perfection. Killian states that he wanted to take his own life because of this bitter jealousy. Although Killian and other antagonists can regrow limbs or remove disabilities through Extremis, they eventually die from its side effects. However, Iron Man also takes the Extremis chemical and develops a cure for his own cardiac injury that neither creates side effects nor results in his death.

Similarly, *Ant-Man and the Wasp* (2018) portrays the antagonist Ghost as villainous only to the extent that her experience with chronic pain makes her embittered. She specifically states that her experience with pain causes her to break laws. When her mentor pleaded with her, saying, "People are getting hurt," Ghost responds, "Everything hurts" and refused to retire from her course of action. The moment Ghost receives a magical cure for her disability through Pym particles, she becomes a sympathetic character who selflessly helps the heroes evade law enforcement. Disabled villains in the MCU experience not just anger but a desire to destroy the non-disabled due to their disability, reinforcing the stereotype of the individual with a disability as the bitter loner (Mitchell and Snyder 2000).

In some cases, these characters do not rise above the status of mere set pieces used to develop the narratives of non-disabled heroes. This lack of development for minor characters becomes problematic when it reduces certain characters to nothing more than stereotypes rather than creating individuated minor roles. This can be perceived quite easily within the agentic behavior of men who are expected to follow gendered expectations of being forceful, aggressive, and strong. Agentic stereotypes for gender lead one to believe a character is competent and confident. However, the unagentic character plays into another ableist stereotype: that disabled individuals are helpless, sometimes even to the point of being less than human (Wolbring 2008). This type of character prevents awareness of how society-wide dehumanization of individuals with disabilities can actively prevent their expression of agency (Alaniz 2014).

For instance, in *Iron Man 3*, several veterans with disabilities appear only long enough to receive an Extremis cure and then die. The camera focuses on their disabled bodies, lingering on shots of one woman's residual limb rather than showing her face, emphasizing that these individuals are props rather than characters. Their deaths drive the plot forward, and most of them never speak a single line onscreen. Audiences are encouraged to feel pity for these individuals as they are shown strapped down and screaming and to feel fear as one by one they suffer catastrophic explosions due to the Extremis side effects. This framing reinforces the ableist construction of disability as pitiable fearsome, and loathsome (Mitchell and Snyder 2000). By contrast, the non-disabled minor character Ho Yinsen speaks only two lines in *Iron Man 3*, yet he is likable and sympathetic. The camera lingers on Yinsen's face as Iron Man sweeps by with barely a word of acknowledgment, and one of his two lines ("Another time, perhaps…?") makes a humorous allusion to his future friendship with Iron Man. Even Yinsen's death in *Iron Man* emphasizes his agency, de-emphasizing the physical reality of his wounds. Notably, non-disabled minor villains receive greater individuation, as when an unnamed guard at an AIM facility humorously states, "The people who work here are so weird," before immediately quitting his job (*Iron Man 3*). Thus, characters' roles do not need to be limited to their use as props to drive the plot, but the problem persists.

Arguably more problematic still is *Guardians of the Galaxy*'s mockery of its only known character with a disability. An extended joke rouses the audience to laugh along with the heroes as they barter for an unnamed minor character's prosthetic leg simply for the sake of depriving him of said leg. By way of explanation, protagonist Rocket says, "I thought it'd be funny [...] what'd he look like hopping around?" At no point does the film individuate the character beyond his prosthetic, nor does it condemn the heroes' actions. This motif of protagonist Rocket hoarding unneeded prostheses returns more than once. In *Avengers: Infinity War* (2018), Rocket offers a cybernetic eye (one that renders Thor a supercrip) and explains that he stole it to collect a gambling debt, despite not needing the eye himself. Later, he attempts to purchase Bucky Barnes's prosthetic arm simply for the sake of owning it. Neither case condemns these actions, outside of the brief look of disgust that Bucky directs at Rocket after hearing his offer. The MCU does not show the original owner of the prosthetic leg "hopping around," nor does it offer any consideration of the immediate threat to Bucky's life if he were deprived of his arm mid-battle. Instead, the tone of this running joke mocks and dismisses the actual need for prostheses as mobility aids. The implied message here is that characters with disabilities exist to be gazed upon—and mocked—by Rocket and an assumed non-disabled audience. The result is that it momentarily acts to objectify even a relatively complex character such as Bucky.

However, these stories are not just fictional but fantastical. The Marvel Cinematic Universe, and the comics that inspired it, imagine the impossible. These are stories in which the dead rise, gods walk the earth, humans fly, and sorcerers travel in time. It nevertheless matters that they imagine impossibly effective prostheses and disability-nullifying superpowers because the MCU acts as such a foundational cultural artifact for contemporary audiences. Viewers know that MCU depictions are fictional, but that does not prevent such stories from influencing their perceptions of what is right and true (Appel and Malečkar 2012).

Social psychologists studying the impact of stories have overwhelmingly found that American individuals derive stereotypes as much from fictional media as from human interaction, if not more so. Melanie Green and Timothy Brock (2000) gave a group of participants either a story that contained a stereotypical depiction of a man with schizophrenia as dangerously violent or a story that made no mention of schizophrenia (704). Participants who read the story with negative stereotypes about schizophrenia rated developmentally disabled individuals as more dangerous and supported involuntary institutionalization more than participants who read the unrelated story. Fictional works, including the show *24* (2001) and the novel *State of Fear* (2004), have been used to support arguments during Congressional and presidential debates (Vaughn, Childs, Maschinski, Nino, and Ellsworth 2010, 1181; Leggett 2005; Bradner and Jaffe 2015). Much of what contemporary Americans think they know comes from mass media such as television.

Journalist Manohla Dargis (2018) may have said it best: "movies get into our bodies, making us howl and weep, while their narratives and visual patterns, their ideas and ideologies leave their imprint." Not only do immediate portrayals of stereotypes reinforce these stereotypical beliefs, but they build up over time. Suppose individuals with disabilities are only shown as virtuous overcomers or embittered villains. In that case, the harmful stereotypes that bar people with disabilities from participating fully in society will continue to gain new life. Even superhero stories, with all their flash and glamor, have the potential to be more than moral pornography. Marvel comics can grapple with disturbing questions of morality and personal identity, and the MCU is beginning to do the same. For instance, *Black Panther* (2018) and *Avengers: Infinity War* both portray Bucky Barnes as competent and sympathetic without his prosthetic arm, neither minimizing nor fetishizing his amputation but rather focusing on the character as a human individual whose disabilities contribute to but do not define his narrative. *Agent Carter* (2015) gives complex agency to disabled protagonist Daniel Sousa while resisting and even interrogating the supercrip narrative, like when Sousa talks about his coworkers' tendency to applaud him as a "war hero" for his disability in the absence of any information about his actual service record ("The Blitzkrieg Button").

Nevertheless, the MCU must do better. It must cast disabled actors to play disabled characters, allow disabled characters to have narratives not defined by disability, and break the stereotype of physical beauty indicating inner goodness. The groundwork has already been laid for characters such as Bucky Barnes and Daredevil to become positive disability icons. Marvel only needs to embrace these characters' disabilities to transform these narratives beyond the stereotypes they currently enforce and break those stereotypes down.

REFERENCES

Agent Carter. 2015. "The Blitzkrieg Button." Season 1, episode 4. January 27. ABC. https://abc.com/shows/marvels-agent-carter.

Alaniz, José. 2014. *Death, Disability, and the Superhero: The Silver Age and Beyond.* Jackson: University Press of Mississippi.

Appel, Markus, and Barbara Malečkar. 2012. "The Influence of Paratext on Narrative Persuasion: Fact, Fiction, or Fake?" *Human Communication Research* 38 (4): 459–484. doi: 10.1111/j.1468–2958.2012.01432.x.

Black, Shane, dir. 2013. *Iron Man 3.* California: Walt Disney Studios and Motion Pictures.

Boden, Anna, and Ryan Fleck, dir. 2019. *Captain Marvel.* California: Walt Disney Studios and Motion Pictures.

Bowman, Rob, dir. 2005. *Elektra.* California: 20th Century Fox.

Bradner, Eric, and Alexandra Jaffe. 2015. "Ben Carson Apologizes for Comments on Gay People." *CNN,* March 5. https://www.cnn.com/videos/us/2015/03/05/ctn-sot-lemon-ben-carson-apology-gay-choice.cnn.

Branagh, Kenneth, dir. 2011. *Thor*. California: Walt Disney Studios and Motion Pictures.

Buss, David M., and Douglas T. Kenrick. 1998. "Evolutionary Social Psychology." In *The Handbook of Social Psychology*, edited by Daniel T. Gilbert, Susan T. Fiske, and G. Lindzey, 982–1026. Hoboken, NJ: Wiley.

Coogler, Ryan, dir. 2018. *Black Panther*. California: Walt Disney Studios and Motion Pictures.

Daredevil. 2015. "Into the Ring." Season 1, episode 1. April 10. Netflix.

_____. 2015. "Nelson V. Murdock." Season 1, episode 10. April 10. Netflix.

_____. 2015. "The Ones We Leave Behind." Season 1, episode 12. April 10. Netflix.

Dargis, Manohla. 2018. "What the Movies Taught Me About Being a Woman." *The New York Times*, November 30. https://www.nytimes.com/interactive/2018/11/30/movies/women-in-movies.html.

De Waal, Frans B. M. 2008. "Putting the Altruism Back Into Altruism: The Evolution of Empathy." *Annual Review of Psychology 59*: 279–300. Doi: 10.1146/annurev.psych.59.103006.093625.

Denavas-Walt, Carmen, and Bernadette D. Proctor, 2014. "Income and Poverty in the United States: 2014." *Current Population Reports*, September 2015: 60–252. United States Census Bureau. Washington, D.C.: U.S. Department of Commerce.

Dion, Karen, Ellen Berschild, and Elaine Walster. 1972. "What Is Beautiful Is Good." *Journal of Personality and Social Psychology 24* (3): 285–290. doi: 10.1037/h0033731.

Duggan, Gerry, Aaron Kuder, and Ive Svorcina. 2017. *All-New Guardians of the Galaxy*, vol. 1, no. 1, "#1." Comic. New York: Marvel Entertainment, LLC.

Favreau, John, dir. 2008. *Iron Man*. California: Walt Disney Studios and Motion Pictures.

Gavaler, Chris. 2015. "A Parliament of Monsters." *On the Origin of Superheroes: From the Big Bang to* Action Comics No. 1, 75–102. Iowa City: University of Iowa Press.

Green, Melanie C., and Timothy C. Brock. 2000. "The Role of Transportation in the Persuasiveness of Public Narratives." *Journal of Personality and Social Psychology 79* (5): 701–721. doi: 10.1037//0022–3514.79.5.701.

Gunn, James, dir. 2014. *Guardians of the Galaxy*. California: Walt Disney Studios and Motion Pictures.

Iron Fist. 2018. "The Dragon Dies at Dawn." Season 2, episode 6. September 7. Netflix.

Jessica Jones. 2015. "AKA It's Called Whiskey." Season 1, episode 3. November 20. Netflix.

_____. 2015. "AKA 99 Friends." Season 1, episode 4. November 20. Netflix.

_____. 2015. "AKA I've Got the Blues." Season 1, episode 11. December 20. Netflix.

_____. 2018. "AKA God Help the Hobo." Season 2, episode 4. March 8. Netflix.

Johnson, Mark Steven, dir. 2003. *Daredevil*. California: 20th Century Fox. Film, 2003.

Johnston, Joe, dir. 2011. *Captain America: The First Avenger*. California: Walt Disney Studios and Motion Pictures.

Lee, Stan. 1962. *Journey Into Mystery*. Vol. 85, no. 1, "Trapped by Loki, God of Mischief!" Marvel Comics. Comic, 1962. New York, NY: Marvel Entertainment, LLC.

Lee, Stan, and Jack Kirby. 1963. *The X-Men*. Vol. 1, no. 1 "The X-Men." Marvel Comics. New York, NY: Marvel Entertainment, LLC.

Leggett, Will. 2004. "Social Change, Values, and Political Agency: The Case of the Third Way." *Politics 24* (1): 12–19. doi: 10.1111/j.1467–9256.2004.00200.x.

Luke Cage. 2016. "Step in the Arena." Season 1, episode 4. September 30. Netflix.

Lyubansky, Mikhail. 2013. "Seven Roads to Justice for Superheroes and Humans." In *Our Superheroes, Ourselves*, edited by Robin S. Rosenberg, 175–202. Oxford, UK: Oxford University Press.

Marvel's Agents of S.H.I.E.L.D. 2015. "Melinda." Season 2, episode 17. April 14. Netflix.

McMillan, Graeme. 2019. "5 Comics to Read After Seeing *Avengers: Endgame*." *Wired Magazine*, April 26. https://www.wired.com/story/avengers-endgame-reading-list/.

Mitchell, David T., and Sharon L. Snyder. 2000. *Narrative Prosthesis: Disability and the Dependencies of Discourse*. Ann Arbor: University of Michigan Press.

Murnen, Sarah K., and Bryan Karazsia. 2017. "A Review of Research on Men's Body Image and Drive for Muscularity." In *The Psychology of Men and Masculinities*, edited by Ronald F. Levant and Y. Joel Wong, 229–257. American Psychological Association.

Patel, Jugal K. 2019. "Where the Subway Limits New Yorkers with Disabilities." *The New York Times*. February 11. https://www.nytimes.com/interactive/2019/02/11/nyregion/nyc-subway-access.html.

Pizarro, David A., and Roy Baumeister. 2013. "Superhero Comics as Moral Pornography." In *Our Superheroes, Ourselves*, edited by Robin S. Rosenberg, 19–36. Oxford, UK: Oxford University Press.

Punisher. 2017. "3AM." Season 1, episode 1. November 17. Netflix.

Ratner, Brett, dir. 2006. *X-Men: The Last Stand*. California: Marvel Enterprises, The Donners' Company, Dune Entertainment, Ingenious Film Partners, and 20th Century Fox.

Reed, Peyton, dir. 2018. *Ant-Man and the Wasp*. California: Walt Disney Studios Motion Pictures. Film.

Russo, Anthony, and Joe Russo, dir. 2019. *Avengers: Endgame*. California: Walt Disney Studios and Motion Pictures.

_____. dir. 2018. *Avengers: Infinity War*. California: Walt Disney Studios and Motion Pictures.

_____. dir. 2016. *Captain America: Civil War*. California: Walt Disney Studios and Motion Pictures.

_____. dir. 2014. *Captain America: The Winter Soldier*. California: Walt Disney Studios and Motion Pictures.

Schalk, Sami. 2016. "Reevaluating the Supercrip." *Journal of Literary and Cultural Disability Studies 10* (1): 71–86.

Smith, Kevin. 1998. *Daredevil*, vol. 2, no. 1, "Guardian Devil." Marvel Comics. Comic. New York: Marvel Entertainment, LLC.

Tartaglione, Nancy. 2019. "Oh Snap! 'Avengers: Endgame' Rises to $1.22B+ Global and $866M Overseas Record Bows; Climbs All-Time Charts—International Box Office." *Deadline Magazine*, Box Office Breaking News, April 10. https://deadline.com/2019/04/avengers-endgame-opening-weekend-record-global-china-international-box-office-1202601752/.

Vaughn, Leigh Ann, Kathryn E. Childs, Claire Maschinski, N. Paul Niño, and Rachel Ellsworth. 2010. "Regulatory Fit, Processing Fluency, and Narrative Persuasion." *Social and Personality Psychology Compass 4* (12): 1181–1192. doi: 10.1111/j.1751–9004.2010.00325.x.

Vrij, Aldert, and Mark Baxter. "Accuracy and Confidence in Detecting Truths and Lies in Elaborations and Denials: Truth Bias, Lie Bias and Individual Differences." *Expert Evidence 7* (1): 25–36. doi: 10.1023/A:1008932402565.

Waititi, Taika, dir. 2017. *Thor: Ragnarok*. California: Walt Disney Studios and Motion Pictures.

Watts, Jon, dir. 2017. *Spider-Man: Homecoming*. California: Walt Disney Studios and Motion Pictures.

Whedon, Joss, dir. 2012. *Avengers*. California: Walt Disney Studios and Motion Pictures.

Wolbring, Gregor. 2008. "The Politics of Ableism." *Development 51* (2): 252–258. doi: 10.1057/dev.2008.17.

Living in the Mutant Underground

Marvel's The Gifted

SUE SCHEIBLER

This essay examines the Fox TV series *The Gifted* (an alternate timeline in which the X-Men have disappeared) through the lens of both disability and media studies, bringing the two together to examine the complicated ways in which broadcast television represents disabilities. It begins with the assumption that disabilities are socially constructed. The world in which the X-Men find themselves is ideally suited for exploring how disabled characters are portrayed as dangerously deviant and needing policing, surveillance, experimentation, rehabilitation, and, at its most extreme, extermination. Human variety is suppressed and greeted with suspicion rather than acceptance in the X-Men archetype, such that difference becomes impairment, and then perceived as dangerous. The fear of mutants has reached such an extreme that they are hunted by Sentinel Services, a government agency, neutralized, and placed in camps. The series focuses on two "ordinary" parents, one of whom works for Sentinel Services, who, on discovering that their two children are mutants, go on the run and connect with a mutant underground whose members are, to varying degrees, conflicted about their genetic variations. In these internal and interpersonal conflicts, the tensions between a text that, on the one hand, offers a constructivist argument about disability and, on the other hand, is still grounded in fundamental ableist assumptions. It is for these reasons, this analysis will investigate the ableism present in this series, along with ways for developing anti-ableist representations.

In his book, *The New Mutants: Superheroes and the Radical Imagination of American Comics*, Ramzi Fawaz (2016) observes that a radical transformation took place in superhero comics during the late 1950s,

30

continuing into the '60s and '70s, namely that superheroes were now "framed as cultural outsiders and biological freaks capable of upsetting the social order in much the same way that racial, gendered, and sexual minorities were believed to destabilize the image of the ideal U.S. citizen. Rather than condemn these figures, superhero comics visually celebrated bodies whose physical instability deviated from social and political norms" (4). Classical superheroes such as Superman and Wonder Woman could blend in with society because their bodies aligned with social norms that defined the "normal," even "average" person. Silver Age superheroes, on the other hand, "gained their abilities from radioactive exposure, technological enhancement, and genetic manipulation" (Fawaz 2016, 4), resulting in corporeal transformations, or what Fawaz (2016) calls their "monstrous biology" and "monstrous difference" (5).

Pointing out that "postwar superheroes emerged as the monstrous progeny of atomic and genetic science, no longer legitimate citizens of the state or identifiable members of the human race," Fawaz (2016, 8) argues that the reinvention of the superhero "as a biological misfit and social outcast whose refusal or failure to conform to the norms of social legibility provided the ground for a new kind of political community" (9). If this was true of mutants such as Spiderman, Bruce Banner/The Hulk, and the Fantastic Four, all of whose bodies were destabilized through genetic manipulation caused by exposure to external sources, then it was even truer for mutants whose powers and abilities emerged from within their own genetic makeup.

Mutants were introduced into the Marvel Universe in 1963 via the X-Men, "five suburban teenagers gifted with extraordinary abilities stemming from an evolution in their genetic makeup" (Fawaz 2016, 144). While the original series was cancelled in the late 1960s, it was revamped in 1975 and soon became one of Marvel's most successful comic book series (Alaniz 2014, 116). The proliferation of movies, video games, and television series (live action and animated) has proven a very lucrative property. This success is due, in part, to how the stories and characters have resonated with readers/viewers/gamers who identify with a variety of marginalized and underrepresented groups, including women, people of color, LGBTQIA+, non-gender conforming, and genderqueer. As Fawaz (2016) suggests, "by popularizing the genetic mutant as a social and species minority, the series laid the foundation for reimagining the superhero as a figure that, far from drawing readers to a vision of ideal citizenship through patriotic duty or righteous suffering, dramatized the politics of inequality, exclusion, and difference" (144). Because their social and species minority status rests on a physical and cognitive difference, mutants are especially rich terrain for exploring how people with disabilities experience oppression.

All mutants carry the X-gene. It lies latent until puberty, when it manifests through special powers and abilities. Since the non-mutant defines the norm, mutants and family members are caught off guard when someone's X-gene manifests. Because the x-gene is triggered by heightened emotional states such as anger, fear, or anxiety, the powers that manifest are heightened and uncontrolled, just as the emotional, physical, and psychological stress that produces them. This results in confusion and fear on the part of the mutant and family members and friends. While some powers and abilities leave no physical trace on the body, others result in bodily transformations, adding to the fear and concern created by the activation of the X-gene. If all mutants are considered "monstrous" and "uncanny" by a fearful non-mutant public, those whose bodies carry visible evidence quickly become abject objects, labeled as "freaks," "deviants," and other such terms.

Powerful minorities tend to elicit fear in the majority. As the majority, non-mutants have the power and privilege to respond to the mutant minority. They could accept mutations as natural human variations and accommodate and integrate mutants into their families and larger political-social order. But in the mutant story world, much like the real world with which it resonates, acceptance and accommodation do not prevail. Amy Wilkerson (2015) observes, "[o]ne of the earliest goals of disability studies was to expose the various methods by which some bodies are marked as different and deviant while others are marked as normal" (67). Stories about mutants can further that goal to the extent that they narrativize how non-mutant society identifies and responds to the mutants among them. As Mitchell and Snyder (2000) suggest, "[b]ecause narrative involves the production of stories that shape our lives and help determine possibilities for creating ways of living together, the understanding of narrative plays a crucial role in how we imagine social worlds" (126). In these stories, mutants become subject to various levels of discrimination, oppression, and harassment. This makes them ideal texts for readers and viewers to recognize their own social worlds.

José Alaniz (2014), reading comics through a disability studies lens, observes that "the Silver Age introduced disability as a major and consistent component of superhero comics […] The characters now interact with their shifting bodies as bodies, with all the complications involved" (40). He notes that fans "came to read the series as a mirror for U.S. race relations and identity politics, with mutants as the beleaguered minority struggling for inclusion in a world predisposed to fear them" (Alaniz 2014, 117). Furthermore, he observed that "*X-Men* has earned a reputation as the preeminent disability allegory in superhero comics" (Alaniz 2014, 134). It is through the narrative acts of character and story that the X-Men texts can, in the words of David Mitchell and Sharon L. Snyder (2000), "pursue the subject of disability from multiple directions: as a character-making trope in the writer's and filmmaker's arsenal, as a social category of deviance, as a symbolic vehicle for meaning-making and cultural critique, and as an option in the narrative's negotiation of disability subjectivity" (l). If this is true of the X-Men movies, it is even truer of the television series *The Gifted* precisely because it adopts what Jason Mittell (2015) refers to as the poetics of complex television.

In his book *Complex T.V.: The Poetics of Contemporary Television Storytelling* (2015), Jason Mittell defines a television serial as that which "creates a sustained narrative world, populated by a consistent set of characters who experience a chain of events over time" (10). He goes on to point out that complex T.V. can "create compelling, complex characters" in series that often embrace "antiheroes as lead characters, using the long-form narrative structure to layer psychological traits and key elements of backstory" (Mittell 2015, 13). Television series can do this because a "television program is suffused within and constituted by an intertextual web that pushes textual boundaries outward, blurring the experiential borders between watching a program and engaging with its paratexts" (Mittell 2015, 7). To this end, "texts only come to matter in their consumption, circulation, and proliferation, and thus […] as part of a lived cultural practice, not a static, bounded, and fixed creative work" (Mittell 2015, 7). Reading *The Gifted* through the lens of disabilities studies and its resonances with the real experiences of disabled people make it part of a lived cultural practice. It can draw attention to strategies and structures by which variations among humans become classified as deviations, abnormalities and disabilities.

Mittell (2015) argues that "over the past two decades a new model of storytelling has emerged as an alternative to the conventional episodic and serial forms that have typified most American television since its inception," a mode he identifies with "narrative complexity" (Mittell 2015, 17). For Mittell (2015), complex T.V. is determined through a variety of "different storytelling strategies used by serial television to create engaging storyworlds through a range of complex techniques of narrative discourse, including playing with temporality, constructing ongoing characters, and incorporating transmedia" (10). *The Gifted* fits securely within Mittell's concept of complex T.V. Its format is highly serialized, demanding that its viewers watch every episode in sequence to make sense of the story world, characters, events and themes with which it deals.

The series provides and complicates allegories of disability precisely because it is a transmedia, serialized, television text whose story unfolds over twenty-nine episodes rather than the two to three hour running time of movies. Its structure allows it to intensify and deepen the exploration of a world where the social order can construct genetic variations as dangerously deviant, in need of policing, surveillance, experimentation, rehabilitation, and, at the most extreme, extermination. With its focus on characters and their intra- and inter-relationships, the series explores the complicated and, at times, conflicted ways in which mutants view and relate to their own mutated bodies, often through an internalized ableist lens that interprets bodies such as theirs as "abnormal," "abject," "monstrous," and "freakish."

The series uses multiple flashback sequences to give each character a compelling backstory that depicts psychologically and emotionally complex individuals. They also allow the series to establish complex character arcs, tracing how each character has accepted and fully inhabited their mutated bodies. The flashbacks explain how they came to form the communities where they find physical, emotional, and material support and protection, identity, and a sense of belonging that has empowered their active resistance.

The series, created by Matt Nix (2017), tells the story of the Struckers, a seemingly ordinary, middle-class family living in suburban Atlanta. Reed, the father, is a district attorney, while Caitlin, the mother, has given up a career as a nurse to raise their two children, Lauren and Andy. The world in which they live is one in which mutants, who have always been subject to various forms of discrimination and harassment, are now the targets of systematic violence and eradication due to a cataclysmic event that occurred four years before the series' events.

Known simply as 7/15, the date marks when the ideological conflict between two groups of mutants escalated during a Mutant Rights March in Dallas, Texas. A physical confrontation between the two groups resulted in a horrific explosion that killed hundreds of people, mutants and non-mutants alike. Sentinel Services agent Jace Turner represents the views of many, if not most, average citizens when he points out to former federal prosecutor turned detainee Reed Strucker, "I lost my daughter in the July 15th incident. She was seven years old. Her name was Grace. People talk about the X-Men; they talk about the Brotherhood. I'm never going to know if the blast of energy that killed my kid came from a good mutant or came from a bad mutant, and guess what: I don't care" (*The Gifted* season one, episode two, "rX").

Declared a terrorist act, the event has provided the federal government with the rationale it needs to justify using any means necessary to solve the "mutant problem." The government has proceeded to suspend mutant civil rights and declare any use of mutant powers, no matter how benign, illegal. The post 7/15 enlarged Patriot Act has given the police the authority to detain, imprison, and institutionalize any mutant they find, whether the mutant is engaged in criminal activity. To augment overwhelmed local police forces, Homeland Security has created a special force known as Sentinel Services (a term familiar to readers of the comic books and the Marvel Cinematic Universe) and empowered it to use any means necessary to locate, hunt down, and neutralize mutants. Sentinel Services has been armed with an array of mutant-hunting technologies: small spider-like machines called sentinels after the old mutant hunting robots, drones, and dampening collars which, when placed around a mutant's neck, neutralize their powers. The government has also funded scientific research that has produced various mechanisms to deal with the mutant problem. These include genetic manipulation and prosthetic devices that can weaponize mutants against other mutants when combined with medical interventions.

The mutant response to these conditions is varied and complex. The world they inhabit is one in which the X-Men, Professor Xavier and his School for Gifted Children, along with Magneto and his Brotherhood, have disappeared, leaving in their wake a void into which have stepped three Mutant groups. The Mutant Underground, led by John Proudstar (aka Thunderbird), Lorna Dane (aka Polaris) and Marcos Diaz (aka Eclipse), was established by the X-Men before they disappeared. As the name suggests, it works as an underground network for identifying, rescuing, and transporting mutants to Mexico or Canada, where the anti-mutant laws are less draconian. The Inner Circle, stepping into the void left by the absence of Magneto and the Brotherhood, intends to fulfill Magneto's vision for a separate mutant homeland where mutants will be free to use their abilities whenever they wish. The Morlocks comprise the third group. Morlocks are those mutants whose mutations do not allow them to pass as "ordinary humans." They live in the sewers and tunnels that run under the city and keep separate from both the Underground and the Inner Circle.

Through official propaganda mechanisms, the 24/7 news cycle, T.V. and radio talk-shows, "reality shows," and popular movies, non-mutants have been persuaded by the argument that mutants are a distinct species, as distinct from humans as the Neanderthal was from *Homo sapiens*. While some mutants have accepted this distinction, reveling in their self-identified classification of *Homo superior,* they are a minority within a minority. In the eyes of non-mutants that take the non-mutant as the norm and therefore superior beings, mutants are not just nonhuman but less than human. The non-mutant majority has been convinced that since only humans can be citizens, and mutants are not humans, then mutants are not citizens. If only humans can be considered "persons," then mutants, by not being human, are not "persons." Since they are not citizens, they are not eligible for legal protections extended to citizens. As disability scholar Lennard Davis (1995) would state, since they are not persons, they are not entitled to the rights extended to non-citizens (71–71). They have been denied the right to work, have a fair trial, access to education, housing, and medical care.

The driving force of the series is, in some sense, an illustration of what Rachel Adams, Benjamin Reiss, and David Serlin (2015) observe, namely that "hierarchies of race, class, gender, and sexuality proceed, in large part from a set of presumptions about 'normal' mental or physical capacities" (2). The characters experience the impact of what D. Christopher Gabbard (2015) points out when he notes that the "concept of personhood legitimizes an agent to enter into contracts (such as the social contract), make claims to justice, and participate in the public sphere" (99). In this way, the fictional world of *The Gifted* resonates with the real world experiences of people of color, women, LGBTQIA people, and people with disabilities who have found themselves, at various times and in various social-cultural contexts, classified as less than human, not quite a person, abnormal, deviant, deformed, mentally or emotionally inferior, and, therefore, not entitled to the rights afforded to persons.

While the various mutants and their landscape provide a point of identification for disabled viewers, Caitlin Strucker offers a point of identification for non-disabled viewers of the series. At the beginning of the series, Caitlin's world is turned upside down when she discovers that her children are mutants. The activation of Andy's x-gene is one of the inciting incidents that set the series' events into motion. Triggered when threatened by a group of bullies at a school dance, Andy's potent abilities nearly destroy the school. Lauren, who has known about her mutant abilities for several years, outs herself when she rescues Andy while protecting her classmates from the falling debris. By the time they arrive home, they have been tagged as terrorists, and targeted by Sentinel Services. Caitlin's sense of privilege is shattered on several fronts: the discovery that both of her children are mutants; the fact that Lauren kept it secret for years; and that, as mutants, her children can be arrested and imprisoned without a trial.

After escaping Sentinel Services, the fugitive family eventually lands among the Mutant Underground, where Caitlin's nursing training is useful. Living among and eventually fighting alongside mutants allows Caitlin to hear about the realities of mutant life from mutants themselves. She soon realizes that her naïve belief that mutants had rights and were legally protected is symptomatic of her own privilege. If Lauren and Andy must learn to use their abilities, Caitlin must grapple with the profound cognitive dissonance she finds herself. As the series progresses, Caitlin's white, middle-class, progressive, ableist, stable world is destabilized further when she pays attention to the "real world" around her. Talking to the mutants she encounters, she understands the discrimination, harassment, and violence each has experienced. She begins to understand that their suffering has little to do with their mutant abilities. They suffer because of social-legal-medical structures that declare them as "unfit," "disabled," and "unnatural" beings. As events unfold, she learns firsthand the extreme measures that the non-mutant world is prepared to use to eradicate mutants and the x-gene. Surrounded by "fluxable" bodies and minds, Caitlin, by virtue of her own stable body and mind, offers the abled viewer a point of identification to understand how abled privilege and power support it.

Fawaz (2016) argues that neoliberalism, in its "imposition of market demands on all aspects of American culture, politics, and social life […] has encouraged the development of the 'flexible subject'" (10). The flexible subject is someone "who exhibits the capacity to flexibly adopt every aspect of her identity to accommodate the demands of neoliberal capital and its periodic crises, including recessions, market fluctuations, and increased economic risk" (Fawaz 2016, 10–11). The fluxable figure, on the other hand, is one whose body is "unruly and in flux" (Fawaz 2016, 11). Fluxability, then, is "a state of material and psychic *becoming* characterized by constant transitions or change that consequently orients toward cultivating skills for *negotiating* (rather than exploiting) multiple, contradictory identities and affiliations" (Fawaz 2016, 11) (emphases in the original). It is through their "monstrous powers and bodies" that post-superheroes "exhibited a form of fluxability" (Fawaz 2016, 11).

Lorna's capture and imprisonment in season one, episode two, "rX," also serves to establish the reality of mutant life in a post 7/15 world. Captured while attempting to help a young mutant, Clarice (aka Blink) escape from the police, Lorna is sent to prison. Her disorientation is represented through a combination of subjective point of view shots, slow motion, and canted angles as she walks down the corridor to her cell to the taunts of all the inmates she passes. Entering her cell, she attempts to use her power, only to learn that the collar around her neck is a device that shuts off her mutant abilities while causing immense pain when she uses them. She collapses in pain on the cell's floor as the inmates closest to her mock and taunt her.

Later, on the way to the showers, inmates mock her with cries of "mutie" and spit on her as she passes their cells. In the shower, she washes off the dark hair dye, revealing her green mutant hair. The camera pans across the other inmates as they turn away in their shower stalls to stare at her as the dye runs down her body. The canted angles and slowly panning camera that picks out each inmate while multiplying the number of stares is juxtaposed with Lorna's unknowingness. Her back is turned to them and the camera. All they can perceive is the black dye running down her back as she continues to wash her hair. She turns and is caught in a relay of stares through a series of one-shots that isolate each person. She refuses to look away but stares back. The last shot is a closeup of her walking past them, almost, but not quite staring into the camera.

In her essay on stigma, Heather Love (2015) references the work of Erving Goffman (1963), Lennard Davis (1995), and Rosemarie Garland-Thomson (2009) to draw the connection between visibility, staring, and stigmatization. Lorna's shower scene provides an example of what Love (2015) refers to as Goffman's "emphasis on live interaction" to construct disability (Love 2015, 174). The way the sequence foregrounds both the starers (the other prisoners as well as the viewer) and the staree (Lorna) through intercutting creates a relationship and interaction between them and us. As Love (2015) points out, "scenes of staring produce conditions of vulnerability for people with visible differences; however, under usual conditions not only the staree but also the starer is exposed to view" (174). As viewers, we are also staring at Lorna and the women who are staring at her. In the exchange of stares, we locate our own relationship to the characters. Because our sympathies lie with Lorna, we want her to stare back, to reclaim her subjectivity to become something other than a passive object of stigmatization. What is more difficult to acknowledge is our own complicity with the curious non-mutant inmates who perceive her green hair as the mark of something other to them(our)selves. While we want to identify with Lorna as an "us" against the "them" of the inmates, our position as viewers consuming the spectacle of her unveiling situates us as "us" with the inmates against Lorna, as one of "them."

Lorna is revealed as a mutant to the inmates and correctional officers by two means: the green hair and the dampening collar. She illustrates and complicates Mitchell and Snyder's argument (2000) that "disabled people are encouraged to 'pass' by disguising their disabilities. Prosthetic devices, mainstreaming, and overcompensation techniques all provide means for people with disabilities to 'fit in' or to 'de-emphasize' their differences" (3). While the hair dye has allowed Lorna to pass, the dampening collar locked around her neck identifies her as a mutant to everyone within the prison system. An inmate explains the collar to Lorna when she is knocked to the ground by a powerful electric shock when she tries to use her abilities.

In some sense, the collar functions as a prosthetic device that disables Lorna's abilities and renders her "normal" and "manageable." As Mitchell and Snyder (2000) point out, a "body deemed lacking, unfunctional, or inappropriately functional needs compensation, and prosthesis helps to effect this end" (6). Lorna's body, like that of all mutants, is "inappropriately functional." It requires a "prosthetic intervention" to "accomplish an erasure of difference" or, "failing that [...] to return one to an acceptable degree of difference" (Mitchell and Snyder 2000, 7). From the perspective of Lorna and the viewers, she is abled without the device and disabled with it. The viewers want her to rip it off to restore what is, from the mutant perspective, full functionality appropriate to a mutant.

Marked and targeted by inmates and guards, Lorna's isolation is intensified when other mutant inmates rebuff her. They have found a community, of sorts, by passively accepting their status and actively performing it through servitude to the non-mutant inmates. In their essay "Community," the authors argue that the "extent to which a community recognizes, accepts, supports or affirms disabled persons says much about the potential of that community. The community is an essential other against which to understand and locate one's self. Recognizing one's self in a community or finding that the community recognizes one's self pulls at the very heart of what it means to be human" (Goodly, Liddiard, and Runswick-Cole 2017, 147). They argue that disability communities need to become less normative, more accessible, and more inclusive (Goodly, Liddiard and Runswick-Cole 2017, 147). They observe that disability has a "troubled history with the category of the human being" because it is both troubled by the human in that it risks being "cast-off as non-human" and troubles the human in that it challenges narrow and exclusionary notions of the human. Based on these observations, they argue for what they call the Dis-human position. The Dis-human rejects the category of the human while promoting other post-human communities (Goodly, Liddiard, Runswick-Cole 2017, 148).

While suspicious of community, mutants in *The Gifted* find that their survival depends on forming communities. In this way, they model the Dis-human. While some mutants have joined the Mutant Underground, other mutants have literally gone underground, setting up communities in the sewers. Known as the Morlocks, they have created safe spaces for those mutants deemed unfit to live among non-mutants because of their physical mutations or other conspicuous manifestations of their mutant genetics. Tired of being subjected to disgust, fear, and hate due to their "deformed," "monstrous," and "freakish" appearances and stigmatized as outcasts and misfits, they have withdrawn from the world above and created a home with one another. Suspicious of all non-mutants, they do not allow any to live among them and require all "normal" looking mutants to be branded with an "M" on their faces, marking their bodies in solidarity with their mutant brothers and sisters and ensuring that they can no longer "pass" in the "human" world. In this way, they embody what Mitchell and Snyder (2000) observe as "the power of transgression" that "always originates at the moment when the derided object embraces its deviance as value. Perversely championing the terms of their own stigmatization, marginal peoples alarm the dominant culture with a canniness about their own subjugation" (36).

The third group of mutants, the Inner Circle, heirs of Magneto's Brotherhood and the Hellfire Club, lives in luxury, in a penthouse high above the city. The group is led by Reeva Payge, and their goal is to realize Magneto's dream of a mutant homeland—a utopia where mutants can live safely, openly, and comfortably. Since they have wealth and social power, they work primarily by pulling the strings of politicians and media personalities, manipulating them to lay the groundwork for their master plan. Similar to the Underground that identifies, locates and, when necessary, trains mutants to help the cause while holding out hope for a utopian future where mutants are fully accepted and embraced by mutants, the Inner Circle is hard at work, identifying, locating, recruiting, and training mutants who share their assumption that mutants are a superior species that will never be able to co-exist with non-mutants.

Since not all mutants have bodies or abilities that allow them to be readily identifiable, the fear that there might be "mutants living among us" has led politicians, with the support of their constituents, to press for legislation that would require everyone to be tested for the X-gene, calling to mind Siebers' argument that "identifiability is tied powerfully to the representation of difference. In cases where an existing minority group is not easily identified and those in power want to isolate the group, techniques will be used to produce identifiability" (Siebers 2008, 17). He continues by noting that it "is not the fact of physical difference that matters, then, but the representation attached to difference—what makes the difference identifiable. Representation is the difference that makes a difference [...]. Identity must be representable and communicable to qualify as identifiable" (18). Mandatory testing coupled with the promise of a serum that can "cure" mutants by eliminating the X-gene has fostered conflicting responses among mutants. While many who embrace and even revel in their mutant abilities are fearful that they may soon be identified through testing and, once identified, eradicated through genetic manipulation, others perceive the promise of a cure as a relief. For these mutants, the lure of the "normal" is too great to pass up.

The conflicting attitude towards their mutations is perceived in a flashback sequence when Marcos first joins the Mutant Underground. Alone with Lorna, he asks, "ever wonder what you did in a past life to deserve this? Have a gene that forces us to live this way?" To which Lorna responds, "is that really what you think? I wouldn't change who I am or what I can do for anything. Tell me this, when you discovered your ability, what is the thing you did that gave you joy?" She flies up into the air and hovers over him, telling him, "your turn." He reaches down and picks up some glass which he breaks, and then, aiming at the light that bursts from his hands, he turns the glass into a prism. Lorna descends and uses her ability to control the magnetic field to turn the prism into a replica aurora borealis (Later in the series, when their daughter is born, they'll name her "Dawn" [*The Gifted* season one, episode 3, "eXodus"]).

If Lorna and Marcos celebrate their fluxable bodies, Reed's reaction to his mutations is one of horror and fear. As the series progresses, Reed finds the body he has assumed to be the stable body of the non-mutant is a fluxable, unruly, mutant body. Reed is terrified and confused when his hands and arms begin to burn with fire, melting everything he touches. Unable to manage his abilities, Reed decides to seek out Dr. Madeline Garber, who is reported to be working on a drug that will suppress the X-gene. In this way, the series exemplifies what Mitchell and Snyder (2000) observe: nearly "every culture views disability as a problem in need of a solution" (48).

It is at this point in the series, season two, episode eight, "the dreaM," and episode nine, "gamechanger," that the subtext of disabilities becomes text by two means: the reference to "real disabilities" and Dr. Garber's use of disabilities as a metaphor for the X-gene. As Dr. Garber shows her lab to the Struckers, she comments that "people talk about the manifestation of the X-gene as powers, but for many people who have the X-gene, they have serious problems that can better be described as disabilities. Those are the people we help here. We genetically tailor treatments for each patient" (*The Gifted* season two, episode eight, "the dreaM"). Reinforcing the symbolic use of disabilities, Dr. Garber, when asked by Lauren if their powers will be gone, responds, "no, it's like giving a diabetic insulin. The device we use is much like an insulin pump. Her X-gene will be active but she'll finally be able to be in control of her own body" (*The Gifted* season two, episode eight. "the dreaM").

On their tour of her lab, Dr. Garber points out Shana, a young woman who has both Down syndrome and the X-gene. Her powers allow her to promote plant growth. As Dr. Garber reports it, when Shana's parents told Dr. Garber that they wanted a cure (what they aim to cure is not clear), she told them that there is nothing to cure (again, it is not clear if she's referring to Down syndrome, the X-gene, or both). She has given Shana a job and "the plants have never been happier." She continues, "for some the X-gene is a blessing. When it's a curse, we find the answers" (*The Gifted* season two, episode eight "the dreaM"). Noah, Dr. Garber's assistant, is one of those for whom the X-gene is a curse. He has named his pump "Norm" because it has given him a "normal" life.

The second reference to a "real disability" occurs via a flashback in the episode twelve years earlier. A young Lorna, sitting in a field, uses her power to drive nails from a fence into a tree. Her aunt Dane, with whom she lives, warns her about using her powers. Lorna responds, "I'm already the bipolar girl with the green hair and the dead parents. So what if they know I'm a mutant?" (*The Gifted*, season two, episode eight, "the dreaM"). Another flashback in the same episode shows Lorna in a bar where a guy confronts her, asking if she is Lorna whose dad is the guy from the news (a reference to Magneto). When he asks her to use her abilities to show him a trick, she uses her power to hoist his car, which is parked outside, into the air, turn it upside down, and drop it on the pavement. He calls her a "crazy bitch." When her aunt shows up to bail her out of jail, she asks Lorna, "what is going on with you, Lorna? This is the fourth time you've been arrested this year. And it's not just the police. You've stopped taking your meds, you're fighting with the psychiatrists." Lorna replies, "maybe I am a crazy bitch." Her aunt responds, "you have so much potential" (*The Gifted* season two, episode eight, "the dreaM"). Later in the episode, Lorna returns to her hometown and asks her aunt to take care of Dawn. She tells her aunt, "I need her to be safe. I need her to be here" to which her aunt replies, "but you hated living here." Lorna says, "no, I hated being a bi-polar kid with green hair. I hated being different" (*The Gifted* season two, episode eight, "the dreaM").

If the episode brings together allegorical and "real" disabilities, it also brings together the medical and social models of disabilities. Watching images of mutant protests against the new curfew laws on T.V., Dr. Garber comments that "they oppress mutants for years then act shocked when they stand up for themselves" (*The Gifted* season two, episode eight, "the dreaM"). This would seem that, while she considers the X-gene to be a medical problem, to be treated on an individual level through medical intervention, she also understands that it is a "curse" due to social-political structures.

The series intensifies its commentary on disabilities when Dr. Garber's true intentions are revealed. The Struckers discover that Dr. Garber does not want to suppress the X-gene in those mutants who want to stabilize their fluxable bodies. She wants to eliminate the gene altogether. Dr. Garber's research will open the door to its use by the government and families who do not want mutant children. When the Struckers discover the truth, they hatch a plan to destroy her research and all of their blood samples that she is using to create her serum. Dr. Garber discovers them:

> DR. GARBER: Reed, I was trying to save your life. Why would you do this?
> REED: Madeline, what you're doing is wrong. You're talking about ending an entire race.

DR. GARBER: No. I'm rescuing the human race.

CAITLIN: With scientific genocide?

DR. GARBER: Reed's grandparents were monsters. They murdered thousands. Do you want that potential in your family? In anyone's?

CAITLIN: You have no right to do this. God made them this way.

DR. GARBER: God! What kind of God would curse their family with a son like Noah? Or Andrew?

REED: The X-gene is not a curse. You have seen who my daughter is and what she can do. The world is a better place for her in it.

DR. GARBER: We both know what your children did in Atlanta. I'm sorry but your daughter should have never been born. We can succeed where Otto failed. We can save future generations from this curse. (*The Gifted* season two, episode nine, "gaMechanger")

Siebers (2008) defines the medical model of disability as one that "lodges defect in the individual body and calls for individualized treatment" (72). He points out that medicalization "has at least two unsettling effects as a result: it alienates the individual with a disability as a defective person, duplicating the history of discrimination and shame connected to disability in the social world, and it affects the ability of people with disabilities to organize politically" (Siebers 2008, 72).

The Struckers, thinking that the logical extension of the medical model is euthanasia and genocide, reject it. They have personally experienced the realities of mutant life. From experience and the stories told them by other mutants, they know that the real conditions of mutant life are due to political-social-cultural attitudes that have shaped the environment within which mutants live. They know that mutants are not defective citizens. They have found a common cause, in the community with other mutants, around which to organize politically. The story-world, events, and characters have encouraged the Struckers and, by extension viewers who identify with them, to understand the medical model for what it is. They understand that the social model, as defined by Siebers (2008), "challenges the idea of defective citizenship by situating disability in the environment, not the body" (73). They, and the viewers who identify with them, understand that "gender, race, sex, nationality, and ability are heterogeneous, indeterminate, and artificial categories represented as stable or natural by people who want to preserve their own political and social advantages" (Siebers 2008, 73).

With its subtext made text, *The Gifted* accomplishes what Dan Goodley describes as the function of disability studies (Goodley 2017), namely, to point out that

Disability is about the social world in which we live. Disability is part of life. Disability is part of the human condition. Disability is a socio-cultural phenomenon and a personal, embodied physiological or psychological one.

> Disability studies encourage us to ponder how we normally (or normatively) understand our bodies, minds, relationships, communities and economic priorities. And we are encouraged to think of living non-normatively [1].

The series does this precisely because of its status as complex T.V. The serialized, long-form narrative structure allows the story to deepen, broaden, enrich, and complicate the characters, the story-world, and story-events. By rejecting a straight linear story in favor of a chronological structure that uses a complex flashback structure, the series can include real disabilities such as bi-polarism, PTSD, Down syndrome, and blindness as one aspect of personhood. Doing so can probe each character's back story, including their struggles with their impairments, the construction of communities that embrace and empower them, and the realities of living in a non-mutant (ableist) world.

While Caitlin offers the viewer an ableist perspective, the complex narrative explores multiple characters and perspectives that change over time as relationships develop, modify, fall apart, and are restored. In this way, as a media text, it has the potential to be

> a site of continual struggle, a space in which the relationships of power and oppression in a society can be exposed, challenged, reinforced, and rearticulated by those who find power and pleasure within cultural artifacts. It can also provide resources for identity formation, coalition and capacity building, and collective political action [Ellcessor et al. 2017, 12].

REFERENCES

Adams, Rachel, Benjamin Reiss, and David Serlin. 2015. "Disability" In *Keywords for Disability Studies*, edited by Rachel Adams, Benjamin Reiss, and David Serlin, 5–11. New York: New York University Press.
Alaniz, José 2014. *Death, Disability, and the Superhero: The Silver Age and Beyond*. Jackson: University Press of Mississippi.
Davis, Lennard. 1995. *Enforcing Normalcy: Disability, Deafness, and the Body*. London: Verso.
Ellcessor, Elizabeth, Mack Hagood, and Bill Kirkpatrick. 2017. "Introduction: Towards a Disability Media Studies." In *Disability Studies Reader*, edited by Elizabeth Ellcessor and Bill Kirkpatrick, 1–4. New York: New York University Press.
Fawaz, Ramzi. 2016. *The New Mutants: Superheroes and the Radical Imagination of American Comics*. New York: New York University Press.
Gabbard, Christopher. 2015. "Human." In *Keywords for Disability Studies*, edited by Rachel Adams, Benjamin Reiss, and David Serlin, 98–102. New York: New York University Press.
The Gifted. 2017. "rX." Season 1, episode 2. October 9. Fox.
_____. 2017. "eXodus." Season 1, episode 3. October 16. Fox.
_____. 2018. "the DreaM." Season 2, episode 8. November 27. Fox.
_____. 2018. "game Changer." Season 2, episode 9. December 4. Fox.
Goodley, Dan. 2017. *Disability Studies: An Interdisciplinary Introduction*. Los Angeles: Sage Publications.

Goodley, Dan, Kirsty Liddiard, and Katherine Runswick-Cole. 2017. "Feeling Disability: Theories of Affect and Critical Disability Studies." *Disability and Society* 33 (2): 197–217. doi: 10.1080/09687599.2017.1402752.

Love, Heather. 2015. "Stigma" In *Keywords in Disability Studies*, edited by Rachel Adams, Benjamin Reiss, and David Serlin, 173–176. New York: New York University Press.

Mitchell, David T., and Sharon L. Snyder. 2000. *Narrative Prosthesis: Disability and the Dependencies of Discourse*. Ann Arbor: University of Michigan.

Mittell, Jason. 2015. *Complex TV: The Poetics of Contemporary Television Storytelling*. New York: New York University Press.

Siebers, Tobin. 2008. *Disability Theory*. Ann Arbor: University of Michigan Press.

Wilkerson, Abby. 2015. "Embodiment." In *Keywords for Disability Studies*, edited by Rachel Adams, Benjamin Reiss, and David Serlin, 67–70. New York: New York University Press.

Isolation, Overcoming, and the Filmic Stare in the Marvel Cinematic Universe's *Iron Man* Films

"It is a high-tech prosthesis. That is actually the most apt description of it," says Tony Stark (played by Robert Downey, Jr.) to the Senate committee in *Iron Man 2* (2010). Stark's description of his Iron Man suit is greeted by laughter from the crowd and incredulity from Senator Stern. Both reactions stem from the seeming contradiction of describing a suit that, in its infancy, decimated the terrorist organization responsible for Stark's acquired physical disability as simply an artificial body part. The incredulity is underscored by the fact that Stark appears able-bodied in the hearing, the development of similar suits by enemy countries, and Stark's refusal to turn the proprietary technology over to the U.S. military. However, all grandstanding aside, defining the Iron Man suit as a prosthesis might be the most vulnerable, revealing statement Stark makes because it is a tacit admission of his own impairments and a public acknowledgment of disability. Stark's message is worth taking seriously, particularly because he entered a crucible of trauma, violence, and desperation and emerged as a superhero with a disability.

Ronald Berger (2013) defines the field of disability studies as "an interdisciplinary field of inquiry that includes representation from the social sciences, the humanities and the medical and rehabilitation and education professions" (3). Catherine Kudlick (2003) adds that disability studies "invites scholars to think about disability not as an isolated, individual medical pathology but instead as a key defining social category on par with race, class and gender" (qtd. in Hobgood and Wood 2013, 3–4). Disability studies has evolved from a medical model (where an impairment is individual deviance and therefore heavily medicalized and stigmatized) to a social model (which posits that it is socially imposed barriers, not a particular impairment, that constructs disability), to a cultural model (wherein disability is embraced as a matter of group identity) (Berger 2013, 26–28). While this evolution may seem deceptively linear, the evolution of disability studies has had a rocky history. To this day, the United States and the United Kingdom disagree on whether the social or cultural model is more effective. Disability theorist Martin Norden (1994) traced the development of disability stereotypes and the increased isolation of disabled characters onscreen, while Rosemarie Garland-Thomson (1997) explored the intersections of disability theory with feminist theory and other critical paradigms. Given the breadth of disability studies, narrowing the field to examine the representation of disability in the Marvel Cinematic Universe's (MCU's) three standalone *Iron Man* films (2008, 2010, 2013) requires a new critical framework.

This new framework must encompass Stark's isolation due to his physical and mental impairments and the "overcoming" narrative that spans the three films. An overcoming narrative is when a character with a disability accepts a given impairment's physical and emotional consequences. By the end of the film, the character no longer experiences stigma or practical inconvenience related to navigating a world not designed to access all abilities. Overcoming narratives frame disability as a lack of personal fortitude and acceptance of an impairment that should not be a significant problem from an able-bodied point of view (Norden 1994, 3–4). Overcoming narratives also feed into Garland-Thomson's (1997) assertion that an out-of-control body or mind is dangerous to the social order; if a character is in control of themselves, they should overcome their disability (37). This essay will use the filmic stare (McCarthy 2021)—a new critical framework inspired by Laura Mulvey's (1975) male gaze and Rosemarie Garland-Thomson's (1975, 1997) theory of the stare—to analyze the representations of Stark's physical and mental disabilities. The filmic stare is neither proscriptive nor prescriptive, but rather descriptive and analytical. It explores the interconnected web of shots, angles, and cinematographic techniques that comprise a filmic stare. Additionally, it examines the choices made by the director and actors that highlight or suppress impairments and disabilities. The filmic stare demonstrates how Stark's seclusion, efforts to pass as able-bodied, and final overcoming of his impairments before his traditional happy ending (a stable, happy relationship with Pepper Potts) indicate an ableist undertone in the portrayal of Stark's disabilities.

Stark's isolation throughout the three films, first in a cave in Afghanistan, then in his workshop, and finally in a garage in Tennessee, parallels the taboo around publicizing disability and the tradition of the cinematic isolation of disabled characters as described by Norden (1994) in *The Cinema of Isolation*. These spaces of isolation are contrasted with the public appearances Stark makes as CEO of Stark Industries, during which he hides the damage the arc reactor has done to his body, enabling him to pass as physically abled despite the physical consequences. The Iron Man suit is itself simultaneously an isolated space and an instrument for passing in public spaces, as it weaves in and around both the public and private spaces of the film as well as Stark's body. As such, the destruction of the symbolically resonant suits, the cure for the physical disability, and the disappearance of any PTSD symptoms at the end of *Iron Man 3* (Langley 2013) suggest that, despite the privilege and merit that Stark has as a genius-billionaire-philanthropist-playboy and superhero, he must nevertheless overcome disability before gaining a traditionally happy ending. The films underscore disabilities and isolation by using the filmic stare to visually highlight Stark's impairments.

Defining disability is challenging, and definitions can change depending on medical, governmental, and social contexts. For this analysis, the only division made is between mental and physical disabilities. This analysis will not distinguish between chronic illness, congenital physical or psychological disability and acquired physical or mental disability to align with the filmic stare's resistance to diagnosing fictional characters. Therefore, the Americans with Disabilities Act (ADA) broadly defines non-normative bodies and minds that substantially limit one or more major life activities as bodies and minds with disabilities. The ADA's definition also prevents falling into the trap of diagnosing a comic book character who has no life outside of the diegetic world to disrupt. The ADA's definition of disability is not the only source of disability definitions, and there has been resistance to the implicit medicalization within the definition (Brown 2015). By avoiding a strict diagnosis and using a broad understanding of disability, it is possible to investigate the film representations of Tony Stark through a lens of realism without inviting counterfactual thinking, propagating popular culture understandings of disability, or assuming medical knowledge. Film is a representation, and true-to-life accuracy is not the goal. Stark has been "diagnosed" with everything from PTSD to being "mentally unhinged" (Foundas 2013). The goal is to neither refute nor support these diagnoses but rather explore a nebulous set of disability representations on film.

In terms of a formal theoretical structure for analyzing disability, Mitchell and Snyder's (2000) theory of narrative prosthesis is often used. Their theory argues that disability is historically perceived as a mystery requiring an explanation, and therefore disability is itself the inspiration for narrative. Mitchell and Snyder (2000) also argue that disabled bodies function as a narrative crutch, whereby the text avoids discussing disability. Norden lays out a formal structure beyond the common metaphoric understandings of disability (e.g., the dichotomy between disabilities denoting a "pure" vs. a villainous character). Norden (1994) argues that, between the birth of cinema and the passage of the ADA in 1990, representations of disability in film overwhelmingly isolate the impaired individual both visually and geographically within the narrative. Isolation then leads either to exploitation, "kill or cure," or the impaired—and usually secondary—character becoming a prop for the protagonist's emotional journey (Norden 1994, 106). Norden's (1994) conclusions about the outcomes of isolation are practical in wider discussions of film and disability, particularly in "kill or cure" contexts.

The Oxford English Dictionary (OED) dates the phrase "kill or cure" to the mid–1700s. The phrase refers to last-ditch attempts to heal patients; these cures were often so extreme that the patient would either be cured or the treatment would prove fatal ("kill, v." OED Online). Norden (1994) uses the term to describe films in which a character with a disability is either cured of their disability or dies at the end of the film (106). Death may be due to the disability itself, but, more commonly, death is a sacrifice that buoys the development of the abled protagonist. Norden's (1994) kill or cure dovetails nicely with Mitchell and Snyder's (2000) theory of narrative prosthesis. As such, the development of the narrative and disability are tied together; when the story ends, the disability is resolved—either through a miraculous cure or death—simultaneously with the central narrative conflict. Kill or cure is so prevalent in narratives that feature disability that it becomes the basis for criticism regarding the oversimplification of disability. Often, the plot frames a disabled character's death in terms of a useful death instead of a useless (or burdensome, restricted, or painful) life, which elides kill or cure with the death of a secondary character to forward the protagonist's development. The false binary—abled life or disability and death—creates emotional moments in narratives (especially narrative arcs that become generic conventions), but critics argue that it fails to consider that a person with a disability's life is worth living (Berger 2013, 2–3). The stakes are somewhat different for Tony Stark. Nobody explicitly suggests that Stark's life as a superhero with a disability is not worth living, but multiple characters surrounding Stark wish that he be "cured" of the disability. Ironically, had Stark not been kidnapped, Iron Man would never have come into being, and Stark's isolation during the development and habitation of the suit might have been avoided. Ultimately, in all three films, Stark spends a lot of time isolated in and around the suits, which leads to tension with his assistant-turned-girlfriend, Pepper Potts.

Potts is the driving force behind Stark's decision to destroy the suits and have surgery to remove the shrapnel; she explicitly frames Stark's focus on the suits as a detrimental "distraction" to their relationship and something to be "cured" (*Iron Man 3* 2013). While this conflict is framed as a romantic subplot in a superhero film, on closer examination, the result of Stark's isolation and focus on developing his high-tech prosthesis is a kill or cure scenario: either the disability is cured, thus removing the bar to a successful relationship, or the relationship dies. While Stark's life is not on the line in this specific case, Marvel is certainly not above requiring Stark to sacrifice his prosthesis for Potts's sake. The overall *Iron Man* arc experiences both a metaphorical kill—the destruction of the suits—and a literal cure—the surgery to remove the shrapnel. The kill and cure that underpins the overall narrative arc reveals the broad strokes of the film's ableist tendencies. By incorporating a close analysis of the construction of Stark's impairments through the filmic stare, however, one can analyze visual representations of disability. Understanding the construction of onscreen representations of disability is critical because it allows scholars to pivot away from the restrictive discourse of asking only if a representation is accurate and then either giving the film an Oscar or dismissing the film as "negative" without exploring the impact of the represented disability.

The Filmic Stare

Filmic representation of disability has received many of the same criticisms as the cinematic film adaptations' literary antecedents: there is a fundamental difference between disability as a character attribute and the experiences of real people (Garland-Thomson 1997, 9–10; Norden 1994, 3–4). Scholars argue that film representations have historically been used to marginalize people with disabilities by oversimplifying disability onscreen and using it as a shorthand for villainous or helpless characters (Garland-Thomson 1997, 36, 47; Norden 1994, 11). Inherent in these criticisms is the assumption that literary and film representations of disability must be true-to-life. The slippage between marginalization and nuance, as well as between reality and realism, is addressed in the filmic stare, which is inspired by Rosemarie Garland-Thomson's (1975, 1997) concept of the stare.

Like Mulvey's gaze (1974, 6–18), Garland-Thomson's (1975, 1997) stare is inherently ideological and based on unconscious but pervasive socio-cultural assumptions about disability. Garland-Thomson's (1975, 1997) theory of the stare describes an interpersonal interaction in the real world. A normate—defined by Garland-Thomson (1997) as a white, heterosexual male in his mid-twenties who is fit, successful, and physically normative—stares at a person with a disability and acknowledges discomfort because they lack knowledge about people with disabilities. The discomfort and lack of knowledge lead to an unconscious, negative othering of the person with a disability (Garland-Thomson 1997, 8–9). Garland-Thomson (1975, 1997) argues that these real-world interpersonal interactions are always dynamic, whereas literary interactions between a reader and a character with a disability are always static (10–11).

The filmic stare focuses on constructing a visual synecdoche and the visual fragmentation of a character, both of which are achieved through an interconnected web of cinematographic techniques (primarily but not exclusively shot distance and framing). These are used to highlight or suppress a character's impairment, and assume an audience composed of straight, white, physically abled heterosexual men, and often—but not always—asexually objectify the character with a disability. Shot distance and framing are critical in highlighting or downplaying the visual impact of an impairment. While there may be no such thing as a truly invisible impairment in film, if the impairment is out of frame or consistently hidden by shot distance or composition, then what is literally out of sight is largely out of mind. While some shots are used to highlight an impairment or a break with social and behavioral scripts, others suppress the visibility—and therefore the impact of—those same impairments (McCarthy 2021).

Close-ups and extreme close-ups emotionally affect audiences in addition to focusing on critical details. Garland-Thomson (1997) argues that part of literature and film's compression of narrative into a two-hour feature film is that a character with a disability is reduced to the stereotype of their impairment (10–11). However, close-ups work for characters with disabilities onscreen in three ways: (1) "Focusing on a body feature to describe a character throws the reader into a confrontation with the character that is predetermined by cultural notions of disability" (Garland-Thomson 1997, 11). This confrontation is even more visceral with an image onscreen than words on a page because the cognitive schemata that viewers bring with them are very visual (2). The impairment (and assistive device) is highlighted, causing visual fragmentation and objectification of the (disabled) character (3). The close-up contributes to the creation of a visual synecdoche for the character. These shots create an emotional reaction to an obvious facet of a character that often becomes the shorthand for stereotypes about disability. For example, the image of the miniaturized arc reactor shining through a black or dark-colored shirt becomes shorthand for Stark as Iron Man, a partial synecdoche supplemented by the now iconic extreme close-ups of Stark's face when he is in the Iron Man suit.

In addition to creating a visual synecdoche, close-ups in the filmic stare function to fragment and objectify characters with disabilities (McCarthy 2021). The filmic stare is analogous to Laura Mulvey's (1975) male gaze, described in "Visual Pleasure and Narrative Cinema." Given an aesthetic approach to disability in film, however, the fragmentation of a non-normative body complicates Mulvey's (1975) gendered reading. For Mulvey (1975), the fragmented female body is a part of the fetishistic, scopophilic pleasure a heteronormative male audience takes from looking (6–18). In the context of the filmic stare, disability often takes erotic appeal out of the equation. Garland-Thomson (1997) argues that many social meanings attached to women's bodies are also attached to disabled bodies, including the individual being cast as deviant while being excluded from full participation in public and economic life (19). She takes Harlan Hahn's terms—asexual objectification and inappropriate—to highlight the assumption that sexuality is inappropriate for people with disabilities (Garland-Thomson 1997, 25). The idea that bodies with disabilities are not eroticized might hold up in some films, but Robert Downey, Jr., has significant erotic appeal attached to his celebrity persona, which carries over into his portrayal of Tony Stark. Underlining Downey Jr.'s, appeal and adding to Iron Man's visual synecdoche, Stark's "high-tech prosthesis" required a style of filming that could switch between the external view of the Iron Man suit and Stark inside the suit. Thus, whenever Stark is inside the suit, the framing switches between wide shots of the suit in action and close-ups of Stark's face behind the suit's head's up display (HUD) in front of a black background. These tightly framed close-ups and the miniature arc reactor's light work together to form Stark's visual synecdoche. Stark's visual synecdoche is also unusual in that it includes his face, largely preventing the fragmentation and objectification effects of a missing limb or an assistive device. Because Stark's impairment is literally in his chest and his prosthesis requires a tight focus on his face, the *Iron Man* films (2008, 2010, 2013) are unusual in that they insist on the protagonist's humanity and identity, despite fragmentation and the creation of a visual synecdoche. An insistence on humanity also subverts the asexual objectification that often comes from the filmic stare. Close-ups are also helpful for underscoring small impairment details, affecting audience emotions, and serving as the anchors for the construction of the stare.

In the filmic stare, medium and wide shots establish larger-scale visual impairments (e.g., Stark inside the Iron Man suit) and make visible the breaking of social and behavioral scripts that often accompany the representation of mental impairments. Close-ups might affect the viewer and draw their attention to a specific impairment or prosthesis, but staring requires the visibility of the impairment in a wider frame. In a close-up of a non-normative body or assistive device, it is impossible to ignore the visual reality of disability. Wide and medium shots allow directors to compose the mise-en-scène to subtly highlight disabilities or downplay them by removing them from the frame. The techniques for stressing or suppressing a disability and impairment are slightly different depending on whether the impairment and disability in question is physical or mental (McCarthy 2021).

For physical disabilities, the medium and wide shots serve to contextualize a character's impairment. The *Iron Man* films (2008, 2010, 2013) are centered on the visibility of Stark's suits, so the wide and medium shots serve as action shots, and as the wide/medium highlight of Stark's prosthesis in action. Referring to the suits as prostheses and then using them to perform heroics, however, creates a visual foundation for the overcoming narrative that surrounds Stark. Narratively, the suits allow Stark to overcome his selfish lifestyle and become a superhero; as a high-tech prosthesis, they allow Stark to overcome the blow to masculinity that so often accompanies a physical disability and the stigma that accompanies an acquired physical disability.

Because mental impairments are "invisible," directors fall back on breaking verbal and behavioral social scripts to show these disabilities. Behavioral abnormalities require a wide frame in which the actor can move freely, so when a mental impairment is involved in a scene, the shot is often framed loosely. A clear example of the need for a wider frame and depth of field is the high angle, medium shot of Stark and Potts in bed, when Potts wakes up and tries to wake Stark from a night terror in *Iron Man 3* (2013). There is so much distance between Stark and the camera in this shot, even though a sleeping Stark does not technically need the loose framing and depth of field to express the behavioral break. A second example is when Stark is in Tennessee exploring the explosion that was thought to be a suicide bomb, and he experiences another panic attack. In a shot with deep focus, loose framing, and a significant depth of field, Stark runs down an alley toward the camera, bounces gently off the wall, and then sinks to his knees in the snow. These cinematographic techniques underscore the fact that the mental impairment exists only in Stark's mind; it is not visible to Potts, director Shane Black, or the viewers. The impairment is entirely Stark's, and it isolates him significantly. The disability comes from the sudden shift in Stark's inability to adhere to society's largely unspoken verbal and behavioral scripts. Since mental impairments are problematic to show in a visual medium, medium and wide shots are critical to the filmic stare because they explain the disruption of behavior highlighted by loose framing, deep focus, and depth of field.

Ultimately, both prosthesis and disability must be overcome for Stark to get the traditional happy ending. At the *Iron Man 3* (2013) conclusion, Stark detonates all his suits and undergoes surgery to remove the shrapnel in his chest from the first *Iron Man* (2008) movie. As the film wraps up with these concluding scenes, *Iron Man 3* (2013) suggests that Stark and Potts will finally have a successful romantic relationship because Stark has moved beyond his disability through a kill or cure logic.

Iron Man in Isolation

Garland-Thomson (1997) argues that persons with disabilities cannot win because they either suffer privately for passing or they end up as "supplicants and minstrels" (13). Stark, dying of palladium poisoning in *Iron Man 2* (2010), exemplifies the cost of passing as he alternates between "expert showmanship"—a kinder term than minstrel—and still, silent moments alone backstage checking his blood toxicity levels during the opening ceremony of the Stark Expo. These contrasted sequences early in the film neatly encapsulate Norden's (1994) general thesis for physical disability in film: "most movies have tended to isolate disabled characters from their able-bodied peers as well as from each other" (1). Stark is the only character with a disability in the first two films, and when viewers meet Aldrich Killian in film three, Stark himself dismisses the physically non-normative man. In doing so, Stark creates resentment and the Mandarin, and the film perpetuates the trope of casting characters with orthopedic impairments as villains, which Norden (1994) argues became entrenched in film in the early-to-mid 1910s (51). However, if critics focus only on the accuracy of a representation, the conversation stops at "yes, give them an Oscar," or "no, burn the witch." Especially for medically inaccurate representation, it is critical to understand how the representation is constructed cinematographically and how filmic stare elements reconnect to thematic arcs. For example, in *Iron Man* (2008), Obadiah Stane (played by Jeff Bridges) leverages the tendency to stop the conversation to increase the imbalance of power and control between himself and Stark. When Stark returns to the U.S. from Afghanistan, he only has a physical disability. Stane invents a case of PTSD, misrepresenting Stark's lived (and living) experience of acquiring a physical disability to have an injunction granted that removes Stark from the power structure of his own multi-national, multi-billion-dollar weapons corporation. Extradiegetic consequences are rarely as steep as losing control over an entire company. Still, stigma and a social taboo against in-depth discussions of the way disabilities—or representations of disabilities—are constructed increase the power imbalance between temporarily able-bodied individuals and individuals with disabilities. Due to the sudden betrayal from a close associate,

Stark becomes even more reclusive about his impairments. The added reclusiveness is reflected in how Stark's visual synecdoches are integrated into the narrative arc of the three films.

Stark's visual synecdoches are typically only visible in private spaces after Stane's betrayal, often in intimate moments. The contrast between these private moments and the very public events where the glow of the arc reactor is hidden—e.g., the senate hearing, the infamous "I am Iron Man" press conference, and the opening of the Stark Expo—reinforces Stark's attempts to pass as physically abled. Thus, the privacy of the impairments and their consequences are witnessed primarily by Potts and viewers, and even Potts is not privy to the extreme close-ups on Stark's face when he is inside the Iron Man suit.

Since no other character in the film can witness the synecdoche that humanizes Stark inside the suit, this second synecdoche reflects how the suit is both a space of isolation and an instrument for passing. The high-tech suit allows Stark to do tasks that even the U.S. Army struggles to accomplish and creates a mythology around the suit that also changes the mythology surrounding Stark Industries and Tony himself. Characters who perceive just the Iron Man suit, not the pilot inside, may assume that the pilot is in some way superhuman. The same elision of pilot and suit occurs in Rhodes' assumption of the Iron Patriot and War Machine personae. Diegetically, this elision masks both Stark's physical impairment and the mental impairment present in Stark during the bar scene at the beginning of *Iron Man 3* (2013), when Stark, experiencing a severe panic attack, runs for the suit and hides while JARVIS runs diagnostics. Outside the suit, neither Rhodes nor the gathered crowd understand what Stark is experiencing; the suit isolates the pilot from the rest of the world. Viewers are privy to the events taking place inside the suit, and in frame is Stark's in-suit synecdoche: his own face in extreme close-up, behind the suit's faceplate's HUD. As Stark grapples with his mental impairment inside the suit, the film insists on humanizing Stark for the extradiegetic audience; his visual synecdoche keeps viewers right in Stark's face, resisting fragmentation.

In resisting fragmenting Stark, however, the film also isolates him. Cutting away from Stark's face during his panic attack at the bar, Rhodes perplexedly knocks on the suit, waiting for Stark to snap out of it. Rhodes even attempts to call Stark back to socially normative behavior by saying, "Come on man, this isn't a good look, open up" (*Iron Man 3* 2013). Optics are prioritized over the individual's well-being in the public space, both within the film's diegesis and in the extradiegetic cinema space, from wherein the viewers watch the film. Rhodes' attempt to nudge Stark into keeping up appearances comes from the same fundamental place that the "Ugly Laws" (Berger 2013, 7–8) in the U.S. did: privileging able-bodiedness and maintaining the status quo of compulsory able-bodiedness in public spaces. Even though Stark is isolated within the privacy of the Iron Man suit, the suit itself is in a public parking lot, and the suit can and does mimic the physical collapse Stark experiences in the wake of his panic attack. Stark gets to the suit, gets inside it, and falls to one knee because he has entered a private space. The fact that the private space telegraphs body language and signals distress is what invites a diegetic version of Garland-Thomson's stare (1975, 37–38). Iron Man is the object of the stares from the crowd and Rhodes; these stares reflect confusion at unusual behavior that breaks social scripts, and they make Rhodes, at least, visibly uncomfortable. In this case, the suit is doing double duty: it is a private space that isolates Stark in the aftermath of a panic attack while simultaneously serving as a prosthesis that elicits stares from onlookers and signals the presence of mental impairment. The film represents the stare diegetically but extradiegetically uses the filmic stare to humanize Stark. In essence, the filmic stare is here being used to construct a relationship with a popular character with a disability in a way that seems disability positive. Ultimately, however, the filmic stare also reveals that the *Iron Man* films (2008, 2010, 2013) reproduce ableist narrative patterns.

Viewers witness ableist narrative patterns through Stark's relationship with Rhodes (one of his best friends and supporters) and the differences in how Rhodes addresses Stark's physical and mental impairments. When Stark is rescued from Afghanistan, Rhodes insists that next time, Stark "ride with [him]" (*Iron Man* 2008). Rhodes' response is playful, relieved, and tacitly acknowledges Stark's physical and emotional trauma. When Stark experiences a panic attack, however, Rhodes minimizes it by repeating the tired cliché, "Just calm down" (*Iron Man 3* 2013). Rhodes, however, is not privy to as many private moments as Potts is, and it is in Stark's relationship with Potts that echoes of the kill or cure narrative are present.

The synecdoche that most significantly represents Stark's travels along the kill or cure narrative path and his relationship with Potts is the miniaturized arc reactor. In public (or any time Stark wears a tie), the tell-tale glow from the reactor implanted in Stark's chest is hidden. In private, the reactor is almost always casually visible through Stark's shirts. In the intimate space of Stark's workshop/garage, the reactor and implant apparatus are apparent directly. Rhodes witnesses several significant moments in this personal space (replacing the mark I reactor in Stark's chest after Stane steals the mark II in *Iron Man* [2008]; watching Stark replace a depleted palladium core with a fresh one in *Iron Man 2* [2010]). Besides Stark himself, Potts is the character with the most intimate relationship with Stark's impairments. As Stark's assistant, she manages his playboy lifestyle before his kidnapping, and after Stark returns, Potts assists in swapping out the mark I arc reactor for the mark II (*Iron Man* 2008). She also bears witness to the effects Stark's nightmares have on the autonomous suit in *Iron Man 3* (2013).

As with Rhodes, Potts's response to Stark's mental impairment is significantly different from her reaction to Stark's physical impairment. When Stark lands in California in the first film, Potts, like Rhodes, greets Stark with playful relief, quipping that she "hates job hunting" (*Iron Man* 2008). When Stark accidentally summons a suit in the middle of the night in response to a nightmare, his terrified "Don't go" is met with a hard, "I'm going to sleep downstairs. Tinker with that" (*Iron Man 3* 2013). Arguably, Stark's tinkering with the Iron Man suits and miniaturized arc reactor are coping mechanisms; building the first arc reactor allows him to cope with the shrapnel in his chest, and upgrading it allows him to feel in control of his body and impairment. The first suit initially helps Stark cope with the fact that he is being held by a terrorist cell. However, once Stark is safely stateside again, the need for coping mechanisms still exists. In *Iron Man 3* (2013), however, Potts characterizes Stark's work on the suits as a "distraction" from his responsibilities and relationship. Potts actively minimizes Stark's disabilities by referring to his coping mechanisms as distractions. Although she never explicitly says, "Stop tinkering or I'm leaving you," her minimization evokes the logic of kill or cure. Either Stark cures his need for his coping mechanisms—and by implication cures his impairments—or Potts will kill their relationship.

Norden (1994) discusses kill or cure, the "not-so-hidden philosophy of mainstream society toward its physically disabled minority" (107), in feature-length silent-era films, noting that the perceived threat of the other, in this case, a person with a disability is neutralized either by transforming the other into part of the self or by condemning and (if possible) annihilating the other. Separating Iron Man, the superhero in the "hot-rod red" suit (*Iron Man* 2008), from Tony Stark is how mainstream society transformed a superhero into part of the collective self. Stark is visually and functionally separate enough from Iron Man to also need to be either transformed or annihilated. Potts's minimization of Stark's coping mechanism and her implied threat to end the relationship if Stark does not focus more time and energy on her fundamentally suggests that Stark being disabled is "too other" to make a relationship work. A plot hole augments this sense of being too other, especially when Stark decides to remove the shrapnel from his chest after blowing up his suits. The question of why Stark undergoes the operation in film three rather than film one is interesting. The arc reactor powers an electromagnet that prevents the shrapnel from piercing Stark's heart, but why wait to remove the shrapnel until the end of the third film? The answer has to be because the choice to have the shrapnel removed is motivated by the kill or cure dynamic set up by Potts in *Iron Man 3* (2013) after the symptoms of Stark's mental impairment surface. At the end of *Iron Man 3* (2013), the surgery sequence neatly resolves the kill or cure relationship dynamic of the overall narrative arc of the films.

At the end of *Iron Man 3* (2013), the surgery sequence also uses the filmic stare in some interesting ways to reflect the underlying kill or cure narrative. The first wide shot in the sequence is a high angle shot of Stark lying bare-chested on a surgical table to reveal the arc reactor. This shot recalls a similar moment in film one when Stark wakes up in a cave in Afghanistan, chest covered in bandages. In *Iron Man* (2008), the overhead shot was paired with an extreme close-up on the implanted electromagnet, highlighting the physical impairment and memorably introducing Iron Man's visual synecdoche. Coming full circle in *Iron Man 3* (2013), however, the high angle shot in the surgical suite is wider than the overhead shot in *Iron Man* (2008) to reflect the mental impairment that has been with Stark throughout this film and includes the physical impairment centrally in frame with its own miniature spotlight. The lighting highlights the visual synecdoche of the physical impairment, allowing the mise-en-scène to encapsulate all the disabilities Stark has existed with up to this point in the films in a single image. The next shot is an extreme close-up of Stark's hand giving a thumbs up before the camera racks focus on revealing Potts and Rhodes waiting outside the surgical suite for a fully cured Stark to emerge. The editing of the surgery sequence in *Iron Man 3* (2013) breaks the visual parallel established with *Iron Man* (2008) and highlights that Stark is now being cured of his impairments. Impairments is plural in this instance because although *Iron Man 3* (2013) never explicitly addresses the cure of Stark's mental impairment, the filmic stare and the editing break from the pattern established in *Iron Man* (2008) imply that, with the resolution of the physical impairment, so too is the mental impairment resolved. Essentially, the filmic stare explicates the visual construction of the process of curing Stark as the film's narrative adheres to Norden's (1994) pattern of kill or cure and the last stage of Mitchell and Snyder's (2000) narrative prosthesis, wherein the central conflict of the film is resolved simultaneously with the disability. The filmic stare highlights that, even in 2013, that the kill or cure logic is insidiously interwoven in popular narrative film, even within those narratives that might seem, on the surface, to be disability positive.

Conclusion

As the existence of Superman's Fortress of Solitude and Batman's Batcave testify, the isolation of superheroes is not a new phenomenon.

Norden (1994) and Garland-Thomson (1975, 1997) demonstrate that the othering, isolation, and kill or cure narratives surrounding characters with disabilities are widespread in popular and literary fiction and cinema. The MCU's *Iron Man* films (2008, 2010, 2013) follow these traditions, but it is the filmic stare that allows viewers and scholars to tease apart narrative, story, and superhero mythologies to understand the construction of visual representations of disability. By identifying the visual synecdoches that stand as shorthand for Stark's physical and mental impairments and exploring the interconnected network of cinematographic techniques surrounding those synecdoches, the use of the filmic stare reveals how Stark's narrative arc subtly reiterates ableist assumptions about disabilities and the individuals who live with them.

Overcoming narratives can seem benign; who does not want to witness a charismatic, popular character become more than just an impairment? However, the filmic stare helps to reveal the ableist building blocks behind overcoming narratives, and the layers of privilege built into Stark's life underline how insidious overcoming can be. Without the miniaturized arc reactor, Stark is a billionaire, the genius CEO of a major weapons and technology company, and he has people around him who care deeply about him. The centralization of the impairments Stark deals with throughout the three *Iron Man* films (2008, 2010, 2013) demonstrates how an impairment is assumed to take over someone's whole life. Yes, needing the arc reactor to prevent a painful death becomes a central concern to Stark, but as the development of the Stark Expo and other projects suggest, Stark is still actively engaged in the rest of his life. The assumption that Stark must overcome his obsessive focus on the arc reactor is as ridiculous as the idea that he must overcome his disabilities to have a successful relationship with Potts. Understanding the visual building blocks of an overcoming narrative using the filmic stare underscores how pervasive and ingrained ableist ideas are. Even Iron Man, who is integrated into the cultural mythos, is not immune from the requirements of overcoming narratives in popular culture.

REFERENCES

Berger, Ronald J. 2013. *Introducing Disability Studies.* New York: Lynne Rienner Publishers.
Black, Shane, dir. 2013. *Iron Man 3.* Burbank, CA: Walt Disney Studios Motion Picture.
Brown, Steven E. 2015. "Disability Culture and the ADA." *Disability Studies Quarterly 35* (3). doi: 10.18061/dsq.v35i3.
Favreau, Jon, Dir. 2008. *Iron Man.* Hollywood, CA: Paramount Pictures.
_____. 2010. *Iron Man 2.* Hollywood, CA: Paramount Pictures.
Foundas, Scott. 2013. "Iron Man 3 Review." *Variety.* April 24. https://variety.com/2013/film/reviews/iron-man-three-review-1200413714/.

Garland-Thomson, Rosemarie. 1997. *Extraordinary Bodies: Figuring Physical Disability in American Culture and Literature*. New York: Columbia UP.

_____. 1975. *Staring: How We Look*. New York: Oxford UP.

Hobgood, Allison P., and David Houston Wood. 2013. *Recovering Disability in Early Modern England*. Columbus: Ohio State UP.

Langley, Travis. 2013. "Does Iron Man 3's Hero Suffer from Posttraumatic Stress Disorder?" *Psychology Today*. May 3. https://www.psychologytoday.com/us/blog/beyond-heroes-and-villains/201305/twitter-takes-iron-man-3-why-cant-tony-stark-sleep.

McCarthy, Grace. 2021. *Shakespearean Drama, Disability, and the Filmic Stare*. New York: Routledge.

Mulvey, Laura. 1975. "Visual Pleasure and Narrative Cinema." *Screen 16* (3): 6–18. 10.1093/screen/16.3.6.

Oxford English Dictionary (OED). 2018. "kill, V." OED Online. Oxford University Press.

Mitchell, David T., and Sharon Snyder. 2000. *Narrative Prosthesis: Disability and the Dependencies of Discourse*. Ann Arbor: University of Michigan Press.

Norden, Martin. 1994. *The Cinema of Isolation: A History of Physical Disability in the Movies*. New Brunswick, NJ: Rutgers University Press.

Tech as Ableist Tool

Understanding the Role of Disability
in the Arrowverse Series

Courtney Stanton

The *Arrowverse* is a collection of four television shows and numerous web series broadcast by the CW network and centered on the adventures of various DC Comics heroes. The shared universe began with the premiere of *Arrow*, which follows the transformation of wealthy party-boy Oliver Queen into the eponymous hero of Star City in 2012. Spin-off *The Flash* quickly followed in 2014, followed by *Supergirl* in 2015, and *Legends of Tomorrow* in 2016. The shows have followed the rich tradition within comics of reimagining many of their prominent characters and storylines while remaining true to their conceptual roots. Each has amassed a strong following among viewers. This popularity is furthered by exclusive licensing deals between the CW and Netflix, which began in 2011, allowing Netflix to broadcast new seasons almost immediately after they finish airing in prime time. Akin to the Marvel Cinematic Universe, within which countless characters interact across many films, the *Arrowverse* shows are rich with crossovers and Easter eggs, crafting history and depth which help balance its more fantastical elements. Through twenty combined seasons (and counting), the shows have established an expansive and complex world in which characters combine otherworldly powers with wondrous technology to protect their shared universe.

This analysis focuses on the essential but troubling role that technology plays within this collection of shows. Technology helps characters track, capture, and contain villains and protect their complicated dual identities. In many instances, such as the Flash's protective suit or Felicity Smoak's vast bank of computers, they are nearly inextricable from a character's contributions. The technology of the Arrowverse reveals a glaring omission in an otherwise unique path toward diversity. The shows represent an impressive array of races, genders, ages, sexual orientations, and even spiritualities. Where they are sorely lacking, however, is in their representation of disability identity.

Throughout the *Arrowverse's* prime time run, various characters have acquired disability identities in some form or another, often from injuries sustained during clashes with criminals. However, disability is rarely portrayed as anything other than temporary and easily surmountable via technological intervention. In other cases, disability identity is disguised or—when showrunners take liberties with the original comic material—ignored entirely. Given the broad reach of the shows on the CW and Netflix, viewers must carefully consider how they impact disability identity and representation of disability. To do this, this analysis centers primarily on the Arrowverse's two longest-running shows, *Arrow* (2012–2020) and *The Flash* (2014–present), not only because they offer the most examples but also because *Supergirl* and *Legends of Tomorrow*, interestingly, largely avoid disability altogether. This analysis also focuses exclusively on physical disability, for while the Arrowverse offers examples of intellectual and emotional disability, the complexities of said experiences and the distinctions between realms of disability are beyond the scope of this analysis. These points of focus will hopefully illustrate that despite frequently working at the complicated intersection of disability and technology, these shows do so by devaluing the former.

The shows are analyzed through two controversial frames for disability representation, the freak show, and the transhumanist future, to illustrate fundamental problems with the shows' portrayals that introduce the role technology plays in reinforcing them. The Arrowverse exhibits many of the same dangerous and demeaning tropes as freak shows of old. Using the traits of the freak show outlined by Rosemarie Garland-Thomson in *Extraordinary Bodies* (1997), the analysis illustrates how the shows often stage and sensationalize characters with disabilities in ways that mirror the treatment of "freak"-ivied individuals. The shows deviate significantly from this framework in their general lack of scientific and techno-driven narratives for characters with disabilities. It is from this lack that the dangers of the transhumanist future which these shows project emerge. To more mindfully portray disability within the techno-centric Arrowverse and better showcase the fluidity of human identity, the Arrowverse must move away from transhumanism and embrace a more posthumanism view of body and identity. These concepts along with suggestions for how to enact this change will be discussed later in this essay.

The Influence of Technology and Media on Cultural Conceptions of Disability

From low-tech items like pencil grips and canes to the high-tech world of modern prosthetics and assistive computers, there is a long history of functional relationships between disability and technology (Williamson 2019). Technological advancement is a powerful ally for people with disabilities, not only regarding how it impacts function, comfort, and access. As advances achieved through universal design initiatives become integrated into everyday spaces, for instance, they serve to highlight how the world has for so long been designed with only certain types of users in mind. Universally designed tech impels humans to consider the profound cultural implications of objects and spaces—elevators, hallways, touch screens—that we might otherwise consider culture-free. Thus, perceiving technology through the lens of disability highlights the significant relationship between technological choices and fundamental values like freedom and equity.

This relationship is not without complication, however. Technology helps shape our understanding of what qualifies as a disability, in ways that become less apparent over time. David Braddock and Susan Parish (2001) summarize this reality succinctly by saying, "Throughout Western history, disability has existed at the intersection between the particular demands of a given impairment, society's interpretation of that impairment, and the larger political and economic context of disability" (11). In other words, while impairment refers to a specific biological condition, disability entails a complex web of social factors determining how that impairment is understood, and technology has long played a fundamental role in this perception. For example, a nearsighted individual would be said to have a disability throughout history, but eyeglass technology is now so ubiquitous that the label no longer applies. When someone uses a calculator for simple arithmetic or a car for traversing short distances, such actions are not perceived as a disability, even if their use occurs within the context of cognitive or physical impairment because these technologies are so deeply enmeshed in the broader culture. They have become tools of convenience rather than assistance, reflecting how humans choose to understand the need for them as well as ability more generally. Similarly, as smart technology becomes more innovative and accessible, humans' understanding of visual, hearing, and fine-motor skill impairments will continue to change (Haraway 2006). This is not to suggest that technological advancement will eradicate disability, but to understand that the two are inextricably intertwined. Technology, for better and worse, substantially impacts our broader cultural understanding of disability.

Along with shaping our fundamental definitions of disability, however, technology is often represented within media as a means to reduce or eliminate disability, casting disability identity as a temporary or in-between phase of existence. This portrayal is rooted in a conception of the body as a physiobiological machine, with technology playing the part of the trusty repairman, armed with ableist tools. This understanding of the body is unsurprising. From the Industrial Revolution forward, machines have become increasingly integrated into even the smallest details of our daily lives. Thus, it was inevitable that machines would cross the threshold from influence to embodiment. Yet, the conflation of bodies and machines fails to acknowledge that bodies are malleable, ever-changing, and continually defined by context, in ways that machines are not. While machines *are* designed for specific purposes, and a machine that does not achieve its intended purpose can be labeled broken and in need of repair, assigning such fixed value to human bodies, on the other hand, is an untenable proposition. It leads only to supposedly objective— but in truth, quite arbitrary—scales of physical value. Who is to say that the tactile sensitivity developed by a blind person is inherently less valuable than the visual abilities of a sighted one? Or that the paralympic champion's body is automatically inferior to the able-bodied couch potatos, simply because it was not born with four full limbs? Moving beyond this body-as-machine paradigm clarifies that perceiving technology as a means to break free from disability, rather than as a force that works in tandem with it is problematic. As the subsequent analysis shows, portraying technology as a bodily panacea leads to a harmful understanding of embodiment and a pernicious devaluing of disability identity.

This portrayal can be observed most clearly through mass media representations of disability, such as the shows of the Arrowverse, and a central assumption of this essay is that such media function as much more than a source of entertainment. They are part of what Stuart Hall (1997) calls the "circuit of culture," which entails the interconnected processes of production, consumption, regulation, representation, and identity (1). Television programs, films, graphic novels, comics, music, and literature are produced and consumed to represent various aspects of culture which informs audiences about demographic groups and social practices. The circuit continues as these particular understandings influence the production and consumption of subsequent media, and how they will be regulated and represented. Understanding media through this model illustrates not only the complexity but also the magnitude of media influence.

Moreover, Hall's (1997) conception of media influence also complicates the process of meaning-making. Mary Talbot (2007) explains how his ideas take "issue with the simplistic notion of communication as a sender-message-receiver chain, in which the message being transmitted was assumed to have a transparently recognizable content. A semiotic understanding of language was central to his challenge to the notion of message transparency" (7). What his model illustrates is that meaning is not created simply through explicit, linear communication. Many layers of meaning exist beyond this surface, which audience members can be expected to understand through a culturally specific lens. Hall elaborates: "we give things meaning by how we *represent* them—the words we use about them, the stories we tell about them, the images of them we produce, the emotions we associate with them, the ways we classify and conceptualize them" (1997, 3). At its most basic, the Arrowverse is a network of language acts, dense and complex symbols that convey meaning to viewers. As a prominent contributor to the cultural circuit—prominent in audience size and enduring, culturally iconic narratives—its role in creating cultural meaning is significant.

Disability, within this cultural circuit, has traditionally not fared well. Throughout most of history, popular media has been populated with only the most stereotypical representations of disability identity, ranging from the supercrip, the heroic individual who overcomes all impairments and surpasses expectations, to the burden, an unending source of inconvenience and obligation. In "The Invisible Cultural Group: Images of Disability," Jack A. Nelson (2003) analyzes prominent disability stereotypes to suggest that "Of all the stereotypes about the disabled that plague the public, none is so insidious as the one that dwells inside the mind because of being exposed to all the media stereotypes" (1–2). The most enduring disability stereotypes are those that strip disability identity of political and social context. Such representations are easier to handle narratively and absolve the audience of cultural responsibility for disability experience (Darke 2004; Mogk 2013; Mitchell and Snyder 2000). Given the misrepresentation of disability throughout mass media history, and the harm it inflicts on individuals and the broader cultural conception of disability experience, exploring the meaning behind a popular cultural product such as the Arrowverse is crucial to building an enriched cultural understanding of disability.

The Arrowverse as Freak Show

Fittingly, the first lens through which I view the Arrowverse represents one of the earliest popular exhibitions of disability to the general public: the freak show. Freak shows had their heyday in nineteenth-century America, but as Rosemarie Garland-Thomson (1997) points out, the freak-as-spectacle has been a cultural convention for many centuries. "A fervent and persistent human impulse to account for corporeal exceptions surfaces in nearly every writer who casts his eye on the natural world," she notes, as "Every historical era reinterprets the figure of the prodigious monster or nature's caprice, the freak" (56). They faded out of public view during the twentieth century primarily due to an increasingly medicalized view of disability. Later, the sense of impropriety that came with society's somewhat more nuanced and sympathetic, albeit still very limited, understanding of disability identity lingered. Despite its recession from popular view, however, the freak show continues to be a focal point of critical disability studies, and the Arrowverse, notably *Arrow* and *The Flash*, fits within the modern freak show mold. As programs, they exhibit many characteristics particular to the freak show construct, creating a freak-spectator dynamic through various characters and their relationships to the audience. Just as Christopher Smit (2003) does in his discussion of the Jerry Lewis telethons, I frame my analysis of these shows as freak-centric according to traits suggested by Garland-Thomson in *Extraordinary Bodies* (1997), which serve to define the spectacle of the freak and highlight its impact on disability identity.

The first defining trait is the simplest and most fundamental—the staging of the body to make money. It is not enough for performers' bodies to simply be present and available for viewing; they must be arranged in ways that draw attention to and spectacularize their differences. Taking the form of a spotlighted stage or pit, the "freak platform" displays bodies and "[holds] the observer's gaze like a magnet, not only foregrounding the body on display, but exposing it in such a way that the physical traits presented as extraordinary dominate […] the entire person on exhibit" (Garland-Thomson 1997, 60–61). The performer's body is staged to highlight their otherness as clearly as possible and, in doing so, maintain a substantial distinction between themselves and the audience. Thus, there is a strange confluence of intimacy and distance encouraged by this arrangement, as viewers can visually explore the bodies before them but are also continually confronted with those qualities that distinguish spectacle from spectator.

A similar staging pattern is employed at various points within the Arrowverse, most clearly through *Arrow's* character Felicity Smoak. Felicity, the computer technology genius of *Arrow*, is hit by a bullet during a battle in the fourth season of *Arrow*. Throughout her intense—yet surprisingly brief—tenure as someone with paraplegia, her body and wheelchair are often framed to highlight her disability status. The first time the audience encounters Felicity out of the hospital, for instance, is in a tightly framed shot panning outward as she is slowly carried down her

apartment's stairs (Season 4, episode 11). Her disability is visually introduced through disempowerment, a moment of complete physical dependence on the person carrying her. Despite a long history of sharply
tailored, formal clothing and tidy blond ponytails, she is wearing loose-
fitting lounge clothes, her hair down and slightly unkempt. She is, these
visual clues confirm, not quite herself. Later in this episode, a character
running through a literal war zone is mirrored in the following scene by
Felicity wheeling through her apartment, frantically searching for her
medication, suggesting that she, too, is navigating a new battleground.
Felicity struggles with medication-induced hallucinations throughout
this episode. Somehow, despite the intensity of these visions and the profound disassociation she seems to be experiencing, she nevertheless processes her trauma by the episode's end through visual cues that confirm
this for viewers. She wheels into the Arrow team's headquarters appearing
like her former self, sharply dressed and coifed, indicating she has moved
expressly through her psychological trauma. She has done so entirely on
her own, reinforcing a further misperception that physical disabilities
should be navigated in isolation; she has transitioned through sheer force
of will, with no need for, or acknowledgment of, any broader community
support. Fittingly, the show's staging choices cease to highlight her struggle and instead simply emphasize the presence of her wheelchair. Felicity's
wheelchair is frequently used as a transition device over the next several
episodes, such as when the camera pans into its spokes and then out to a
new setting. Furthermore, when she rolls down a ramp the camera transitions seamlessly to characters on the move in following scenes.

Other disabilities in *The Flash* and *Arrow* are highlighted in similar ways. During the first season of *The Flash*, Harrison Wells is known to
other characters as having paraplegia. As the audience quickly realizes, he
has no disability, and cues similar to Felicity's clothing and hairstyle are
employed to maintain this distinction. While posing as one with paraplegia, Wells wears glasses, and camera shots often pan upward from his feet
on his chair's footrest as he enters a room. In scenes when the audience is
meant to identify him as his "true" self, he inevitably stands and removes
his glasses, even when it seems unwise or unnecessary. He does so, for
instance, when an unknowing character has *just* left the room, and when
he speeds off (he's a speedster just like Flash), he still displays the where-
withal to leave not just his wheelchair but also his eyeglasses behind (Season 1, episode 15). Physical cues are similarly staged in the case of John
Diggle, another member of Team Arrow, who has degenerative nerve
damage caused by a shrapnel injury affecting his right hand and, with it,
his ability to remain a part of the Arrow team. His injury is first intimated
during a moment of hesitation while out in the field with the team (Season

6, episode 1) but is later confirmed by numerous tightly-framed shots of his tremorous hand. In another episode of *The Flash*, the Flash (aka Barry Allen) travels to the future and finds another member of his team, Wally, has been injured; he walks into the man's home only to find him sitting alone and unresponsive in the middle of a room, sunlight streaming through and creating somber shadows all around his wheelchair (Season 3, episode 19). The significance of this visual is meant to be immediately clear—the villain Team Flash seeks has, through inflicting disability, ruined yet another life.

These moments of staging, like those of the traditional freak show, are meant to remind viewers that disability is present and significant. This seems like a positive admission—indeed, the shows *should* present disability as significant to each character's identity. Yet, this display of disability does not necessarily beget a complex representation. As Garland-Thomson (1997) explains, "On the freak show stage, a single, highlighted characteristic circumscribed and reduced the inherent human complexity of such figures as the Dwarf, the Giant, the Bearded Woman, the Armless of Legless Wonder, and the Fat Lady" (61). Through the perverse staging of the freak show, these multifaceted human beings come to be identified only synecdochally through their disabilities. Such extreme representations never occur within the Arrowverse, but the same reductive process worked in the previous examples. When the screen fills with the image of the Flash's old teammate, sunlight and shadows highlighting his disability, audiences are not meant to observe a man; more than anything else in this image, they should notice the wheelchair, and from this wheelchair understand what has happened. The scene is brief and offers almost no explanation of how Wally came to be this way, but the message that the season's villain has struck again is clear.

Along with these basic bodily exhibition techniques, Garland-Thomson (1997) also describes how the freak show is marked by a continual sales pitch that tantalizes and compels the viewer to participate in the spectacle. Furthermore, *Flash* and *Arrow* repeatedly use characters' disability status to increase dramatic tension and pull viewers along from one episode to the next. In the very first episode of *Arrow's* fourth season, viewers are shown a distraught Oliver standing at a fresh gravesite, and the identity of the unknown person within becomes an intense point of interest for countless fan sites and the season's "overarching mystery" (Leane 2016). In the episode immediately after Felicity is shot, the scene opens with a flashforward to the same graveside scene, as mourners stand over the grave and discuss an unnamed woman who has died. This suggests that perhaps Felicity is the one who has died, especially since the episode focuses on her time in the hospital. At the very end of the episode, viewers are shown that Felicity is still very much alive, waiting in a car at the cemetery. Withholding the revelation of Felicity's survival plays directly into fans' desire for answers, and the injury which disables her is merely a red herring in the larger gravesite mystery.

Similarly, *The Flash* emphasizes Wells' disability status, specifically its artificiality, to reveal his "true" character. By confining these glimpses almost exclusively to closing scenes, they compel viewers forward, and as countless reviews of the first season can attest, Wells' identity and motivation is the overarching mystery of the first half of season one. In the second episode of the series, he stands, much to the surprise of the adversary he proceeds to stab; in the very next episode, he is shown sitting cross-legged in his wheelchair, and by the end of the seventh episode he is shown walking about in his secret headquarters. These moments build suspense and are crucial to the season's narrative, but they unfortunately relegate disability as a cloaking device. Rather than a genuine facet of Wells' character, disability again becomes a mere narrative marker, a set of symbols—wheelchair, eyeglasses—for viewers to track, for hints of where the plot will take them next.

Also important to the freak show, Garland-Thomson (1997) explains the presence of an empathy-inducing, but often largely fabricated, personal narrative. Such stories amplify the impact of the spectacle, "transfigur[ing] what, for example, would have been in a mundane context an ordinary 'deformed darkey' into the 'Beast of Borneo,'" and, as a result, funneling more money into the pockets of those putting on the show (Garland-Thomson 1997, 61). Felicity's struggle with medication-induced hallucinations is a prime example of such narrative manipulation. She specifically hallucinates her younger self—again distinguished visually through brunette locks and goth-inspired style choices—who mocks her "pity party" and the life choices bringing her to this moment. Before this, Felicity had little struggle with her former life as a brunette, goth/punk hacker. Viewers are given only fleeting glimpses of her former lifestyle, and there is no suggestion that she longs to return to it. The severity of her hallucinations, then, is surprising and, quite simply, out of character. They may develop from her new medications, which is understandable. However, given that she presumably continues these medications well past a single episode, along with her remarkably complete emotional recovery during this episode, it is more likely that these scenes are a poorly-executed attempt to illustrate the emotional weight of Felicity's transition into disability status. Instead of following this journey more honestly, gradually and in ways more consistent with Felicity's backstory, the writers create an altogether too melodramatic experience that suggests disability is a brief, easily contained experience.

A similar use of personal narrative occurs with *Arrow's* Diggle, as another contrived storyline is imposed on his experience of disability. Diggle is generally presented as a man of great integrity, noble almost to a fault. Yet, almost immediately after Diggle's tremulous hand is revealed, he is also shown buying illegal drugs to treat it (Season 6, episode 3). Again, this is understandable to some extent, as he feels an intense responsibility to his team and, as a man of extreme stoicism, would prefer others not know about his injury. His reluctance to disclose his disability aligns with what has been written about disability and hegemonic masculinity (Brian and Trent Jr., 2017; Shakespeare 1999; Shuttleworth et al. 2012). Yet, as with Felicity, not only does this string of bad decisions not seem to track with what viewers already know about Diggle, but this experience with illicit drugs adds nothing but an extra bit of drama to his disability storyline. There is no ensuing addiction or confrontation over his drug use, and just as abruptly as it began, it falls completely out of the story, never to be mentioned again. The show identifies—most likely unintentionally—the ludicrousness of his behavior when another character jokes that he is quite offended that Diggle did not come directly to him for help with his injury. At this point in the show, multiple seasons after Felicity's quick bout of paraplegia, it stands out as quite odd for another major character not to seek the medical advice of the team's science and technology gurus. In both examples, it seems as if the show feels compelled to spice up the storylines, as if disability experiences alone will not be enough to compel viewers.

Before moving on to the final trait discussed by Garland-Thomson (1997), another should be considered as crucial to the freak show framework: transience and escape. From their early beginnings, freak shows have not been places of repose or rootedness. The traditional freak show was constructed as a temporary and uncomfortable experience, and the audience could view the spectacle always with an eye toward the exit. Immersed in the spectacle of disability, there was an ever-present sense of impermanence, as at any moment they could choose to retreat to the "real" world and leave the spectacle safely behind the curtain. Garland-Thomson (1997) describes the experience, saying, "The American [onlooker] is mobile, entering and exiting the show at will and ranging around the social order, but the freak is fixed, confined by the material structures and the conventions of the staging and socially immobilized by a deviant body" (65). One enters the performance space with the expectation of near-revulsion, and the urge to flee or avert one's eyes—and the thrill of resisting this urge and perhaps, to the contrary, allowing oneself to stare—is a crucial part of the experience. The show's architecture also plays into this sense of temporary thrill, as troupes traveled continuously, never staying in any one village or city for too long.

Likewise, the Arrowverse shows never focus all that long on any character's impairment. In reality people who acquire disabilities often face months and years of physical therapy, a steep learning curve for navigating a world that is generally not designed with them in mind, and a complex web of psychological and emotional responses to understand. Yet, while the Arrowverse narratives sometimes hint at these gradual realities, they generally adhere to the traditional medical model of disability, showing a consistent impatience toward fixing or curing characters' disabilities. For instance, after only a handful of episodes, Felicity is offered the opportunity to use an "implantable biostimulant" to restore the full use of her legs (Season 4, episode 14). Curtis, a colleague who develops the technology, and her physical therapist warn Felicity that restoring her full nervous system function will be a slow process. Yet, it is shockingly fast from the viewer's perspective. In the very next episode after learning of the biostimulant option, viewers witness her in an ostensibly arduous physical therapy session. Still, at the end of the episode, she slowly rises from her wheelchair and (after a fight with Oliver) walks out of their apartment, as steadily as if she had never missed a step (Season 4, episode 15). Not surprisingly, in the episodes that follow, no one seems to notice Felicity's lack of a wheelchair; it is as if her disability experience never occurred.

This and other examples suggest that the shows intend to present disability only when it works conveniently within current storylines and can be, as the need arises, dispatched easily. Fittingly, the only time that Felicity's disability reemerges is during season five, when an electromagnetic pulse disables the chip implanted in her spine. Yet, while her paralysis makes her escape from the team's headquarters all the more harrowing, she is mobile again by episode's end, having had a temporary replacement chip put in place even before she has had the time to wash the blood from her face (Season 5, episode 20). John Diggle's recovery period—if it should even be called that—is astonishingly brief as well. Curtis creates another implant similar to Felicity's to place in John's tremulous arm, and with little more than a swab of alcohol and a quick injection, Diggle's chip is in place. Later in the same episode, Curtis finds John doing handstand push-ups, a clear signal that he is now back to his exceptionally fit form (Season 6, episode 7). Moreover, in this same episode Diggle confides in Oliver that the nerve damage in his arm has spread to his back and, because of his drug use, has caused some permanent damage, yet nothing comes of this information. Diggle is shown going back into the field seamlessly, and, as with Felicity, his disability is never mentioned again.

Curtis's role as the inventor of all these gadgets serves as a metaphor for the oft ableist medical model of understanding disability. Within the medical model, individuals are encouraged to cure or fix their "broken" bodies through science and medicine. One has to wonder whether Curtis participates in this process of creating implants to "restore" the disabled body? Does he want to perpetuate ableist beliefs about the need to rehabilitate "abnormal" body types, or might he genuinely be seeking to remove one's pain?

Other characters like *The Flash's* Cisco Ramone and Malcolm Merlin experience disability in similarly fleeting ways. In the same episode during which Barry/Flash encounters the catatonic Wally, he also runs into a future version of teammate Cisco who has had both his hands removed by an accomplice of the season's reigning villain. This detail goes largely unnoticed for much of their encounter, however, as Cisco has somehow acquired, or perhaps constructed, a set of cybernetic prostheses that when covered with gloves are, both in form and function, indistinguishable from actual hands. Similarly, villain Malcolm Merlin has one of his hands cut off during a confrontation with Oliver, yet a few episodes later he reappears with a new cybernetic hand in place, again with unknown origins and hyper-realistic capabilities (Season 4, episode 18). Through these momentary glimpses, subsequently viewers experience a truncated, tempered form of disability. Like the traditional freak show audience, viewers of the *Arrowverse* shows are conditioned to perceive disability in impermanent terms only. In particular, the creators of the *Arrowverse* shows suggest that technology is the key to sidestepping the narrative and conceptual complexity of disability.

This leads to the final trait defining the freak show, according to Garland-Thomson (1997), which is science-based narratives, typically used to legitimize the disability on display—i.e., highlight the exotic and titillating qualities of the freaks themselves. Couched in descriptions filled with technical jargon and language meant to sound foreign to the casual spectator, performers became alluring. Unlike the previous freak show qualities, however, the shows of the *Arrowverse* shy away from this particular trend, generally offering viewers minimal explanation of the science behind characters' disabilities and their technology. Almost no details are shared about the chips implanted into Felicity and Diggle. As mentioned previously, the shows never even attempt to explain the prostheses acquired by Cisco and Malcolm; they simply appear, integrated seamlessly into their everyday lives. Likewise, when Barry/Flash finds teammate Wally using a wheelchair in a future timeline, there is no narrative attempt to explain why the man, as a fellow speedster, previously exhibited the ability to heal even severe injuries to his body at super speeds but now, for some reason, must use a wheelchair. As usual, the disability is convenient to the storyline, and consideration of the scientific or technological particulars is perceived as an unnecessary distraction.

The lack of scientific and technological dialogue surrounding characters' disabilities is significant and troubling for several reasons. Techno-driven dialogue is simply part and parcel of the Arrowverse, for one thing, as all of the shows are filled with, and appeal to, proud science and computer brainiacs who are continually MacGyver-ing their ways out of seemingly impossible jams. Thus, the lack of scientific or technological context to support the disability storylines is out of character. Perhaps this originates from narrative laziness or is to be expected from fantasy writing of this sort. It is certainly not the show's responsibility to make all of its science explicit and verifiable; therein, lies the fantasy. Still, the obvious eschewing of this responsibility in the face of disability suggests an uncritical transhumanist ideology which can be extremely dangerous to disability identity. The lack of explanation for implants and prostheses, for lightning-quick recoveries and a complete lack of residual trauma, gives clues to how the Arrowverse depicts reality and envisions science and technology—as well as the bodies upon which they act—of the future.

As this section ends, it is worth noting that while some may argue that the freak show can be reappropriated as an empowering disability identity, this claim is suspect. In his discussion of the Lewis telethon, Smit (2003) argues that there "is a discourse of power between the spectacle and the spectator wherein both the observer and the observed share the power of the telethon event. The spectacle has shown its power by raising a pledge vis-à-vis its allure, and the spectator feels it by making the pledge itself." While he is right to point out that this effect is "neither permanent nor fixed," it is questionable that any such empowerment occurs at all given that power resides with the able-bodied creators and producers of the telethon. Amy Vidali (2007) critiques Smit (2003) directly, rightly pointing out that his "slip from seeing the spectacle as empowered to imagining the people who participate in, or are represented by, the spectacle as empowered is erroneous. The Jerry Lewis telethon is perhaps empowering only because it earns money; it is largely disempowering because of the message it sends about and to people with disabilities" (633–4). While freak shows may have offered individuals with disabilities a means to earn a wage, and thus exhibit autonomy and self-reliance, such gains carry little weight in the face of the broader cultural ramifications of such representations of disability. Likewise, David Mitchell and Sharon Snyder (2005) examine the potential space for performer agency within the freak show and conclude that "even a systemic critique of the freak show offers little salvage from its dehumanizing effects." Thus, it comes as little surprise that characters with disabilities never seem to last very long in the Arrowverse. Only when they find ways to ditch their impairments are they folded back into their respective teams.

Taking the view that freak shows do not offer narratives of empowerment, there is little for the Arrowverse to do with this frame but to resist it, perhaps using Garland-Thomson's (1997) traits as a starting point. Its writers must incorporate disability for purposes other than to build suspense or emphasize character drama, and they need to stop portraying disability as an essentially temporary experience and be willing to develop a character who views the world through the lens of disability identity—which will, through the circuit of culture, encourage viewers to do the same. As the next section will discuss, they also need to think carefully about the ideal future which they choose to portray.

Making the Shift from Transhumanism to Posthumanism in the Arrowverse

While the concepts of transhumanism and posthumanism are often discussed in overlapping ways, there are significant distinctions between the two that must be fleshed out within discussions of disability representation. Transhumanism refers to the basic belief that humans can evolve beyond their strictly biological capacities, through technological and scientific intervention (More and Vita-More 2013; Manzocco 2019). In contrast, posthumanism refers to an ideology that questions the basic definitions of humanness, what it means to be, and what qualifies as, human (Nayar 2014; Braidotti 2013). Both concepts deal with human beings' relationships with science and technology, but whereas transhumanism explores ways that these forces can work to fortify and enhance the human experience, posthumanism seeks to disrupt and potentially redefine the boundaries between humans and nonhumans. Subsequent analysis aims to show that while the Arrowverse currently tends to project a transhumanist view of humans and their relationships between science and technology, this disruptive essence of posthumanism makes a more productive framework for representations of disability.

From the perspective of disability, one might argue that while the Arrowverse examples discussed thus far are examples of attempts to fix disability, they are not strictly transhumanist. Scholars (Hall 2017; Fletcher 2014) have written about the important distinction between therapy and enhancement, explaining a difference between *restoring* one's natural/original capabilities and *adding to* one's natural/original abilities. The latter is, they claim, more properly labeled transhumanist. One could, for instance, view Felicity's spinal chip and Cisco's prostheses as examples of simple therapy, meant to restore initial abilities and not transhumanist. Yet, they do not know what these fixes are capable of and, more importantly, they endow the bodies with invulnerability and regenerative quality that they would not have had otherwise. This is, in and of itself, transhumanistic. The quickness with which Curtis whips up a new spinal chip for Felicity after her first one was damaged, for instance, suggests that she will be forever privy to a fully functioning spine. In an immediate sense this may qualify as therapy, but the lasting promise of functionality—not to mention affordability and easy access—certainly qualifies as an enhancement.

A transhumanist lens need not explicitly or intentionally conceive of technology as a means to eradicate disability—a ticket out, within the freak show narrative—to carry with it the potential implication of a future in which disability does not exist. How a culture defines and values disability stems largely from fundamental assumptions about the body itself, and the transhumanistic perspective is typically one which views the body as a fragile construction and science and technology as the means to overcome this fragility. This set of beliefs, for many, positions transhumanism in direct odds with the efforts of critical disability theory. In "Transhuman Perfection: The Eradication of Disability Through Transhuman Technologies," David-Jack Fletcher (2014) discusses the transhumanist striving for bodily perfection and argues that disability may be a primary impetus for this transhumanist vision, as viewing disability "as a threat to the mythical 'pure human' can ultimately position the human as fragile," and "it is possibly this fear of fragility that drives the human to pursue the dream of perfection through technology" (82). Melinda Hall (2017) likewise asserts that transhumanism "plays upon fears of disablement" and that "transhumanist thinkers emphasize the facility of the body and its susceptibility to *risk*" (23). "Instead of seeing disability as a complex interrelationship between the body, social structures, and social norms," she argues, "disability becomes the outcome of a too-complacent posture toward death and 'technophobia'" (24). This assumption of a link between disability and technophobia communicates deeply held beliefs about disability's categorically negative value, that disability is inferior to ability. For the transhumanist, then, its persistence is merely a sign of Ludditism that can hopefully be overcome. Joel Michael Reynolds (2017) refers to these assumptions about disability as the "ableist conflation," which he defines as "the conflation of disability with pain and suffering," through which "disability is both a sign and cause of existential dis-ease and dis-order" (150). Through the transhumanist lens, disability is often conceived of as unquestionably undesirable and crucial evidence of the need for transhumanist innovation.

The shows of the *Arrowverse* unfortunately draw upon and support this understanding of disability. Along with the habit of addressing characters' impairments so quickly, never allowing for long-term experiences of disability, the Arrowverse also suggests that characters' lives simply fall apart in the wake of their disabilities. As discussed previously, Felicity begins to deteriorate mentally and make unprecedented mistakes while guiding other team members (Season 4, episode 11). Diggle becomes a liar and illicit drug user with great speed as well. After Barry/Flash has his back broken in the second season of *The Flash*, he descends into self-pity and shows little interest in the team's current mission. He perks up only slightly after another character reminds him that his brain, if not his legs, is still valuable for the team (Season 2, episode 7). It is reasonable for a character to feel a sense of defeat on many levels, including a sense of personal loss. However, this experience reinforces a general pattern of discounting disability identity and how these characters are *never* shown to accept or understand their disabilities in any lasting sense.

Another significant example of this fleeting portrayal is the story of Devoe, the villain of *The Flash's* fourth season, who devises a means to exponentially enhance his brain power but soon finds that his mind has begun siphoning energy from his body in ways that mimic the symptoms of amyotrophic lateral sclerosis (ALS). Through flashbacks viewers are shown his moment of diagnosis as well as a single instance of bodily struggle, as he falls from his chair while attempting to reach a book. As his wife tries to console him, he tells her that her husband is "gone" and pleads with her to let him die (4.7). Again, the problem here is not that Devoe and other characters struggle. The shows should not necessarily suggest that disability is *easy*. However, they never seem to present disability as anything *but* life-shattering and steeped in despair. When these individuals acquire disabilities, they seem to simultaneously lose their summative value as characters, which, along with the unwavering pattern of "fixing" their impairments, suggests that disability has little enduring functional, social, or personal value in the Arrowverse.

Just like the freak show genre is inevitably stigmatizing, there is little potential space to value disability within a transhumanist frame. Transhumanist philosophy relies on dangerous assumptions about the body, and a deeper concern is that it typically does so uncritically, which is the flaw that makes posthumanism the stronger choice. Hazem Zohny (2018) argues, for instance, that "for proponents of enhancement, there may be an assumption that greater capacities tend to enable more life opportunities and having more of those is good for well-being in some objective sense—that is, regardless of how they impact our sense of happiness or satisfaction." Because this implicit linking of ability and value, what Reynolds (2017) calls the "ableist conflation," feeds into more fundamental assumptions about what makes for a good life, critical disability studies has long considered the disruption of this link a central pillar of disability identity assertion (153). Whereas transhumanism embraces these assumptions in the interests of building a "stronger" or "better" human being, posthumanism challenges the usefulness of these basic terms. As Pramod K. Nayar (2014) puts it, the ideology of posthumanism entails a "radical decentering of the traditional sovereign, coherent and autonomous human to demonstrate how the human is always already evolving with, constituted by and constitutive of multiple forms of life and machines" (2). Whereas, as Reynolds (2017) explains, transhumanist philosophy "functions in part through capitalizing upon the ambiguity of its terms [...] [and] leaving the meaning of disability, harm, pain, and suffering all uncritically underdefined," posthumanism views this ambiguity as an opportunity for analysis and reason to challenge traditional notions of body and identity (153).

Not surprisingly, much is vague and implicit in the transhumanistic Arrowverse, and this is part of what makes its projected future so dangerous. There are no explicit discussions of how things "should" be for characters with disabilities within the Arrowverse. Rather, there is a clear pattern of framing disability as an opportunity for technological intervention, a pattern which expresses the pervasive assumption that disability is inherently undesirable. Whenever characters are introduced they have the means to potentially address their impairments—Felicity and Diggle with their chips, for instance, or Devoe with his hover chair—neither they nor those they love weigh their various options or even question the basic safety of the proposed procedures. In other instances, like those of Malcolm Merlin or future Cisco, the incorporation of prostheses is treated as a foregone conclusion and simply skipped within the narrative. This assumption influences even those characters who seemingly have no need for, or interest in, addressing their impairments. In *Legends of Tomorrow*, for example, a character with a long-established vision impairment is found in the future with his vision fully restored. There is no narrative explanation or justification for this change, except that, as the character explains, "The future is full of marvels" (Season 2, episode 12). This line about the future and its marvels seems, in some sense, to be the central message of much of the Arrowverse's presentation of disability. Rather than a complex identity, an intricate mix of not just pain and disappointment but also triumphs and growth and deliberateness, disability too often becomes, for characters of the Arrowverse, merely an opportunity to innovate. It acts as an occasion to invent rather than a chance to understand, and dream up a future of (supposed) perfection rather than explore the intricacies of identities in the present.

To move away from the more reductive assumptions of transhumanism and toward a posthuman representation of disability, there are at least two changes the creators of the Arrowverse need to consider. First, they need to examine how they have, intentionally or not, coupled disability and transhumanist belief and make it clearer that bodily alteration and enhancement are not exclusive to characters with disabilities. While characters of all sorts get fun and fantastic technology to use—the Flash has his suit, the Arrow has various gadgets, and each team their groundbreaking tracking devices—these enhancements are not embodied ones; they are temporary, external additions. They are not incorporated as *a part of* the character in the same way that Cisco's prosthetic hands or Diggle and Felicity's chips are. Those behind the Arrowverse need to consider the implications of this pattern and develop a more flexible and diverse set of relationships among humans, science, and technology. As discussed earlier, the current disability-innovation link not only frames disability as an opportunity for intervention but also communicates an implied future in which disability no longer exists, since by providing only characters with disabilities with permanent, embodied technologies, the shows' creators reinforce the dangerous link between transhumanism and bodily vulnerability.

A second change the shows' creators must consider is clarifying that technological advancement is a choice, not a path to perfection or necessarily the best or most logical choice in any situation. Transhumanism supports an objective understanding of the body and disregards the subjectivity of experience in achieving mechanical perfection. Embracing instead a more posthumanist philosophy, one that directly challenges traditional ideas of the body and embraces subjectivity, would allow the Arrowverse to more clearly acknowledge the value of disability identity by presenting it as one among many options. One crucial—not to mention relatively easy and obvious—stride toward clearer acknowledgment is to foster greater bodily diversity across all shows. The able-bodied portrayal of Lena Luthor in *Supergirl*, for instance, is a glaring example of a missed opportunity to incorporate bodily diversity. There are various iterations of Luthor in other media, one of the most prominent versions being a wheelchair user after contracting an illness in her youth that her brother, notorious villain Lex, cannot treat. Despite this rich backstory from which to draw, and a general faithfulness to other characters' comic legacies, the series creators decided to present Lena as fully able-bodied and with no hint whatsoever of any experience with disability. Moreover, as with previous examples, there is seemingly no narrative need for this change. Yet, disability was left out for reasons unknown, contributing to a long line of ableist missteps in the Arrowverse.

Conclusion

The goal of the argument here is not to condemn the shows of the *Arrowverse* or diminish their popularity; rather, it is to drive their portrayals of disability forward by acknowledging that the mere presence of characters with disabilities is not enough to achieve progressive representation. Perhaps the most fundamental assumption of the current argument is that only through critical engagement can representations of identity be fully understood and improved. As Reynolds (2017) puts it, "without a critical analysis of disability, one will likely end up unintentionally conceptualizing disability on faulty grounds, ultimately contributing to rather than countering or mediating disability stigma" (151). This is what the shows of the *Arrowverse* continue to do in their attempts to represent disability. Thus, only close examinations like this can illustrate how the mere presence of characters with disabilities is not nearly enough. Instead, the producers and writers need to reevaluate their portrayal of disability to reflect its long, complicated—and often constructive and empowering—relationship with technology. Moreover, they need to offer a more balanced view of this relationship, exploring the technological advances and the complex identities of characters with lasting disabilities. Given the shows' growing popularity, bolstered significantly by exclusive licensing deals with Netflix, and the CW's domination of DC-based television, such changes are necessary and overdue. Critical analysis of the *Arrowverse* shows, as with other artistry dismissed as mere science fiction fantasy, is more essential than realized. When the ideals reflected through this constructed world—along with the limitations and exclusions formed by these ideals are investigated—audiences learn what needs to be accomplished in the real one.

REFERENCES

Arrow. 2015. "Green Arrow." Season 4, episode 1. October 7. Netflix.
_____. 2016. "A.W.O.L." Season 4, episode 11. January 27. Netflix.
_____. 2016. "Code of Silence." Season 4, episode 14. February 17. Netflix.
_____. 2016. "Taken." Season 4, episode 15. February 24. Netflix.
_____. 2017. "Underneath." Season 5, episode 20. May 3. Netflix.
_____. 2017. "Fallout." Season 6, episode 1. October 12. Netflix.
_____. 2017. "Next of Kin." Season 6, episode 3. October 26. Netflix.
_____. 2017. "Thanksgiving." Season 6, episode 7. November 23. Netflix.
Braddock, David, and Susan Parish. 2001. "An Institutional History of Disability." In *Handbook of Disability Studies*, edited by Gary Albrecht, Katherine Seelman, and Michael Bury, 11–68. Thousand Oaks, CA: Sage Publications.
Braidotti, Rosi. 2013. *The Posthuman*. London, UK: Polity.
Brian, Kathleen M., and James W. Trent, Jr. 2017. *Phallacies: Historical Intersections of Disability and Masculinity*. New York: Oxford University Press.
Campbell, Fiona Kumari. 2009. *Contours of Ableism*. London, UK: Palgrave Macmillan.
Darke, Paul Anthony. 2004. "The Changing Face of Representations of Disability in the Media." In *Disabling Barriers, Enabling Environments*, 2nd edition, edited by John Swain, Sally French, Colin Barnes, and Carol Thomas, 100–105. London, UK: Sage Publications.
The Flash. 2014. "Fastest Man Alive." Season 1, episode 2. October 7. Netflix.

_____. 2014. "Things You Can't Outrun." Season 1, episode 3. October 21. Netflix.

_____. 2014. "Power Outage." Season 1, episode 7. November 25. Netflix.

_____. 2015. "Out of Time." Season 1, episode 15. March 17. Netflix.

_____. 2015. "Gorilla Warfare." Season 2, episode 7. November 17. Netflix.

_____. 2017. "The Once and Future Flash." Season 3, episode 19. April 25. Netflix.

_____. 2017. "Therefore I Am." Season 4, episode 7. November 21. Netflix.

_____. 2018. "Lose Yourself." Season 4, episode 18. April 17. Netflix.

Fletcher, David-Jack. 2014. "Transhuman Perfection: The Eradication of Disability Through Transhuman Technologies." *Humana Mente: Journal of Philosophical Studies 7* (26): 79–94. http://www.humanamente.eu/index.php/HM/article/view/116.

Garland-Thomson, Rosemarie. 1997. *Extraordinary Bodies: Figuring Physical Disability in American Culture and Literature.* New York: Columbia University Press.

Hall, Melinda. 2017. *The Bioethics of Enhancement: Transhumanism, Disability, and Biopolitics.* Lanham, MD: Lexington Books.

Hall, Stuart. 1997. "Introduction." In *Representation: Cultural Representations and Signifying Practices,* edited by Stuart Hall, 1–12. London, UK: Sage Publications.

Haraway, Donna. 2006. "A Cyborg Manifesto: Science, Technology, and Socialist-feminism in the Late Twentieth Century." In *The Transgender Studies Reader,* edited by Susan Stryker and Stephen Whittle, 103–118. New York: Routledge.

Leane, Rob. 2016. "Arrow Season 4: Who Is in the Grave?" *Den of Geek.* https://www.denofgeek.com/comics/arrow-season-4-who-is-in-the-grave/.

Legends of Tomorrow. 2017. "Camelot/3000." Season 2, episode 12. February 21. Netflix.

Manzocco, Roberto. 2019. *Transhumanism—Engineering the Human Condition: History, Philosophy and Current Status.* Cham, NY: Springer Praxis.

Mitchell, David, and Sharon Snyder. 2000. *Narrative Prosthesis: Disability and the Dependence of Discourse.* Ann Arbor: University of Michigan Press.

_____. 2005. "Exploitations of Embodiment: *Born Freak* and the Academic Bally Plank." *Disability Studies Quarterly 25* (3). https://dsq-sds.org/article/view/575/752.

Mogk, Marja Evelyn. 2013. *Different Bodies: Essays on Disability in Film and Television.* London, UK: McFarland.

More, Max, and Natasha Vita-More. 2013. *The Transhumanist Reader: Classical and Contemporary Essays on the Science, Technology, and Philosophy of the Human Race.* West Sussex, UK: Wiley-Blackwell.

Nayar, Pramod K. 2014. *Posthumanism.* Cambridge, UK: Polity Press.

Nelson, Jack A. 2003. "The Invisible Cultural Group: Images of Disability." In *Images That Injure: Pictorial Stereotypes in the Media,* 2nd edition, edited by Paul Martin Lester and Susan Dente Ross, 175–184. Westport, CT: Praeger.

Reynolds, Joel Michael. 2017. "'I'd Rather Be Dead Than Disabled'—The Ableist Conflation and the Meanings of Disability." *Review of Communication 17* (3): 149–163. Doi: 10.1080/15358593.2017.1331255.

Shakespeare, Tom. 1999. "The Sexual Politics of Disabled Masculinity." *Sexuality and Disability 17* (1): 53–64. Doi: 10.1023 /A:1021403829826.

Shuttleworth, Russell, Nikki Wedgewood, and Nathan J. Wilson. 2012. "The Dilemma of Disabled Masculinity." *Men and Masculinities 15* (2): 174–194. Doi: 10.1177/109718 4X12439879.

Smit, Christopher R. 2003. "'Please Call Now, Before It's Too Late': Spectacle Discourse in the Jerry Lewis Muscular Dystrophy Telethon." *Journal of Popular Culture 36* (4): 687–703. https://doi.org/10.1111/1540-5931.00041.

Talbot, Mary. 2007. *Media Discourse: Representation and Interaction.* Edinburgh, UK: Edinburgh University Press.

Vidali, Amy. 2007. "Performing the Rhetorical Freak Show: Disability, Student Writing, and College Admissions." *College English 69* (6): 615–641. Doi: 10.2307/25472242

Williamson, Bess. 2019. *Accessible America: A History of Disability and Design.* New York: New York University Press.

Zohny, Hazem. 2018. "Competition, Cooperation and Human Flourishing: Commentary on Koch." *Journal of Medical Ethics 44* (8): 581–582. Doi: 10.1136/medethics-2017-104426.

Cultural Appropriation and Ableism

Dr. Strange's Strange Concoction

SHANTI SRINIVAS

When *Doctor Strange* hit theaters in 2016, the Marvel Cinematic Universe (MCU) gathered praise for giving audiences a hugely entertaining film, fully equipped with a star-studded cast of A-list celebrities and stunning computer graphics to showcase Marvel's magic. The storyline reads somewhat like other Marvel character arcs; a white man named Dr. Strange goes from being a renowned neurosurgeon to a disgruntled person with a disability, only later to transform into a superhero who saves the world. Critics hailed this film as "diverging in tone and ideas" typical of MCUs films to provide audiences with "a relatively thoughtful meditation on what it means to live with a disability" (The *Washington Post* 2019). The social construction of various social identities within the film, most notably a more empowering image of a superhero with a disability, coupled with its box office earnings, was believed to make *Doctor Strange* one of MCU's more socially progressive productions (Ahlgrim 2020). Despite its popularity, the film still presents ableist perspectives that are coupled with racist, classist, and sexist viewpoints as well. Given these facts, audiences must understand that *Doctor Strange* does perpetuate harmful stereotypes and engage in cultural appropriation that demonstrates inauthentic depictions of cultural identities based on disability, gender, and race in superhero media. This essay exposes the MCU's apparent and hidden representations of cultural identities that propagate stereotypical and prejudiced representations. The MCU could have used its immense global influence to accurately represent the fullness of diverse lives of those residing in our communities, whether real or imagined, but it failed to do so.

Before the release of *Doctor Strange* (2016), the MCU got to witness the powers of *Spiderman* (2002, 2004; 2007; 2012; and 2014), *Incredible Hulk* (2008), *Iron Man* (2008; 2010; and 2013), *Captain America* (2011; 2014), *Thor* (2011; 2013), and *Ant-Man* (2015). They also watched Hawkeye and Black Widow in action in the *Avengers* movies (2012; 2015), in addition to a distinct group of heroes fighting for justice in *Guardians of the Galaxy* (2014). A new superhero film was released almost every year, and their box office success demonstrated the MCU's popularity. Fitting into this genre, *Doctor Strange* presents the story of another superhero, with a disability, determined to save the Earth and earthlings from a dark universe supervillain, Dormammu, who wants to control the entire universe (Marvel 2021).

Who Is a Superhero?

Before dissecting Strange's character through the lens of ableism, cultural appropriateness, and other 'isms, it is imperative to clarify how this analysis interprets the superhero concept. For a brief background on superheroes and their evolution over the past several decades, the Cambridge Dictionary's definition provides a good start. It defines a superhero as a character in a story with strength who uses it for societal benefit (Cambridge Dictionary 2021). This broad definition is all-inclusive because it is non-specific to strength type, gender, age, race, species, or other identifying factors. For a superhero to be heroic, they must also have an aggressor/villain or threat to protect. An entry about superheroes in the Britannica Encyclopedia expands this definition to include the presence of superhuman strengths and alter-ego states (Eury et al. 2021). Superheroes typically use their superpowers to save humanity or protect "good" against evil. *Doctor Strange* is no exception from this trope; he uses magic, not muscle, to save the earth from Dormammu, an evil force from beyond the time dimension. He also chooses to give up his past life in exchange for the superhero life's calling.

According to creator Stan Lee (2013), given the confines of our limited, non-superhero abilities, people often desire to be and do more than their human condition allows. This desire, coupled with the relatable nature of a character like Strange, who leads an everyday but successful life with a stable career, home, and personality quirks, is a cinematic recipe for success. Therefore, fans identify with superheroes, often to the point of experiencing their joy, pain, and disappointment while undergoing tragedy, performing heroic acts, and saving the world (Rosenberg 2013). Stan Lee infused realism into characters by giving them families, friends, enemies, and people they love, reflecting our lives and social ills from which we can improve society (Lee 2013). This rationale makes studying modern comics and superhero movies a rich arena for understanding popular culture and the human condition.

Events Leading Up to Dr. Strange Becoming a Superhero

The original Dr. Strange character originated from the comic strip series created by Stan Lee and artist Steve Ditko in 1963 (Marvel Comics 1963). The original strip and film version is about an arrogant, yet talented surgeon who acquires a disability from crashing his car. The film version had Strange texting while driving, at a high rate of speed, traveling on curvy roads in rainy weather, late at night (Marvel Studios 2016). When he regains consciousness after the accident, he does not express an ounce of gratitude for being alive. Instead, he gasps in anger, looking at his hands, which resemble those of a robot. He has broken nearly all bones in both his hands and cannot control the nerves in his fingers. The outrage he experiences at the revelation of what had happened to his hands is not surprising, given the numerous steel rods and joints that hold his fingers in place. However, it is shocking to watch him roar in agony, not from physical pain, but mental unacceptance of his condition. His emotional state seems to stem from the demise of his physical, and hence, social status.

While audiences cannot disregard the range of emotions people with disabilities might face, and each person with a disability can experience acquiring a disability differently. Strange's reaction to his disability falls somewhere on the continuum. However, the glaringly visible embitterment Strange feels at losing his hands' functionality indicates a distorted view of the disability experience. The anger and dissatisfaction at his disability seem normal yet, wildly out of place. Such a narrative falls into the existing tropes of showcasing human existence as worth living only when everything is "normal." Disabilities, when presented as unbearable burdens, often get stigmatized. Ava's character in the *Ant-Man & The Wasp* and Charles Xavier's in *X-Men* are designed from a similar mold. They become obsessed with treating their pain and paralysis, respectively, as Strange did (Jackson 2018). Parading disabilities with a casual carelessness as unwanted aspects of life and "afflicted" individuals spending their remaining time obsessing over the mishaps, as in the case of Strange, is troubling.

Witnessing Strange cope with his newfound physical disability, one cannot help but notice the social and emotional pressures of hegemonic masculinity, which demand he is strong, independent, and successful.

Hegemonic masculinity requires that "being a real man" means possessing and performing certain masculine qualities that reinforce men's domination over women and those who identify as LGBTQIA in society. The physically disabled man's media image is often feminized, perceived as incapable of autonomy, strength, and aggressiveness associated with hegemonic Westernized masculinity (Manderson and Peake 2005). The linkages among disability, feminization, and the loss of masculinity resulting from acquiring a disability harm not only people with disabilities but also women and LGBTQIA individuals. To live in a patriarchal culture means internalizing the devaluing of femininity and describing undesirable individuals or actions by using feminine terms, especially terms for women's anatomy. It is also attached to perpetuating homophobia and reinforcing heterosexist ideals, suggesting that to be a real man, one must avoid being perceived as gay or lesbian and deny anything associated with LGBTQIA culture. Thus, ableism meets genderism to suggest that disability is undesirable because it does not conform with the hegemonic masculine image; it makes the person effeminate (Morettini 2016; Reynolds 2017).

Furthermore, the connection between the cultural construction of disability as vulnerable, passive, helpless, and hence undesirable mirrors how women and LGBTQIA individuals are often perceived. Strange's identification with hegemonic masculinity stands in direct conflict with his new experience with disability (Fannon 2020). Thus, Strange not only seeks to affirm himself as able-bodied but also seeks to reinstate his status as an alpha man to restore his lost masculinity (Berger 2018). His gendered, ableist characterization implies that impairment makes men lose their masculinity, making him less of a man (Shuttleworth et al., 2012). As with other man characters, Strange's access to superpowers enables him to reacquire masculine strength, dominance, and admiration for "overcoming" his acquired disability (Wilson 2004).

Despite these facts about the emasculation of the newly disabled Strange, only three women have "screen-time" in the film (e.g., The Ancient One, Dr. Palmer, and a physician on the medical board/consulting team). This film fails what media and literature studies refer to as the Bechdel-Wallace test, which measures the representation of women in fiction (Bechdel 1985). To pass this test, a film must have at least two women characters who have names; these women must communicate with each other; and they must communicate about something other than a man. Like most Marvel films, *Doctor Strange* does not pass this test because the women never communicate with each other, and only one woman (Dr. Palmer) has a given name. Additionally, Dr. Palmer's leading utility in the film is to support Strange, not be an independent character in her own right.

The film also fails the Vito Russo test, which requires there to be an identifiable lesbian, gay, bisexual, intersex, or transgender character (Russo 1981). This character must be defined by identities outside of their sexual orientation, gender identity, or having an intersex condition. And the character must play a significant role in the plot to where their removal would vastly change the storyline. Like many other MCU films, *Doctor Strange* fails this test because no characters identify as LGBTQIA, despite having LGBTQIA characters in the graphic novels and comic strips from which the films are based.

Passing the Fries Test for disability representation requires that a film has more than one main character with a disability, and the disabled character must do something other than educate or assist a nondisabled character, and the character's disability cannot be managed through curing or killing (Fries 1997). *Doctor Strange* has several dominant ableist undertones, which makes it fail this test as well. Strange continues to live within and be defined by the nondisabled gaze, spreading stereotypical and harmful depictions of disability (Garland-Thomson 2009).

Strange, a man of science and medicine, adopts a medical model mindset when he perceives his impairment as a personal failing that requires medical intervention (Hogan 2019). As one might expect, his fall from being a renowned neurosurgeon to a person no longer capable of performing his passion is met with anger, sorrow, and frustration. His inflated ego and arrogant personality posed additional challenges to adjusting to his disability. Like many other people who acquire a disability later in life due to injury or disease, he feels pressured to "overcome" his limitations and find a cure. Naturally, he also experiences depression when the physical therapy from top-notch experts and his wealth fail to restore his hand's functionality.

Strange's desolation and hopelessness to live unless he becomes "whole" again echo the medical model of disability. Often, disabilities, disease, and death are used interchangeably, and hence, people without disabilities try to avoid them at all costs. People's reaction to disability is pity due to "suffering" from having a disability (Reynolds 2017). This convoluted logic disparages any efforts for inclusivity and empowerment. Due to stigmatization, people with disabilities may confer to "passing," nullifying the purpose of the medical model. Although Strange did not "pass" or "cover" his disability, he conformed to the medical model with his single-minded focus on becoming "normal" again by constantly rallying to "fix" his disability.

Some critics suggest that Strange's portrayal of a person with a newly acquired disability goes beyond what other representations would afford the character. Strange becomes emboldened to cure his disability by never giving up; this is perceived as an inspiring persona. One critic suggests that "Strange's mentality mirrors one common to many Hollywood productions: that we are the sum of our bodies, and that people who become disabled in some capacity will either have to live with diminished expectations or find relief through suicide" (The *Washington Post* 2019). However, just because Strange avoids contemplating suicide does not negate that the image of disability being projected is ableist. As commonly noted, disability scholars suggest, this portrayal situates disability as an undesirable deviance from normative existence (George and Schatz 2016). It also indicates that a person with a disability, such as Strange, cannot have an adequate quality of life or provide any value to society given his new situation with his hands. Perhaps he cannot perform surgery anymore, but could he still teach others to perform surgery? Although the disability propels him to become a superhero, the emotional roller-coaster he goes through cannot be generalized to reflect every individual's experience when their abilities change.

After months of rehabilitation, physical therapy, and counseling from experts worldwide, his hands stay less than "perfect" because they still shake, which prevents him from performing surgeries. The medical model interpretation of disability continues, as Strange's characterization implies that his identity draws from him being a world-class surgeon and not much else. And when he becomes disabled, his identity crisis is like no other. It is difficult to say if self-reflection would have soothed his grief and resentment. Prior to the accident, his demeanor becomes so poisonous that he ends his relationship with Dr. Christine Palmer, his implied love interest. Showcasing a physical disability to have a domino effect on all life, robbing it of wholeness, can be an inaccurate and offensive projection in a film with a global reach (Griffith 2016).

Woven into this ableist rhetoric are classist ideologies as well. Individuals who are not as successful and wealthy as Strange may not react to their situation as he did, demanding every known specialist from all over the world cure him. The facts remain that most people who have or acquire injury related disabilities do not have access to world-class, high-tech healthcare like Strange. Additionally, not all individuals get so utterly intolerable to consider their lives not worth living when disability affects them unsolicited and suddenly.

Further, it is presumptuous to make general claims about the challenges people with disabilities encounter, as stigma surrounds almost all aspects of everyday life (Ali 2020; CDC 2020). Going by how Strange reacts to his newly acquired disability, audiences may not realize that people with disabilities need accommodations to accomplish their goals and contribute to society. Social support, acceptance, and love are required far more than cures after one acquires a disability. Nevertheless, Strange's desire to fix his hands leads him to travel to Nepal for a cure.

Cultural Appropriation: Orientalism and Whitewashing

It seems very curious that a man of rationality, science, and medicine would search the world for a miraculous cure only to find one in the Far East, specifically the Himalayan mountains. Strange is so desperate to erase any association with a disability that he turns to mystical worlds, phantasmic psychic powers, and remedies that defy his medical training and all that he used to believe. If not for his disdain, embarrassment, and anger about acquiring a disability, how else can one explain why he suddenly turned to alternative meditative practices for help? This abrupt turn was even odder, considering that Strange held Orientalist prejudices about Eastern medicine and mysticism before the accident. Yet suddenly, his strong binary associations that posit the West (taken to mean European and American cultures) as superior to the East fade away, all in pursuit of eliminating his disability. This hegemonic binary of understanding how East is pitted against West defines the Orientalist practices in the film.

Eventually, Strange learns that former master of the mystic arts, Jonathan Pangborn cured his disability (paralysis) through what he assumes is a back-alley, underground experimental treatment facility called Kamar-Taj. Pangborn draws on familiar Eastern stereotypes when he romanticizes the treatment options as more spiritual and less regulated. Pangborn had internalized ableist beliefs about his own body, and in a bid of desperation, attempted to "heal" his mind. He states, "I had given up on my body. I thought my mind was the only thing I have left, so I might try to enlighten that" (Doctor Strange 2016). Strange also seems to internalize ableism and confront his Orientalist perceptions when he shares that he has "given up on Western medicine" for finding a cure.

When Strange travels to Kathmandu, Nepal, audiences get their first glimpse of Orientalist perceptions of Asian culture on full display. Curiously, the storyline does not adopt any concept or term explicitly related to Nepalese religion or culture. Instead, "East" becomes a catchall, generalized term that identifies for viewers anything related to Asian religions and cultures. This generalizing, or even going a step further, stereotyping an entire landmass of cultures is Orientalist.

Audiences understand Nepal and Kamar-Taj (the mystical training center) through Strange's Western perceptions of what the East should be (read: Orientalist ideologies). On-screen, Strange is met with beautiful, exoticized, mystical landscapes that are quite different from what Strange is accustomed to in the familiar United States landscape. This aligns with traditional Euro-American conceptions of the Orient as romantic, exotic, and "other" (Said 2019). The Kamar-Taj presents a mixture of several Asian architectural styles that exemplifies Edward Said's (2019) conception of orientalism. According to Said, orientalism is a "created body of theory and practice" which constructs images of the East for those in the West to consume. Representations of the East mirror how the West perceives itself as powerful, masculine, and rational. These idealizations pervade all aspects of behavior including language, history, customs, and religion to create a dichotomy between two geographical entities (Said 2019). The characters' costumes come together to craft an Asian aesthetic to satisfy Western expectations for the East. True to form, the creators of *Doctor Strange* "created" a version of the "Orient" to be stereotypical enough to be recognizable yet inferior to Western culture and identity.

Cultural appropriation and "whitewashing" are when the presence or achievements of people of color are erased and stolen by those seeking to fulfill a particular plan. Examples include appropriating hairstyles (adorning cornrows, locks), skin color (yellow for Asian and brown for Latino characters), Black music, Black voices for white actors, attire, imagery, symbols, and roles. Despite intense public outrage and criticism against whitewashing characters and storylines, *Doctor Strange* engaged in ableist whitewashing when Tilda Swinton, a white British woman, was cast to play the Celtic character known as the Ancient One. The Ancient One appropriates Asian-like mysticism to restore Strange's normality, a very medical-model-like agenda (Yamato 2017). Interestingly, in the original comic series for Doctor Strange, the Ancient One was cast as an older Asian man. The Media Action Network for Asian Americans (MANAA) criticized replacing the character with a white woman citing Orientalist intent to erase Asian culture from the film (2021).

Meanwhile, other fans hailed this as a noble effort to avoid typecasting an offensive Asian stereotype, such as The Dragon Lady, Anna May Wong (Alexander 2019; Women and the American Story [WAMS] 2021). Derrickson also argued that changing the gender of the Ancient One promoted gender inclusion (Yamato 2017). While the newer version of the Ancient One from 2016 is miles away from the original stereotypical comic book version from the 1960s, it still falls short on many accounts. For Derrickson to fear repeating another Dragon Lady stereotype and thereby reassigning a Tibetan man's role to a Celtic woman typifies stealth racism (Ronald 2018). Eurocentric schemes undermine the ownership and contributions of non–Western cultures and their knowledge. Additionally, they muddle the injustices and inequities created and perpetuated by European colonialism, thus preserving racial hierarchies (Ahlberg et al. 2019). Not only was this choice in poor form for people of color, but also for women of all races. It suggests that race and gender are mutually exclusive, whereby adapting one stereotypical portrayal by inserting another will eliminate stereotypes.

Further, one might take issue with transporting a white, upper-class, highly educated cis-gender man of medicine to Asia to meet with an influential spiritual leader situated in Tibet. After decades of study, ascetic training and practice are used as a token of gender equity. No one wants their identity and culture to be used in such a manner; it is insulting to Asians, for it passes them off as "others." Even more offensive is the Ancient One's hollow showcasing of her knowledge. In an initial conversation with Strange, the Ancient One flips a page and Strange notes that he has seen it (the image of Kundalini) in gift shops, as if what she studies is nothing more than a cheap trinket to buy. Strange has no initial interest in learning the Ancient One's beliefs, and he's only there to learn mystic arts for selfish reasons—to heal his disability and return to his pre-disability lifestyle.

It is worth noting that Kundalini references may be found in different cultures, including Egyptian and Native American, but are closely associated with Hinduism and later Buddhism (Keutzer 1996). Hinduism considers Kundalini shakti (power) a very secret and powerful form of yoga. When fully awakened, it bestows a person with abilities beyond human perception and enlightenment, including curing disabilities (Sri Swami Sivananda 1999). However, Hindu Veda Puranas mention that awakening should be done under a fully enlightened guru and can take many years, if not lifetimes, of practice. The process requires internal cleansing and strong faith in Kundalini's power. Therefore, Strange's reference to it as an item he saw in gift shops is disrespectful. The fact that he can suddenly become a powerful superhero with a time stone and a cape, discredits the years that other spiritual practitioners dedicate to learning these crafts. No religion or spiritual symbols should be used as a narrative plot to assist a person with a disability to overcome their obstacles. Furthermore, no religion should be used to wield one's influence or position to prey upon people. Some Eastern based religions and practices, such as yoga, already suffer from cultural appropriation by wealthy, Eurocentric men who use their power as charismatic figures to abuse people, most especially women. For the last decade, media has been saturated with stories about sexual assault perpetrated by white, cis-gender men posing as spiritual gurus, most especially within cult-like retreats they have created in far East lands, such as Thailand (e.g., Swami Viekananda Saraswati) (CBC Radio 2018). Thus, the point remains that East and South Asian symbolism should not be appropriated because it is often misinterpreted or used for sinister gains which discredits the religion, its practitioners, and those potentially victimized by it. There was no need for the MCU to stay true to Stan Lee's and Steve Ditko's (1963) original character formulation which sent a privileged white man, with a disability to the East to acquire magical superhuman powers to save the world.

Just as with the other two tests that seek gender, sexuality, and disability equity in media representation, there is a person of color test as well. To pass this test, the film must have at least two people of color characters, these characters must communicate with one another, and they must discuss something other than a white person. *Doctor Strange* fails this test because while there are two prominent people of color characters, Benedict Wong as Wong, the librarian at Kamar-Taj, and Chiwetel Ejiofor as Baron Mordo, they both remain as tokens of Asian and African American representations, respectively. These characters never talk to one another, let alone discuss anything other than things related to Strange. They are cast as supporting characters, experts in the mystic arts, but not as powerful as Strange. Strange, who has nothing but ridicule and disrespect for their magical skills, learns from them because of their potential to cure his disability. He treats his newfound superpowers like feathers in his cap and as items to add to his repertoire of skills, with little mention of his "limits" from his disability. What the knowledge ascetics and scholars take decades to learn, Strange learns in a shockingly short time, which even Wong or Mordo cannot accomplish. This implies that whites are better than Asians and Blacks, even at their own art, which lends Strange to fully embracing the white savior narrative. Under the tutelage of another white person, a white superhero reigns high to save the world with the help of ancient eastern knowledge. At the same time, Mordo and Wong remain supporting characters.

Even when people wear the white savior robes or such roles become part of major Hollywood productions with good intentions, they are highly problematic because they focus on the savior instead of the people they save. The grandiose bestowing of the liberator image on white people is ill-intentioned. Strange and the Ancient One are white saviors, replacing Asianness and cultural heritages, rich knowledge, and existence, with a blatant disregard for venerated mystic arts. Nowhere in the films does he demonstrate his appreciation for what he has learned. His character remains unidimensional with or without the disability and before and after gaining mystical powers.

Gender equality is neither justified nor equated by appropriating a person of color character and substituting it with a white woman. Unfortunately, the Ancient One remains only a namesake replacement in *Doctor Strange*. Although projected as the supreme sorceress, she is not a trailblazer for others to follow, and her character's inspirational value is questionable (Women and Family Life Center 2021; Zimmer 2017). She also draws her power and extended life from the dark dimension and remains inferior to Strange by not defeating Dormammu.

Concluding Thoughts

Doctor Strange is a heartwarming film because its male lead, the superhero, has a disability. However, it is worth noting that his disability is never cured or healed. Even in the following iterations of his character in *Avengers: Infinity War* (2018) and *Avengers: Endgame* (2019), his hands still shake, and the scars are still visible. Regardless, he does embody a powerful masculine persona when he saves the earth from a formidable dark enemy, Dormammu. However, the message from the film does not suggest that a powerful superhero with a disability did the saving; rather, it suggests a man who has overcome his disability through the unrealistic means of acquiring superpowers. The MCU had a wonderful opportunity to share a positive message about people with disabilities having the skills to protect Earth from powerful supervillains. But that opportunity was squandered because Strange failed to project himself as a powerful person with a disability. Additionally, the MCU could have also turned the adaptation of the Ancient One into a powerful "shero" (blending "she" and "hero") of color when they changed her gender and race (Zimmer 2017). Seeing how "two prominent African-American women were the first to embrace 'shero' as a term of pride" it makes sense that MCU could have taken this turn toward inclusion and empowerment (Zimmer 2017). The failure of the MCU to meaningfully combat ableism, genderism, elitism, and racism for a more progressive representation reinforces how much media makers should strive to carefully construct superheroes and their supporting cast.

With the proliferation of mass media technologies changing rapidly and individual and institutional ableism, racism, and classism still rampant in society, all aspects of superheroes should be envisioned with dignity and integrity. Strange may be a superhero with a disability, but that should not preclude him from showing respect for the sorcerer skills he gains from another tradition. He projects racist, colonial perspectives when he adopts his powers without respect or humility. Additionally, casting an Asian actor to play the Ancient One, who lives in Kathmandu, Nepal, and teaches traditions that date back thousands of years ago would not have diminished the value of the film. It might have enhanced it by adding a cultural layer of authenticity and respect. Since the MCU has such a wide range of influence, it must acknowledge the cultural heritage on which it bases its superhero narratives.

Films like *Doctor Strange* make it easy to assume that every person with a disability wants to be cured. Furthermore, they make dangerous assumptions about the intersecting experiences of disability as it relates to socio-economic status, gender, and race. We simply cannot afford to have media moguls like MCU producing films about these experiences when there remains so much work to be done to support women, people of color, people with disabilities, and so on. How can we broaden the average viewer's understanding of disability culture beyond perceiving disability as pitiful, tragic, and undesirable when all we have available are characters like the ones in *Doctor Strange*?

With ever-increasing globalization, cultural intermixing, and cross-border exchanges, a clear distinction of ethnic elements' origins may prove challenging at times but not impossible. Writers and producers invest millions in embellishing superhero movies with stellar technological advancements, cutting-edge computer-generated imagery (CGI), and special effects. However, computer-generated grandiose effects should not be the saving grace of a superhero with a disability. The writers and creators of *Doctor Strange* should have applied the iconic statement they gave the ancient one: "Forget everything you think you know" when making assumptions about disabilities and cultures of the Eastern part of the world. Pouring millions of dollars into technical finesse is admirable, but the narrowing of gender and disability identities' characterization restricts our capacity for growth in the direction of equity and inclusion. The stunning visuals should not numb our analytical focus with a careless rendering of contemporary examples of ableism, racism, classism, genderism, colonialism, and cultural appropriation.

Given that fans identify with the superheroes, the writers, and producers must shoulder the responsibility to portray their creations with integrity and authenticity to promote social inclusion. Artistic liberties should not be based on speculations because the propensity to get it wrong and perpetuate oppressive representation abounds. While *Doctor Strange* is a movie based on scientific and mystical fiction, marginalizing social identities for the sake of entertainment must be critically assessed, or else we may never attain respectful and accurate depictions of individuals and their experiences.

REFERENCES

Ahlberg, Beth M., Sarah Hamed, Suruch Thapar-Björker, and Hannah Bradby. 2019. "Invisibility of Racism in the Global Neoliberal Era: Implications for Researching Racism in Healthcare." *Frontiers in Sociology* 14. doi: 10.3389/fsoc.2019.00061.
Ahlgrim, Callie. 2020. "A Definitive Ranking of All the Avengers, from Least to Most Powerful." *Insider*. March 5. https://www.insider.com/avengers-who-is-the-strongest-after-endgame-2019-5.
Alexander, Kerri Lee. (2018–19). Anna May Wong (1905–1961). *National Women's History Museum*. https://www.womenshistory.org/education-resources/biographies/anna-may-wong#_ftn1.
Ali, Safia Samee. 2020. "30 Years After Americans with Disabilities Act, College Students with Disabilities Say Law Is Not Enough." *NBC News*. March 1. https://www.

nbcnews.com/news/us-news/30-years-after-americans-disability-act-college-students-disabilities-say-n1138336.

Bechdel, Alison. 1985. "The Rule." *Dykes to Watch Out for (DTWOF)*. https://dykestowatch outfor.com/the-rule/.

Berger, Arthur. 2018. *Media Analysis Techniques* (6th Ed.). SAGE Publications, Inc.

Cambridge Dictionary. 2021. *Superhero*. https://dictionary.cambridge.org/us/dictionary/english/superhero.

CBC Radio. 2018. "'It Was Brainwashing': Canadian Speaks Out About Yoga Guru Accused of Sexual Assault." *CBC Radio*. September 10. https://www.cbc.ca/radio/asithappens/as-it-happens-monday-edition-1.4817159/it-was-brainwashing-canadian-speaks-out-about-yoga-guru-accused-of-sexual-assault-1.4817163.

Centers for Disease Control and Prevention (CDC). 2020. "Disability Impacts All of Us." September 16. https://www.cdc.gov/ncbddd/disabilityandhealth/infographic-disability-impacts-all.html.

Eury, Michael, Gina Misiroglu, and Peter Sanderson. 2021. "Superhero." *Encyclopedia Britannica*. https://www.britannica.com/art/superhero.

Fannon, Tara A. 2020. "Will's Story: Managing Culturally Irreconcilable Identities in Everyday Life." *Disabilities Studies Quarterly 40* (4). doi: 10.18061/dsq.v40i4.

Fries, Kenny. 1997. *Staring Back: The Disability Experience from the Inside Out*. New York: Plume Publishers.

Garland-Thomson, Rosemarie. 2009. *Starring: How We Look*. New York: Oxford University Press.

George, Amber E., and J. L. Schatz. 2018. *The Image of Disability: Essays on Media Representations*. Jefferson, NC: McFarland.

Griffith, Nicola. 2016. "The Dos and Don'ts of Writing About the Disabled." *Literary Hub*. August 23. https://lithub.com/the-dos-and-donts-of-writing-about-the-disabled/.

Hall, Ronald E. 2018. "Anti-Racist Racism as Millennial Pattern of Prejudice: The Stealth Perpetuation of White Supremacy." *Race, Gender, & Class 25* (1/2), 64–76.

Hogan, Andrew J. 2019. "Social and Medical Models of Disability and Mental Health: Evolution and Renewal." *CMAJ: Canadian Medical Association Journal 191*(1), E16–E18. Doi: 10.1503/cmaj.181008.

Jackson, Chelsea. 2018. "Superhero Movies Should Stop Using Disabilities as Problematic Plot Devices." *The Mary Sue*. August 27. https://www.themarysue.com/superhero-movies-and-disability/.

Keuzter, Kurt. 1996. *Kundalini Yogas FAQ*. University of California, Berkeley, http://people.eecs.berkeley.edu/~keutzer/kundalini/kundalini-yoga.html#1a.

Lee, Stan. 2013. "Stan Lee on What Is a Superhero." Oxford University Press's Blog. November 17. https://blog.oup.com/2013/11/stan-lee-on-what-is-a-superhero/.

Manderson, Lenore, and Susan Peake. 2005. "Men in Motion: Disability and the Performance of Masculinity." In *Bodies in Communication: Disability and Performance* in Carrie Sandhal and Philip Auslander (230–242). Ann Arbor: University of Michigan Press.

Marvel. 2021. *Ancient One*. https://www.marvel.com/characters/ancient-one.

_____. 2021. *Doctor Strange*. https://www.marvel.com/movies/doctor-strange.

_____. 2021. *Dormammu*. https://www.marvel.com/characters/dormammu/on-screen.

Marvel Comics. 1963. "Strange Tales #110." 1(1). New York: Marvel.

Media Action Network for Asian Americans (MANAA). 2021. https://manaa.org/.

Morettini, Frances. 2016. "Hegemonic Masculinity: How the Dominant Man Subjugates Other Men, Women, and Society." *Global Policy*. October 27. https://www.globalpolicyjournal.com/blog/27/10/2016/hegemonic-masculinity-how-dominant-man-subjugates-other-men-women-and-society.

Reynolds, Joel Michael. 2017. "'I'd Rather Be Dead Than Disabled': The Ableist Conflation and the Meanings of Disability." *Review of Communication 17* (3), 149–163. doi: 10.1080/15358593.2017.1331255.

Rosenberg, Robin S. 2013. *Our Superheroes, Ourselves*. New York: Oxford University Press.

Russo, Vito. 1981. *The Celluloid Closet: Homosexuality in the Movies*. New York: Harper & Row.

Said, Edward W. 2019. *Orientalism*. London, UK: Penguin Books.

Shuttleworth, Russell P., Nikki Wedgwood, and Nathan J. Wilson. 2012. "The Dilemma of Disabled Masculinity." *Men and Masculinities, 15* (2), 174–194. doi: 10.1177/1097184 X12439879.

Sri Swami Sivananda. 1999. "Kundalini Yoga." *The Divine Life Society*. https://www.dlshq. org/download/kundalini.htm#_VPID_12.

The Washington Post. 2019. "Marvel's Latest Superhero Doctor Strange Offers Thoughtful Exploration of Disability." April 30. https://www.scmp.com/yp/discover/lifestyle/ features/article/3070798/marvels-latest-superhero-doctor-strange-offers.

Wilson, Daniel J. 2004. "Fighting Polio Like a Man: Intersections of Masculinity, Disability and Aging." In *Gender Disability*, edited by Bonnie G. Smith and Beth Hutchinson (119–133). New Brunswick, NJ: Rutgers University Press.

Women and Family Life Center. 2021. "Celebrating Inspirational Women and Girls…." https://womenandfamilylife.org/shero-awards.

Women and the American Story. 2021. "Life Story: Anna May Wong (1905–1961)." https:// wams.nyhistory.org/confidence-and-crises/jazz-age/anna-may-wong/.

Yamato, Jen. 2017. "'Doctor Strange' Director Owns Up to Whitewashing Controversy." *The Daily Beast*. July 12. https://www.thedailybeast.com/doctor-strange-director-owns-up-to-whitewashing-controversy.

Zimmer, Ben. 2017. "With the Help of Barbie, the Term 'Shero' Gets New Fans." *The Wall Street Journal*. November 24. https://www.wsj.com/articles/the-term-sheroes-gets-new-fansand-adds-barbie-to-the-list-1511536372.

Of Sexism and Ableism

Wonder Woman's (Ab)Use of Disability

Tatiana Prorokova-Konrad

From Captain America to Batman, Hulk to Aquaman, Green Lantern, and beyond, several generations of audiences understand that superheroes come in all shapes and sizes. Superheroes and villains have long since shaped our cultural understandings of binaries such as good vs. evil, femininity vs. masculinity, strong vs. weak, and so on. Unfortunately, when it comes to gender identity, superhero films and comics predominantly focus on *male* heroes, masculine superhero traits, and men's storylines that often replicate patriarchal, sexist plots. The exclusion of empowering, equitable women superhero characters from these narratives is striking. Eventually, Wonder Woman was created as "Earth's first ever female superhero" (Zanin 2017, 57). One assumes that the Wonder Woman character would break this patriarchal practice, embodying what feminists have always wanted—a woman character, equal in skill to men, and caring for herself and the world. As this analysis reveals, the most recent cinematic representation of Wonder Woman, aka Diana Prince in Patty Jenkins' *Wonder Woman* (2017), fails to challenge patriarchy and perpetuates ableist narratives. This essay explores how Wonder Woman (a superhero) and Dr. Poison's (a supervillain) femininity is essentially similar—the women are represented as oppressed subjects who are in possession of the full or partial power of men.

Moreover, their appearances—strong and beautiful, in the case of Wonder Woman, and weak and ugly, as in Dr. Poison's case—are (ab)used to spread the image of an inferior woman. The notion of ableism is used to portray/strengthen the evil nature of Dr. Poison. This analysis examines how the film exploits culturally constructed, negative aspects of disability identity to create the character of Dr. Poison and how ableism promotes sexism and vice versa. Thus, the film reinforces sexist notions of superheroes and ableist conceptions of villainy, which combine to impose false standards for women, people with disabilities, and women with disabilities. Accurate portrayals of empowered women, people with disabilities, and women with disabilities are badly needed today. Thus, the idea that a woman needs to be perfectly shaped, wear minimal clothes, and have certain superpowers to withstand gender and ableist oppression does not positively contribute to the collective effort of various social movements including the #MeToo campaign and disability rights movements.

Wonder Woman: Sexism or Womanly Empowerment?

The original Wonder Woman was created over 70 years ago with her debut in "All Star Comics" (Wright 2017, 5). To specify: "Superman, Batman, and Wonder Woman emerged from the pages of Detective Comics in quick succession, in the summer of 1938, spring of 1939, and winter of 1941, respectively, when humanity was in need of superheroes" (McCrossin 2017, 51). The birth of Wonder Woman during such a difficult time in (American) history as World War II can be interpreted in multiple ways. Perhaps most significant is the societal recognition of women who lived through hard times both on the battlefield and on the home front. Wonder Woman's "female masculinity" (Halberstam 1998) reflected women's transition to witnessing the atrocities of World War II directly or becoming breadwinners due to men's military deployment or death during the war. Yet, Wonder Woman reemerged in both comics and films several times, as her role and the narratives about her changed over time. Labeling every Wonder Woman—from the heroine of the first comic to Gadot's character—as the *same* Wonder Woman would be entirely incorrect. Reading Wonder Woman from the perspectives of feminism and sexism is thus historically and temporarily bound. In this respect, Philip Smith (2018) makes a shrewd observation:

> the question of whether or not *Wonder Woman* can be described as a sexist or feminist narrative (or if Wonder Woman is a sexist or feminist character) is a meaningless one. We must first ask which version of Wonder Woman? Which story? In what context? Whose feminism? Various writers and artists to have tackled the character have swung, pendulum-like, from (sometimes clumsy) attempts to embody different models of feminist ideals to a contrary and strongly-perceived need to serve an adolescent male heterosexual fan-base [1–2].

Wonder Woman has not always been a personification of sexism. "Golden-era Wonder Woman was a feminist icon" (Abadía 2017, 162). She was supposed to "demonstrate to young female and male readers that female strength was not a fantastic supposition" (Matsuuchi 2012, 122). The depiction of Wonder Woman that one finds in comics raises the questions of gender and power, skillfully undermining the idea that the patriarchal world is perfect: "Like the crash of Thunder from the sky comes the Wonder Woman, to save the world from the hatreds and wars of men in a man-made world! And what a woman! A Woman with the eternal beauty of Aphrodite and the wisdom of Athena—yet whose lovely form hides the agility of Mercury and the steel sinews of a Hercules! Who is Wonder Woman? Why does she fight for America?" (Marston and Peter, qtd. in Knepp 2017, 152). Scholars have frequently interpreted Wonder Woman's strength as her primary weapon—the one that helps her address the needs of feminists and fight patriarchy. Mónica Cano Abadía (2017), for example, claims:

> Diana becomes Wonder Woman in this fight against patriarchy. She has all the desired skills for a feminist fighter: she is one of the strongest beings on the planet; she is highly resistant to bodily harm; she is an expert in all forms of armed and unarmed combat; she is a skilled tactician and diplomat (which is one of the most important skills to bring to a feminist fight); she has a magic lasso and silver bracelets that can deflect bullets [163].

As a result, "Through Wonder Woman's story, we can build a feminist epic that depicts women who fight patriarchy" (163). Such was Wonder Woman in the twentieth century.

However, in the twenty-first century, Wonder Woman conveys diametrically opposite cultural values. In Andrea Zanin's (2017) words:

> Wonder Woman was a representation of the unconventional, emancipated woman who darkened the door of a post-war world. [...] And yet, 75 years later, in an ironic twist of culture, America's heroine has become something else, something problematic. In a new millennium, 'wonder woman' is an unattainable ideal. She represents a pressure to be the impossible [58].

I apply Zanin's interpretation to the 2017 representation of Wonder Woman only, suggesting that despite certain similarities in the existing portrayals of Wonder Woman, one needs to consider each representation as a product of its time. The most recent Wonder Woman is, thus, the product of today's sexist world.

Despite making strides in achieving some gender equity, the latest *Wonder Woman* narrative returns to the same problem that Simone de Beauvoir articulated in 1949:

> [...] humanity is male, and man defines woman not in herself but relative to him; she is not considered an autonomous being. [...] And she is nothing other than what man decides; she is thus called 'the sex,' meaning that the male sees her essentially as a sexed being [...]. She is determined and differentiated in

relation to man, while he is not in relation to her; she is the inessential in front of the essential. He is the Subject; he is the Absolute. She is the Other [5–6].

The (ab)use of women based on de Beauvoir's gender and disability binary becomes central to maintaining patriarchy, masculinity, and male social privilege in *Wonder Woman*. Further, the binary opposition of ability/disability is also used to position the women against each other as a mechanism to discredit femininity and disability.

The film tells the story of Diana, aka Wonder Woman, raised by Amazonian warriors (all women) on a hidden island. Since her childhood, Diana is trained for combat. Some of the film's opening scenes include dynamic moments of Diana's fighting, accentuating her strength, beauty, endurance, and physical shape. This can be rather easily grasped by the viewer, for Diana, like the other women on the island, wears rather revealing clothes. As the story progresses, Diana saves the British pilot Steve Trevor, who, during World War I, crashes on the island where the women live. Promising Steve to help end the war, Diana leaves the island with him. As she enters the human world, she encounters several problems, all of which involve her appearance. For example, Diana is no longer allowed to wear her outfit, which is considered too provocative. Together with Steve and his secretary, Diana chooses her new dress. The audience observes an extended comedic scene when the woman warrior tries on several socially acceptable womanly dresses. Diana inappropriately stretches her arms and legs to question whether her new outfit is fit for fighting. Yet, she clearly does not understand that in this society, women do *not* fight. The viewer is painfully reminded that women's support in fighting *every* war—either as nurses, soldiers, or workers—has been ignored due to the belief that war is made by and for men.

As the film proceeds, the viewer witnesses how Diana is barred entry to the war room where *men* discuss the war and combat strategies. When she is noticed, one man says, "There is a woman in here." While Steve escorts Diana out of the room, all attention is directed at the *woman*, rather than the main speaker. After the meeting, Steve is reprimanded by one of the military men: "Trevor, what have you been thinking, bringing a woman into the Council?!" As the group is joined by Sir Patrick Morgan (David Thewlis)—the man who later reveals himself as Diana's archenemy Ares—Diana starts introducing herself as "Diana, Princess of…," yet she is interrupted by Steve who says for her, "Prince. Diana Prince." Diana's femininity is erased on a linguistic level; from a "princess" she is swiftly turned into a "prince," as if to fit the male environment and partake in the discussions conducted by men only. In the scene that follows, Diana tries to contribute to such discussions, yet one of the men asks: "Who is this woman?" Steve answers: "She is my … secretary, Sir." In turn, the man sarcastically questions Diana's knowledge of matters related to the war. Steve responds, "She is a very good secretary," which ultimately provokes laughter in the room. Thus, Diana's ability to understand the issues that, according to the scene, only men can understand is doubted. Moreover, her physical combat ability is later questioned by Steve himself who, despite being aware of her superpowers, says, with the Lasso of Truth around his wrist: "I am taking you to the front, where you're probably gonna die."

Perhaps the most powerful image of Wonder Woman is in the scene when she is finally on the front lines and is allowed to fight. Unlike the men who surround her and perceive war as a job, Diana pays attention to the physically and psychologically mutilated veterans and suffering civilians. The image of the latter is intensified through the woman character holding a baby in her arms and telling Diana about the horrors the people in this place have endured. Deeply moved by these personal, human stories, Diana decides to act without delay. She leaves the trenches and runs towards the enemy, skillfully repulsing the attack with her bracelets and shield. She turns into the leader, as the audience observes the male soldiers first waiting in the trenches and then, realizing that they have a chance to get through No Man's Land now, because Diana is with them, start to attack, too. In this scene, the film attempts to foreground Wonder Woman's femininity to distinguish that it is, indeed, a woman who is the strongest, smartest, and most skilled warrior. Yet, how the scene outlines gender distinction is inappropriate, to say the least, for the film that seeks to empower women. As she decides to leave the trenches and attack, Diana takes a pin out of her hair so that the hair falls loose. She also takes off her coat that fully covered her body. As she climbs out of the trenches, the camera focuses on her high-heeled boots and equipment. When she is out of the trenches, the audience observes the woman's full size; her armor is reminiscent of a body shirt. Her nakedness almost makes the viewer feel uncomfortable, for despite Wonder Woman's physical strength, she, whose image is strongly sexualized in the scene through her outfit and hairstyle, indeed, appears vulnerable.

The viewer's response to this scene is particularly curious to analyze through the concept of staring, as suggested by Rosemarie Garland-Thomson (2017). The scholar is primarily interested in the act of staring that emerges between two agents, one of whom has an "'extraordinary' appearance" (35), like Julia Pastrana, a performer from the nineteenth century, whose face and body were covered with black hair. I argue that it is plausible to apply Garland-Thomson's notion of "extraordinary appearance" to Wonder Woman, too. Her extraordinary appearance is defined by the perfection of the (woman's) body displayed in the scene. Whether female or male—the audience might engage in the process of staring, perceiving

Diana not as a soldier/warrior/fighter but first of all as a *woman*, and then later as a character whose appearance is both inappropriate and unreal for the moment. The viewer cannot imagine one of the male soldiers, for example, Steve himself, looking like Wonder Woman does. Then why do viewers have to imagine a woman in a war like that? Garland-Thomson claims:

> The cultural work of staring is frequently to normalize the viewer by spectacularizing the body on view, fixing it in a position of difference. [...] Staring enacts a cultural choreography between a disembodied spectator and an embodied spectacle that attempts to verify norms and establish differences. Staring is a meditation between viewer and viewed that exaggerates particularly by turning the visible body into a series of theatrical props gestures, or poses imbued with hyperbolic significance. [...] Staring thus produces narratives of the body, such as the deviant, the delightful, the marvellous, the primitive, the exotic, the alarming, or the pathetic [39–40].

The viewer *stares* at Wonder Woman because she appears inappropriate for the moment, unreally perfect which, in turn, communicates a very dangerous message regarding the female sex—that to be a true *Wonder* Woman, a woman needs to be overtly feminine, sexy, and perfect (a term that is perilous enough on its own) in everything. As one of the most extreme situations that a human being can find themselves in, war metaphorically stands for the high (sexist) expectations of a woman. This not only undermines gender equity but drastically widens the gap between media portrayals of femininity and real-life womanhood, suggesting the false and dangerous idea of women doing not enough and thus not deserving to be equitable to men.

Commenting on Wonder Woman's body, Mitra C. Emad (2006) writes:

> In each historical instance, however, Wonder Woman's body is both an icon of the traditionally masculine, public realm of nationhood as well as the traditionally feminine, private realm of female sexuality. As such, her body serves as a site for constantly oppositional encounters between gender and nation, private and public, and bondage and power. Reading Wonder Woman's body is an exercise in swinging between the binaries of women's physical empowerment (and sexual freedom) and representations of a body in bondage, lassoed into submission, sometimes by her own power [955–956].

The problem of combining masculinity and femininity is, indeed, apparent in the character of Wonder Woman. Yet one might wonder whether such a combination is generally needed. One can be feminine, or masculine, or both; the expectation of finding a balance and *thus* turning into a *wonder* woman is in itself sexist. And while J. Lenore Wright (2017) claims that Wonder Woman "navigates male and female spheres of existence to embody a modern American ideal," it is important to question ideals like this, for they only intensify the pressure on women, rather than truly empower them today (6).

Disability in Wonder Woman

Along with sexism, the images of an "ideal" female body promoted in *Wonder Woman* raise another significant issue involving physical appearance, body shape, and ability. This is what classifies the film as not only sexist but also ableist. By exaggerating the power of Wonder Woman, the film not simply uses ability; it abuses it to such an extent that the viewer never has trouble identifying the true *wonder* woman. Such an overt focus on an ideal, physically strong female body invites an interpretation of the portrayal of women in the film from a disability studies perspective. Just as feminism rejects the idea that "femaleness is a natural form of physical and mental deficiency or constitutional unruliness," feminist disability studies refute the view that "disability is a flaw, lack, or excess," and demonstrates that "disability—similar to race and gender—is a system of representation that marks bodies as subordinate, rather than an essential property of bodies that supposedly have something wrong with them" (Garland-Thomson 2005, 1557–58). Thus, combining feminist and disability studies perspectives helps uncover the intricacies and true nature of women's oppression in *Wonder Woman*.

As previously argued in the introduction to this essay, every superhero narrative explores the physical and mental abilities of the human body, thus, explicitly touching upon the problem of disability. Analyzing disability and superpowers from a pedagogical perspective, Lindsey Row-Heyveld (2015) makes an important observation:

> Superpowers may seem like an unlikely topic for a disability-focused course, but they provide a rich, wide-ranging context for the study of non-standard bodies. Pairing superpowers and disabilities makes it easy to discuss physical difference as a spectrum with the normate body at its center. Identified as both "less than" and "greater than" a corporeal norm, superpowered and disabled bodies demonstrate how that norm is not a constant but a construct. Examining the spectrum of physical variation reveals the many forces that shape those constructions and superpowers and disabilities wield genuine power in our world despite the artificiality of those categories. Ostensibly fictional superpowers obsess our culture, influencing everything from medical breakthroughs to the Olympics. In addition, because of this mutual focus on normativity, stories about superpowers are where some of the most exciting and widely circulated narratives about disability emerge [520–521].

Row-Heyveld thus underscores the potental of superhero texts to explore the issues involving disability studies, which makes these narratives an important cultural platform that latently or overtly can help celebrate differences and promote diversity. Yet each example is individual, and ableism is part of some of such narratives, too. *Wonder Woman*, for example, uses disability as a tool to contrast physical weakness with power, on the one hand, and good with evil, on the other. This sleight of hand makes the film ableist.

The energetic engagement with the issue of disability that superhero narratives demonstrate is, at first sight, welcome. Scholars have been lamenting about the neglect that the world generally shows to disability and people with disabilities. For example, in their introduction to *The Oxford Handbook of Disability History*, Michael Rembis, Catherine Kudlick, and Kim E. Nielsen (2018) state:

> For many people, disability history—like disability itself—exists at the outermost edges of their consciousness. This omission is striking, given the ubiquity of disability. According to the World Bank, approximately one billion people, about 15 percent of the world's population, can be defined as disabled. Nearly everyone (including historians) encounters disability in their daily lives. Disability is the one minority anyone can join at any time due to an accident, a disease, or simply by growing older. And all signs seem to indicate that the world's disabled population will continue to grow in the coming decades [1].

In a similar tone, Garland-Thompson characterizes disability as "a significant human experience that occurs in every society, every family, and most every life" ("Disability and Representation" 2005, 524). Indeed, closing one's eyes to the medical, cultural, political, economic, and social difficulties that people with physical and mental impairments face is corrupt in itself. The inspiring images of and for disabled people on the page and screen are necessary for maintaining inclusion on various levels.

These images, however, inevitably engage in a cultural dialogue regarding such issues as normality, ability, and the body. They both *produce* knowledge about diversity and *are* manifestations of variety—cultural, gender, body, or otherwise. Indeed, "what we think of as normal is socially and culturally constructed," and cultural images play a significant role in reinforcing the ideas of what is normal, popular, and welcome, and what is not (Walters 2015, 174). In that respect, "disability aesthetics" is a significant contribution to the cultural imagination of diversity and difference, for it

> seeks to emphasize the presence of different bodies and minds in the tradition of aesthetic representation—that tradition concerned most precisely with the appearance of the beautiful. It refuses to recognize the representation of the healthy body and this body's definition of harmony, integrity, and beauty as the sole determination of the aesthetic [Siebers 2005, 542].

In *Wonder Woman*, disability is a defining feature of several characters. First, Sir Patrick Morgan uses a crutch that explicitly accentuates the man's physical weakness—particularly when surrounded by military men whom the audience perceives as "fit" to participate in war. Crucially, despite the suggested physical impairment, the man turns out to be Ares— the god who poses a mortal threat to humanity and Wonder Woman, and is a very strong character. Second, Dr. Poison is another character with a physical disability that helps reinforce the motif of sexism that runs through the film.

Dr. Poison, as is clear from her name, specializes in poisons. She works for General Ludendorff (Danny Huston), creating a deadly chemical weapon for him. The portrayal of Dr. Poison is sexist in a number of ways. First, despite her intelligence, she is perceived as Ludendorff's subordinate, who is both controlled and manipulated by him. She is forced to work harder until she manages to create the gas that would make Ludendorff even more powerful and invincible. The injury to her mouth can be metaphorically interpreted to represent her inability to speak for herself and be level with Ludendorff or other men. Second, her profession echoes the association of women with witches that comes from the Middle Ages but is still frequently used today to represent a woman working in laboratory science as a wicked and dangerous being. Finally, Dr. Poison's evil nature is further reinforced through three other aspects related to her persona: her accent, her hoarse voice, and her facial impairment that is skillfully covered by a mask/prosthesis. It is crucial that when Ludendorff visits Dr. Poison to convince her to create a deadly biological weapon, he says, *stroking her mask/prosthesis*, "I know that you can and will succeed. It is what you're put on this earth to do." Ludendorff's stroking the injured part of Dr. Poison's face intensifies the deadly nature of the woman, thus displaying disability as a form of an evil trait and suggesting that physical impairment is a sign of one's wicked nature. In addition to that, Dr. Poison's physical impairment only reinforces her weakness, for "[d]isabled women are infantilised and imagined as helpless victims" (Mohamed and Shefer 2015, 5). This is particularly evident in the final scene in *Wonder Woman*, when Dr. Poison is lying on the ground between Wonder Woman and Ares. Dr. Poison's facial mask/prosthesis is off, revealing that part of her face is missing, thus displaying her as an already-injured woman and, hence, weak.

The images of both sexism and ableism in the film are related to the women's appearances. Playing with the issues of perfection and imperfection, the film recreates two polar heroines, one of whom is a "wonder," whereas the other one is pure evil. Lennard J. Davis (1995) calls appearance one of the "major modalit[ies] by which disability is constructed" (12). The scholar continues, "The person with disabilities is visualized, brought into a field of vision, and seen as a disabled person. [...] The body of the disabled person is seen as marked by the disability. [...] Disability is a spectacular moment. The power of the gaze to control, limit, and patrol the disabled person is brought to the fore. Accompanying the gaze are a welter of powerful emotional responses. These responses can include horror, fear, pity, compassion, and avoidance" (12). David Hevey describes a similar process through which the disabled/able-bodied binary was brought to the fore regarding freak shows—"enfreakment" (qtd. in Garland-Thomson 2017, 17). Garland-Thomson (2017) elucidates "enfreakment" by the example of American freak shows, claiming that they "offered to the spectator an icon of physical otherness that reinforced the onlookers' common American identity, verified by a body that suddenly seemed by comparison ordinary, tractable, and standard" (17). Similar emotional responses are expected from the viewer who watches *Wonder Woman*: Wonder Woman's body is used to provoke fascination and admiration, whereas Dr. Poison's body becomes an instrument to stir repulsion, disgust, and fear. This helps the viewer easily distinguish between the two women. Thus, the images of the two bodies generate sexism and ableism and emphasize that both gender and disability are social constructions: they are a mixture of what our bodies and minds can do along with what they are perceived to do.

Garland-Thomson argues: "Representation structures rather than reflect reality. The way we imagine disability through images and narratives determines the shape of the material world, the distribution of resources, our relationships with one another, and our sense of ourselves" ("Disability and Representation" 2005, 523). Dr. Poison's physical impairment that is used to reinforce the character's evil nature, therefore, is a criminal manipulation of disability to promote both ableism and sexism. Ian Williams (2015) contends that "[i]mages do not just 'mirror' the world; they help build it"; yet he adds, "The proliferation of image-based media has also ensured that iconographic representations of health, illness, and disease have become increasingly important in Western societies" (118). Images of disability help audiences worldwide learn more about various impairments and ask even more profound questions about social, political, economic, and cultural inclusion. And while promoting ableist images is discriminating and simply wrong, *recognizing* ableism in such embodiment helps promote tolerance and inclusion. Whereas the images of disability such as Dr. Poison are frequently recurring and construct a distorted reality, where people with disabilities continue to be treated unequally by the able-bodied majority, disability studies seriously engage with the problem, working hard towards achieving inclusion.

Disability studies' project is to weave disabled people back into the fabric of society, thread by thread, theory by theory. It aims to expose the ways that disability has been made exceptional and to work to naturalize disabled people—remake us as full citizens whose rights and privileges are intact, whose history and contributions are recorded, and whose often distorted representations in art, literature, film, theater and other forms of artistic expression are fully analyzed [Linton 2005, 518].

The analysis of *Wonder Woman* and its treatment of disability and gender inequity reveals the recurring painful pattern of cultural ignorance and sabotage that allows images of sexism and ableism to continue to fill the screens, in superhero films or otherwise.

Conclusion

Wonder Woman is a superhero film that undoubtedly deserves attention. As society continues to encounter various types of inequity, the portrayal of a strong woman seems very appropriate. Given the age of the character created and recreated since World War II both on the page and screen, Wonder Woman has stirred multiple discussions among her fans and scholars from different fields—from gender studies to popular culture studies to comics studies and beyond. Depending on the time, the heroine was interpreted as empowering or sexist. Scholars also note that "Wonder Woman's own creation through an independent act by her mother, who made her from clay without any involvement from a man, echoes continuing feminist concerns about the importance of women's freedom to make choices about their reproductive rights" (Curtis and Cardo 2018, 382). Diana Prince, aka Wonder Woman, has provoked heated debates. Today, with the release of Jenkins' *Wonder Woman* in 2017, the superheroine again makes one wonder what her image stands for: is she the sign of female strength and independence, or is she just another cultural/media product that muses patriarchy? While there is an attempt to celebrate women's liberation and gender equity in the film, the image of Wonder Woman is primarily sexist and, in its current form, dangerous. Dennis Knepp (2017) notes, "Wonder Woman's origin story is about history, and she must overcome the traditions of the past to become modern" (155). To recontextualize this statement, Wonder Woman, indeed, must become modern/new/updated to fit the needs of today's society that vehemently fights against sexism and women's oppression.

Along with sexism, ableism is another issue that *Wonder Woman* raises. The discriminating images of physical impairment that the film employs help corroborate *Wonder Woman*'s sexist messages and transform the film into another example of cultural myopia, ignorance, and intolerance. Catherine J. Kudlick (2005) claims:

> The study of disability history shares many threads with earlier explorations of marginal groups. Like other Others, disabled people seem to fit neatly in a counteracademic canon that has developed in opposition to the dead white men of yore. Social history, which provided voices to people who had traditionally been ignored (particularly the working classes), gave birth to the history of women and racial minorities and, more recently, to gay and lesbian history. The historiography of each group follows a strikingly similar path [557].

The images of ableism and sexism profoundly intersect in the film, making each other even more insidious. They painfully remind the audiences about the existing inequalities and become obstacles on the way to freedom, diversity, and the celebration of differences. *Wonder Woman* is, therefore, a film that perhaps attempts to send a powerful message yet dismally fails to do so, falling into the trap of popular mass entertainment that continues to profit from discriminating images, including those of sexism and ableism.

REFERENCES

Abadía, Mónica Cano. 2017. "Wonder Woman and Patriarchy: From Themyscira's Amazons to Wittig's Guérrillères." In *Wonder Woman and Philosophy: The Amazonian Mystique*, edited by Jacob M. Held, 162–70. Hoboken, NJ: John Wiley & Sons.

Curtis, Neal, and Valentina Cardo. 2018. "Superheroes and Third-Wave Feminism." *Feminist Media Studies* 18 (3): 381–96. doi: 10.1080/14680777.2017.1351387.

Davis, Lennard J. 1995. *Enforcing Normalcy: Disability, Deafness, and the Body*. London, UK: Verso.

de Beauvoir, Simone. 2010 (1949). *The Second Sex*. Translated by Constance Borde and Sheila Malovany-Chevallier. New York: Vintage Books.

Emad, Mitra C. 2006. "Reading Wonder Woman's Body: Mythologies of Gender and Nation." *The Journal of Popular Culture* 39 (6): 954–984. doi: 10.1111/j.1540–5931.2006.00 329.x.

Garland-Thomson, Rosemarie. 1997. *Extraordinary Bodies: Figuring Physical Disability in American Culture and Literature*. New York: Columbia University Press.

_____. 2005. "Disability and Representation." *PMLA* 120 (2): 522–27. https://www.jstor.org/stable/25486178.

_____. 2005. "Feminist Disability Studies." *Signs* 30 (2): 1557–87. JSTOR. https://www.jstor.org/stable/10.1086/423352.

_____. 2017. "Julia Pastrana, the 'Extraordinary Lady.'" *ALTER, European Journal of Disability Research* 11: 35–49. doi: 10.1556/022.2019.64.1.4.

Halberstam, Judith. 1998. *Female Masculinity*. Durham, NC: Duke University Press.

Jenkins, Patty, dir. 2017. *Wonder Woman*. Burbank, CA: Warner Bros. Pictures.

Knepp, Dennis. 2017. "Merciful Minerva in a Modern Metropolis." In *Wonder Woman and Philosophy: The Amazonian Mystique*, edited by Jacob M. Held, 151–61. Hoboken, NJ: John Wiley & Sons.

Kudlick, Catherine J. 2005. "Disability History, Power, and Rethinking the Idea of 'the Other.'" *PMLA* 120 (2): 557–61.

Linton, Simi. 2005. "What Is Disability Studies?" *PMLA 120* (2): 518–22.

Matsuuchi, Ann. 2012. "Wonder Woman Wears Pants: *Wonder Woman*, Feminism and the 1972 'Women's Lib' Issue." *COLLOQUY Text Theory Critique 24*: 118–42. https://academicworks.cuny.edu/lg_pubs/3/.

McCrossin, Trip. 2017. "Great Hera! Considering Wonder Woman's Super Heroism." In *Wonder Woman and Philosophy: The Amazonian Mystique*, edited by Jacob M. Held, 44–53. Hoboken, NJ: John Wiley & Sons.

Mohamed, Kharnita, and Tamara Shefer. 2015. "Gendering Disability and Disabling Gender: Critical Reflections on Intersections of Gender and Disability." *Agenda 29* (2): 2–13. doi: 10.1080/10130950.2015.1055878.

Rembis, Michael, Catherine Kudlick, and Kim E. Nielsen. 2018. "Introduction." In *The Oxford Handbook of Disability History*, edited by Michael Rembis, Catherine Kudlick, and Kim E. Nielsen, 1–18. New York: Oxford University Press.

Row-Heyveld, Lindsey. 2015. "Reading *Batman*, Writing *X-Men*: Superpowers and Disabilities in the First-Year Seminar." *Pedagogy 15* (3): 519–26. doi: 10.1215/15314200–2917105.

Siebers, Tobin. 2005. "Disability Aesthetics." *PMLA* 120 (2): 542–46. https://www.english.upenn.edu/sites/www.english.upenn.edu/files/Siebers-Tobin_Disability-Aesthetics.pdf.

Smith, Philip. 2017. "Reading Aaron Diaz's Wonder Woman." *Literature Compass 14*: 1–12. doi: 10.1111/lic3.12384.

Walters, Shannon. 2015. "Graphic Disruptions: Comics, Disability and De-Canonizing Composition." *Composition Studies 43* (1): 174–77. https://www.jstor.org/stable/4350184.

Williams, Ian. 2015. "Comics and the Iconography of Illness." In *Graphic Medicine Manifesto* by MK Czerwiec et al., 115–42. University Park, PA: Penn State University Press.

Wright, Lenore. 2017. "Becoming a (Wonder) Woman: Feminism, Nationalism, and the Ambiguity of Female Identity." In *Wonder Woman and Philosophy: The Amazonian Mystique*, edited by Jacob M. Held, 5–18. Hoboken, NJ: John Wiley & Sons.

Zanin, Andrea. 2017. "Wonder Woman: Feminist Faux Pas?" In *Wonder Woman and Philosophy: The Amazonian Mystique*, edited by Jacob M. Held, 57–71. Hoboken, NJ: John Wiley & Sons.

Assimilating Queer/Disabled Subjects in Marvel Superhero Fanfiction

Divya Garg

Media fan communities have often been lauded as a safe space and support group for many individuals, allowing fans to share empowering fan narratives representing marginalized identities such as sexuality and disability experiences, among others (Dandrow 2016). Media fandom is an interactive community where fans participate in transformative creative activities such as writing fanfiction or "fic," and creating art and videos. Superhero narratives can also provide alternative imaginings of corporate media, such as constructing the superhero figure congruent to disability. This runs counter to the traditional genre, which suggests superheroes are associated with superhuman abilities rather than disabilities. Since superheroes live in worlds that often give rise to war and violence, it makes sense that they experience physical disability, mental health conditions, and trauma that is significant. In sharp contrast to the DC Universe, where disabilities, both mental and physical, are predominantly seen via the villains, the MCU has grappled with disability through its superhero heroes. However, in the case of Marvel superheroes, disabilities are less evident or startling. Audiences may forget that prominent characters like Steve Rogers had disabilities before being converted into Captain America by the super-soldier serum.

The narrative arcs of queered, disabled superhero bodies are investigated in this essay to determine how disability fits into the fan model of citizenship. Bucky Barnes' construction as a queer/disabled character is examined through the fanfiction subgenre of the Winter Soldier trial narrative in the Marvel Cinematic Universe (MCU) fandom (McRuer 2006). Barnes' character is assessed within the context of fandom's subcultural politics, his redemption and reintegration into American citizenship, and the limitations of such models. The dominant perspectives in this research are based on surveys and interviews with Marvel fans who identify as people of color and persons with disabilities. Using an intersectional lens, race and nationality are examined for how they complicate the relationship between sexuality and disability in Marvel fanworks. In some cases, disability is mobilized against racial minorities to signify fandom's inclusive "feel good" diversity.

In political fanfics, one of the most influential fanworks in Marvel fandom is *United States v. Barnes* (2014) by fan authors fallingvoices and radialarch. This fan reinterpretation of the *Captain America* storyline imagines the court trial of the popular disabled character, James Buchanan "Bucky" Barnes, also known as the Winter Soldier. Bucky Barnes (played by Sebastian Stan) is first introduced in *Captain America: The First Avenger* (2011) as Steve Rogers' best friend. In the film, set during the Second World War, Barnes is captured by the Germans and rescued by Rogers in his first (unofficial) mission as Captain America. He then becomes part of Rogers' special unit called Howling Commandos and presumably dies after falling from a train during combat. In the second Captain America film, *Captain America: The Winter Soldier* (2014), it is revealed that after his fall, Barnes was captured by a cult Nazi organization named Hydra, who tortured and brainwashed—through electric shocks that erased his memory—him into becoming the Winter Soldier. After losing his left arm in the fall, he was given a super-soldier serum and fitted with a bionic arm. Barnes was held in a cryogenic cell for more than seventy years, and he was only allowed out for authorized assassinations. At the end of the film, he defies his conditioning by rescuing Rogers when he falls into a river following their fight.

The Winter Soldier trial fics are set mainly in the canon (or official) universe but continue the story differently after the end of *Captain America: The Winter Soldier* (2014). These stories center on how the atrocities of the Winter Soldier would be perceived in the modern world and if Barnes would be charged for his time as the Winter Soldier. The unifying thread in these stories is that Barnes is being prosecuted by the U.S. judicial system for his crimes as the Winter Soldier, including treason and sixty-three counts of murder, while Rogers and supporters construct a defense for him. Interestingly, the "Winter Soldier" title comes from the "Winter Soldier Investigation" initiated by American veterans of the Vietnam War to account for war crimes committed by the U.S. Army in Vietnam (Reisman 2016). Barnes' character arc in the MCU is thus an intriguing mix of espionage, violence, disability, and trauma.

Court trials explicitly trace the trajectory of socio-legal accommodation (or rejection) and ideas of citizenship. The "fanonical"—or widely accepted in fandom—trial of the popular disabled character, Bucky Barnes, frequently read as queer by fans, helps study what "moves" fans politically and how markers of race and nationality circumscribe these movements. As emblematic of the citizenship narrative, the representational politics of the trial subgenre center on *United States v. Barnes* (2014) and briefly discuss related works. Fans' political initiatives and the constraints of their emancipatory imagination are depicted through the lens of Western neoliberal nations and white queer/disabled fans. The goal is to decolonize the concept of disability, which has been conceptualized exclusively in terms of research from the Global North. Theories on the politics of affect are also used to connect issues of representation to the emotions and feelings materialized through fans of color's encounters with these texts in the globally diverse space of media fandom. Thus, the consequences of cultural representation in terms of its political dimensions are also examined.

United States v. Barnes (2014) is one of the most popular fanfics in Marvel fandom based on its statistical demographics on the fanfiction platform Archive of Our Own (AO3) and overall impact. It is recurrent in the top ten in the MCU, Marvel, Avengers, and *Captain America* fandoms when sorted by "kudos" or "likes" (20450) and has the highest number of bookmarks (7770) across these. It is also a common choice on lists of the best Marvel fanfiction: named as number one on the comic's website, comicbook.com's list of "11 of the Best Marvel Cinematic Universe Fan Fictions So Far" (August 2019). The Stucky Library—a popular fanfic recommendation blog that a pinned response describes as "*The New York Times* of gay Captain America literature" (Anonymous n.d.)—features it in its "influential fics for new readers" and "personal favorites" lists. It has inspired 12 derivative works and has over a thousand, largely appreciative, reader comments. Elements such as social media text, images, and court transcripts contribute to the creative format of the mixed media fic and its widespread appeal. These aspects make *United States v. Barnes* a culturally significant and particularly "moving" text.

Political Affect and the Winter Soldier Trial Subgenre

In the Marvel universe, stories often focus on pseudo-fictional events of national and international interest. While certain wars (such as World War II) referenced in the Marvel comics took place, these involved science-fiction elements in the narrative engagement with military themes. Political arcs in the comics and movies also include references to the Cold War, U.S. presence in Afghanistan, and various allusions to the United States government. Political engagement is another popular narrative topic among Marvel fans. Marvel fanfiction covers topics including "veteran issues," "period-typical homophobia," "disability rights," "same-sex marriage legislation," and historical events such as the Cold War and Civil Rights Movement. With characters directly employed by the U.S. Army in the canon, their fan fiction often engage with political topics such as war and terrorism. The *Captain America* fanbase, in particular, uses the Captain America myth in overtly political and affective ways, whether it is rioters on U.S. Capitol Hill utilizing Captain America imagery or left-leaning fans depicting characters as socialist activists.

In my survey and interviews, fans of color expressed their affinity for political themes in the movies and the fanworks they engaged. One Indian participant, Sofia Razvi, who identifies as queer, noted her interest in characters written as politically "woke." She explained her favorite fanfiction narrative as follows:

> [characters] being super political, especially when it comes to queerness—we just want hope that the people we ship like crazy fucks are actually the kind of people we might like to be friends with. Also using your position of power to make important statements [2020].

Razvi's statement reveals her desire for specific characterization in terms of its political appeal. For those occupying marginal positions in real life, characters' political leanings connect to their identity and affiliations. Ms. Andry who identifies as a mixed-Chinese queer person with a disability echoes such a sentiment. They express how fanfics about "forbidden queer love" gives them "feels" or makes them particularly emotional because queer and disabled love is marginalized in many contexts. When queerness is blocked from flourishing within the bounds of national culture, queer identity and desire cannot be separated from politics. Furthermore, ableist beliefs about the incongruency between disabled bodies and love could be holding him back from being truly happy. The language of "feels" connects to affective notions, highlighting the materiality of emotional expression and its embodiment (see Sedgwick and Frank 1995). Affect is also understood in the Deleuzian sense as "changes in bodily capacity" (Hickey-Moody 2013, 80), which highlights the emotions involved in the process of engaging with fanworks.

The social character of fans' feelings for political subjects in fanfiction and those formed through their encounter with them produce fans as affective citizens and their emotions as political affects. Feelings such as happiness, sadness, anger, pity, discomfort, unease, desire, and longing, are linked to practices of (dis)identification and belonging. Several of these emotions are traditionally linked with ableist perspectives about disability prevail such as sadness and pity. Ann-Marie Fortier (2010) describes these practices as "governing through affect" (22). In these practices, emotions function as political affects. Other theorists argue, "feelings of belonging and affective attachments [are] not metaphors for something else, but key conduits of power themselves" (Slaby and Bens 2019, 347). The production of emotions in fan engagement links to power operations—of whiteness, (U.S.) nationality, and ability. For instance, fans feel happy when they witness specific representations because they identify with the characters or situations portrayed and are sad or angry when they cannot. The ableist clichés of the bitter wheelchair user, the mystical blind person, the weak disabled war veteran who cannot live an active life, and the "better off dead than disabled" stereotype persist even in fan fiction. Hence, this analysis pays attention to the emotions of fans, particularly fans of color from the Global South, to materialize how governance practices within fandom reproduce real world hierarchies.

Personal and political desires for queer/disabled happiness and belonging combine to form the fan motivations behind this trial genre. In using the narrative device of a court trial, fans call attention to the democratizing legal apparatus of the United States and a discourse of citizenship through a particular framing of intimacy. This is evident in fan motivations for the Winter Soldier trial narratives, discussed by the popular fanfiction blog, *The Stucky Library*, below:

> These fics often function to an extent as treatises defending Bucky against fans and outsiders alike. At the same time the reality of victim blaming and blame shifting in our own world need to be dealt with. These fics handle the complexities of both the character and real world power structures quite amazingly and in a variety of ways [mods 2016].

Trial fics connect narratives of "real" socio-political significance to fans' lived experiences of victimization, trauma and blame—significant for marginalized people. Barnes' marginalization as a traumatized, disabled, and queered figure speaks to fans' own oppressive realities. The desire to effectuate a "happy ending" through political freedom and social equity points to fans' desires for their own societal belonging and normative happiness. The next section investigates how the trial genre functions as a form of citizenship narrative that generates the aforementioned ends.

Affecting Citizenship: Reading the Trial of the Winter Soldier

In reading the legal trial as a test of Barnes' fitness into the (fan) model of American citizenship, his political rehabilitation and assimilation translates as a practice of citizenship, often denied to racial, sexual, and disabled minorities. Lauren Berlant suggests that citizenship is "produced out of a political, rhetorical, and economic struggle over who will count as 'the people' and how social membership will be measured and valued" (1997, 20). In modern times, Berlant notes a shift from perceived citizenship as a form of state-based political identification to a "culture-based concept of the nation as a site of integrated social membership" (1997, 3) performed through everyday acts of intimacy. Such citizenship practices link the private and public spheres or ideas of domesticity and national belonging, as evident in the framework of fanworks (as romance narratives) that engage with political themes. The question that Winter Soldier trial fics seem to ask (and essentially answer affirmatively) is whether Barnes—and by virtue, queer disabled diverse fans—counts enough as a U.S. citizen to achieve personal happiness.

This is significant considering the particular importance of citizenship narratives at this juncture of history. Over the last few years, protests relating to citizenship and nationality have taken place globally. The citizen protests in Hong Kong and India and the Black Lives Matter protests in the U.S. signal the systemic denial of constitutional rights to minorities. Governmental responses to the Covid-19 pandemic reveal further limitations on who gets counted as a citizen and whose life matters. Projects of governmentality afford citizenship and associated rights to those who contribute economically or militarily to the idea of the nation. In addition, notions of global citizenship dissipate due to the unequal distribution of vaccines and resources amidst the pandemic as evident from the massive death toll and systemic failures in third world countries like India and Brazil. These national and global developments highlight how citizenship is a fraught category for various minorities, often under attack by those in dominant positions of power.

Subaltern populations enact citizenship in alternative spheres of civic participation. These areas are often characterized as "subaltern counterpublics" (Fraser 1990), defined by their opposition to dominant discourses, identities, and interests, part of the "public sphere" (Habermas 1991). Here, citizenship is performed through cultural acts of belonging such as creative arts practices, known as "cultural citizenship" (Rosaldo 1994). Counterpublics provide a sense of belonging and space for the articulation of non-dominant perspectives. Wei (2015) argues that as informal sites of participation countering dominant heteronormative narratives, fan communities function as "virtual counterpublics." However, the fandom counterpublic may reproduce privileges and hierarchies of subordination that obscure membership on the basis of sexuality, disability status, and race. As Holm (2019) argues, not all counterpublics are subaltern, as they may include populations who are not structurally underprivileged.

It is inaccurate to assume fans are subalterns under their subordinate status outside of fandom. Notwithstanding the political transgression of heteronormativity and (limited) tolerance of disability, fan work reproduces systemic imbalances and promotes whiteness, ableism, and nationalism. Disability in citizenship (trial) fanworks operate in ways that align with hegemonic power structures relevant to current citizenship policies. Sara McKinnon argues that "access to U.S. citizenship is increasingly dependent on asylum seekers' ability to appear coherently credible, grounded upon … embodied affect … based in exclusionary discourses concerning the proper performances of U.S. citizenship" (2006, 205). Affect used concerning citizenship performances widens understandings of citizenship beyond the level of formal access to the public sphere. Fortier argues that a key dimension to analyzing affective citizenship is to ask how "the fantasy of state power and desirability" is produced (2013, 700). To do so, disability intersects with race, nationalism, and sexuality to include the queer disabled subject within the parameters of citizenship.

Disability and Race: Whiteness, Disability and Violence

Disability is constructed and explicitly performed to engender the disabled subject as sympathetic, attractive, harmless, and valuable to the nation. Given that the punishment for treason and terrorism in the U.S. can be the death penalty, Barnes' case is a literalization of the process of how certain disabled subjects "are made representative and 'targeted for life' even as others are disabled in different ways, or cripped, or 'targeted for death'" (McRuer 2010, 171). In this section, I analyze the role that whiteness plays in targeting disabled subjects for life.

The visibility of physical disablement works to render Barnes as a sympathetic subject. The first mention of Barnes' physical appearance in *United States v. Barnes* is in a *New York Times* article. The news article mentions that witnesses to the Washington, D.C., massacre described the Winter Soldier as "brutally fit" (fallingvoices and radialarch, 4) and that the court has ordered the removal of Barnes' advanced prosthetic deeming it a weapon. Following his prosthetic limb's removal, Barnes's physical disability becomes pronounced, which humanizes the character and dissociates him from his persona as a violent killer. When the defense lawyer questions a witness, he responds that Barnes appears different in court: "real" and "human" (8), unlike before. This supports the defense's strategy of establishing Barnes' innocence by creating sympathy for the character based on his physical and mental disabilities linked to his torture. The defense next provides extensive documentation of the abuse during

Barnes' imprisonment by Hydra. This leads to much public opinion shifting in his favor—evidenced on social media through trends such as "WS is a victim not a murderer" (15). The defense relies heavily on notions of embodied affect by generating feelings of pity for Barnes and disgust at his captors among the jury and audience. Such negative emotions are utilized to authenticate Barnes' experiences of trauma and place him among the "deserving poor" (Snyder and Mitchell 2010) and use disability to garner sympathy.

Whiteness is essential to this discourse of sympathy and the aestheticization of trauma. In *United States v. Barnes*, other trial fics, and Marvel fanfiction centered on Bucky Barnes at large, torture is a continual motif for humanizing the character and rendering him sympathetic. For instance, there are over 7500 stories involving Barnes with the tag "trauma" and over 4200 tagged "torture" on the AO3. The humanization is partly achieved through the attention paid to Barnes' character and subjectivity outside of his time as a prisoner of war, which serves to construct personhood beyond his abuse and trauma. However, this personhood is consistently not granted to racial and national others in Marvel fandom. While this may be owing to the lack of such characters in Marvel canon, it is telling that even fics set in alternate universe stories involving "real" wars continue to center or include the disablement of white male perpetrator/victims alone. For instance, dreadnought's *Baghdad Waltz* recounts the traumatic experiences of Barnes and Rogers as U.S. soldiers serving in the Iraq War for nearly 700,000 words. While it is important to critique the effect of war and violence on the psychology of (U.S.) soldiers, the absence of any national and racial others from such consideration reveals a critical gap in fan's imaginations; a gap which may be inescapable for fans of color who are the subject of U.S. imperial violence. For instance, when it comes to torture, "transnational and transhistorical linkages … surge together to create the Muslim body as a particular typological object of torture" (Puar 2007, 85–86). However, the Muslim body is conspicuously absent from any such mention in fanworks. It is precisely Barnes' racialized whiteness that allows his torture and resulting trauma to be a worthy subject of aestheticization and exploration.

Whiteness serves to eliminate the threat of mental disability resulting from torture to produce Barnes as a sympathetic abject individual. Barnes' mental disabilities and trauma are affirmed in *United States v. Barnes* by the testimony of Sam Wilson, a Veteran Affairs counsellor and the superhero Falcon. The racialization of mental disability is evident from the legal rhetoric and news media coverage in the text. *United States v. Barnes* (2014) begins with tweets from the American press announcing that the Winter Soldier is set to trial for "massacre and treason" (fallingvoices and radialarch, 2) and allude to the Soldier's mass shootings. This is followed by an excerpt from an interview with a Harvard Law professor discussing the legal precedents of the case and possible arguments by the defense team. The fictional professor explains that the defense's argument rests on a "lack of voluntariness," similar to an "insanity plea" in that Barnes did not possess the awareness or intent to commit the crimes (2). Two important interconnected themes emerge from this opening scene: violence and mental health conditions. The language of news media coverage references contemporary America's significant gun violence problem. Popular and political opinion directly links mental health with violence, including then President Trump's 2018 statement that mass shootings are a mental health problem. Mental health conditions, especially psychiatric conditions, are associated with criminalized violence, and Barnes' case makes for an especially suitable linkage given his history of abuse. This association works in Barnes' favor because of the effect of whiteness. In performances of citizenship, disability is racialized, and (non-white) race is disabling. As Jess Waggoner argues:

> presumed mental disability is not the sole disqualifier of citizenship—the persistent racialization of mental disability contributes to these discourses. Many of the decisions about these exclusions are made judicially, but they are also made in the visual field of media and performance, where viewers encounter images that confirm, extend, or refute their notions of who counts as civically fit [2016, 99].

This is evidenced by the success of Barnes' framing of disability in his defense. Real life news media coverage of mass shootings supports such analyses. Scott Duxbury et al. (2018) found that white and Hispanic populations are more likely to have their crimes attributed to mental health conditions than African Americans. While African American men and Latinos are presented as violently inclined, white men are treated as victims or sympathetic individuals. Disability thus intersects with whiteness to portray Barnes as a compassionate and harmless citizen, integrable into the nation-state.

Disability and Nationalism: The Geopolitics of Disability

The potential harm of disabled subjectivity is further countered through the ideological power of nationalism. Despite Barnes' white privilege, the conflicting discourses about his mental and physical disabilities contribute to his persistence as a violent threat to the nation. Though the metal arm visibly links him with a physical disability, the advanced prosthetic serves as a super-powered weapon increasing his bodily capacity. As Anna Hickey-Moody argues, "violent and competitive masculine subjectivity" (2015, 139) can be performed through the masculinization of carbon fiber prosthetics. To establish Barnes' allegiance, which determines his harm or utility for the nation, both sides of the trial make repeated references to his past service to the state and the subsequent "betrayal" of that state. As an American soldier who fought in World War II, Sergeant Barnes can be viewed as a mistreated veteran and the world's longest prisoner of war. However, his crimes as a Hydra assassin, transferred between different parties of Nazi affiliation—from Germany to the Soviet to the U.S.—make him a figure of domestic and international terrorism. This threat is countered by employing the power of nationalism.

Nationalism is emphasized through the de/legitimization of witness testimonies in the trial. As an ex-weapons manufacturer and billionaire superhero, Tony Stark is a useful witness for Barnes because his nationalism aligns with dominant values such as economic and military prowess. In contrast, Natasha Romanoff's (the Black Widow) testimony is delegitimized because of her questionable history as a cultural "other" given her past as an ex-KGB Russian assassin who now works for a U.S. world security organization. More significantly, as the last witness to speak in his own trial, Barnes himself raises the question of nationalism in his speech to the jury. He admits:

> I was killing people long before I was turned into the Winter Soldier. I killed people during the war [WWII] … I was killing people for the United States government a long time before I fell off that train in the Alps. Maybe part of me was made a weapon the second I set foot in that ol' enlistment center back in Brooklyn.

Here, a national register is invoked not to posit Barnes as a "good citizen" but to construct the nation itself as flawed. Such moments facilitate a critique of nationalism, which condones and valorizes killing. However, these implications are never fully realized in fandom by making the government answer for its culpability. A popular and influential fic—which includes the trial motif—that alludes to American culpability is dropdeaddream and WhatAreFears' massively influential *Not Easily Conquered* (2015). Here, the narrative links the American government with Hydra. And the story ends with Barnes and Rogers uniting instead of holding a legal trial where the government answers for its crimes. Though some fics discuss Hydra's accountability, these are not the subject of the trial narratives, but, at most, revenge stories where Barnes kills everyone involved in his Winter Soldier formation. Such stories work to provide emotional or moral catharsis to Barnes, focusing on his disability rehabilitation and mental health.

The validation of Barnes' lived experiences of torture and mental distress in fics does acknowledge the torture undertaken *by* the (imperial) state on foreign or "othered" populations in the name of national sovereignty. Making only the U.S. subject as the abject dispossessed and relegating wrongdoing to a Nazi organization conceals the imperialist agendas of contemporary America that fail to address structural inequity. This is particularly relevant in remembering the origins of the "Winter Soldier" title in a war crime investigation of American vets following the Vietnam War and later for the Iraq and Afghanistan wars. Fics such as *Not Easily Conquered* series mention this association in their notes to raise fans' awareness of such realities without further exploring their impact (in terms of either physical or mental disablement) on people of color. Thus, "Winter Soldier" is a means for Marvel and its fandom to borrow elements of war, violence, and trauma without exploring how the U.S. perpetuated and profited from this racist and imperialist violence.

Furthermore, fandom is also guilty of ignoring the potential for decolonizing disability identity in its representations. Shaun Grech (2016) argues that disability studies in postcolonial nations perpetuate Eurocentric notions that involve a colonial legacy, resulting from historical processes of slavery and impoverishment. Furthermore, the current geopolitical order suggests that disability is unequally researched. Jasbir Puar contends that disability among the disenfranchised in the Global South, where four-fifths of the world's disabled people reside, is a product of deliberate "population debilitation" (2017, 73) arising from conditions of "poverty, permanent war, racism, imperialism and colonialism" (69). Such aspects are particularly relevant to the political terrain of Marvel storylines which consistently represent superheroes as saviors for third world nations and populations, fictional or otherwise. For fandom to repeat their erasures even in narratives involving a popular character with a disability limits its emancipatory ideology and potential.

Political justice as dealt in fandom is crucial to the appeal of the trial narrative, however, the imbrication of this justice in the erasures of American imperialism is a significant qualification in considering its appeal for diverse fans globally. People of color and non–U.S. fans' affective pleasure may be limited by the knowledge that even the fandom world is largely an imperialist utopia. As Sofia Razvi (2020) admits in her reasons for liking the Winter Soldier trial narrative:

> it makes you think of a world where a prisoner of war can get justice, where torture is seen as the heinous crime that it is (*only when perpetrated by non–US governments, of course*) where the public can be on the good side instead of all of them being a bunch of conservative, prejudiced, oppressive horrible people [emphasis added].

While the idea of political justice is linked with pleasure and happiness, Sofia's Razvi awareness of its roots in American hegemony and its non-availability for national others, simultaneously reduces the resulting pleasure. Further identifying the limits of this justice, another Indian research participant, Sanguinaire, who reported having a disability, felt that "Whenever themes related to terrorism, war, disability or mental health is [sic] covered in Marvel superheros [sic] fanfiction, they rely on american [sic] values. The concept of justice and peace is Western centric." For fans of color, justice and peace are different from that which is effected through the victories of white superheroes, structurally denied to people of color and nations. In addition, the discursive gap in the representation of the trauma of people of color in Marvel fandom signals the "affective burden of archival absence" (Hartman 2008), where the erasure of life stories participates in the systemic devaluation of the lives and trauma of people of color. In this process, non-white fans are produced as "others" through "the learning of place and race" (Stoler 2002, 112). For Sofia Razvi and Sanguinaire, the trial narrative is a reminder of their place and race as non–U.S. and non-white. While they may identify with the white protagonists of these stories, they are nevertheless aware of their own absent utopias, both in fanfiction and real life. To determine who can accumulate queer satisfaction and state-sanctioned happiness, disability and sexuality identities and experiences must be investigated in relation to race and nationalism.

Disability and Sexuality: Homonationalism and Neoliberal Queer/Disabled Subjects

On the surface, disability and queerness operate differently in fandom than on the outside. The *crip* turn in disability scholarship (McRuer 2006) discusses important parallels between queer theory and disability studies, as well as theorizations around queer disabled bodies. Robert McRuer (2006) articulates their shared medicalized history and marginalization, as well as the resistive potential to normative systems of compulsory able-bodied heterosexuality. He argues that "compulsory heterosexuality is contingent on compulsory able-bodiedness, and vice-versa" (2006, 2) and that these systems combine to produce stigmatized "queer/disabled" subjects. However, in *United States v. Barnes* and slash fandom at large, queerness conversely works to destigmatize disabled identity. This is because (a particular type of) queerness is hegemonic in media fandom. In the Winter Soldier trial fics, benign queerness is performed through the romantic support of white characters, predominantly Steve Rogers as

Captain America. In this section, I examine the importance of this nation-alist queering—central to which is the whiteness of the characters—in producing assimilable queer/disabled citizen-subjects.

In reparative trial fics, the realization and outing of the romantic nature of Barnes and Rogers' relationship works in favor of Barnes' case, rather than against legitimizing his potentially transgressive and doubly marginalized queer/disabled identity. While Rogers' shared history with his closest friend makes his connection to Barnes viably romantic, it is the ideological force of the "Captain America" title that helps accommo-date the queer/disabled subject into the strictures of American citizenship. Governmental responsibility is overshadowed by individual responsibil-ity through the figure of Captain America, who unites the two. Going back to Barnes' final speech in *United States v. Barnes* that hinted at a critique of nationalism, it is telling how he ends by calling upon Rogers as a moral compass:

> God knows I'm not a good man.... But we're short-handed on good men—and me, I found one. I found that one kid [Steve Rogers] who didn't know how to run away from a fight, decades ago, the most stubborn kid in Brooklyn. Been following him ever since. Maybe I just wanna [sic] get the chance to follow him again [54].

The repetition of "good" is a reminder of the moral currency of queer-ness in fandom. A historian in the fic provides a clear summary of this alignment in his thoughts on the outing of Barnes and Rogers: "it will make some of them [critics] rethink the way they see, well, soldiers, LGBT people, and *American wholesomeness* in general" (57, emphasis added). Wholesomeness is a category of moral well-being, and its association with queerness seeks to expand the category by incorporating queerness (in soldiers and other people) within normative bounds. These words thus link queer love with American (moral) supremacy through its perceived normativity.

The fandom's inclusion and celebration of queer intimacy favor homonormative relationships that frame queerness in socio-politically acceptable ways. Lisa Duggan coined the term homonormativity to describe a "new neoliberal sexual politics" that "does not contest dom-inant heteronormative assumptions and institutions but upholds and sustains them while promising the possibility of a demobilized gay con-stituency and a privatized, depoliticized gay culture anchored in domes-ticity and consumption" (2002, 179). Demands such as monogamy, marriage and child-rearing are common examples of such state-supported regulatory institutions. Barnes and Rogers' relationship within the trial narrative can be read as homonormative through its construction, for-mation, and function. In fics such as Speranza's *4 Minute Window* (2015),

Rogers and Barnes get married during the trial precisely to acquire legitimacy for their relationship and enable spousal rights that may aid Barnes' case. Though upholding the normative logic of family security regarding same-sex marriage, acknowledging its need in terms of practical necessity rather than a culmination of love facilitates a critique of that logic and the state that necessitates it.

Whiteness is key to developing the nationalism associated with the Captain America role. There are 64 Winter Soldier trial fics on the fanfiction website Archive of Our Own (AO3). Twelve of these do not include Barnes in any romantic pairing, while 52 feature him in a romantic relationship. Forty-five fics pair Barnes with Rogers, four with Tony Stark, two with Natasha Romanoff, and one with an original female character. Most trial fanworks are slash (centered on same-sex pairings) fics that involve Barnes in a romantic relationship with a white male and none with a black male. This includes the absence of any trial stories featuring Barnes with Sam Wilson (a black superhero), even though their relationship follows many conventional terms of male homosocial relations that garner queer readings from fans. Wilson and Barnes share common ground in traumatic combat experiences, are both Rogers' closest friends, and share a lighthearted banter-centered camaraderie onscreen. Significantly, Wilson becomes Captain America after *Avengers: Endgame* (2019) when Rogers passes him the Captain America shield. Since the airing of the Disney+ miniseries featuring the two characters, *The Falcon and the Winter Soldier* (2021), fanworks on their interracial relationship have increased exponentially. However, these are still not as popular as fanworks centering white men and are conspicuously absent from trial narratives. Their viewership and popularity evident from hits and kudos are also much lower. The lack of slash fics featuring Bucky Barnes/Sam Wilson in the Winter Soldier trial stories demonstrate Barnes' political victory in the myth-making process of democratization racially queerness and nationalism. Even the hyper-imaginative discursive space of fandom struggles to imagine a story in which a disabled white man in a love relationship with a black man—even if it is Captain America—emerges triumphant in a public trial facing terrorist charges.

The triumph of white coupledom and sexual normativity manifest in displays of queerness that contribute to homonationalism. Homonationalism is the "collusion between homosexuality and American nationalism generated both by national rhetorics of patriotic inclusion and by gay and queer subjects themselves" (Puar 2007, 39). In evoking an affective relation(ship) with Rogers and/as Captain America, Barnes (and the fandom) is not aligning himself with queerness over nationalism, but rather, queerness *with* nationalism. This is evident not only from Barnes' final speech but also from the last words of the text where an imagined spectator serving as a fandom spokesperson proudly claims: "I think it's good that we've grown as a country to allow them this moment." This frames Barnes' victory as a sign of national progress. Rogers' strong patriotic compass and title of the national hero, Captain America, is not coincidental to the final framing of Barnes' freedom. The new kind of nationalist homonormativity is contingent upon "parameters of white racial privilege, consumption capabilities, gender and kinship normativity, and bodily integrity" (Puar, xii), which demarcate acceptable and assimilable "good gay citizens" (Collins 2004, 74). The inclusion of certain queer individuals into the nation-state functions as a sign of the modernity of the West and its progress towards increasing freedom while constructing third world nations, particularly Islamic countries, as sexually regressive and simultaneously (queerly and debility) monstrous (Puar 2007; Dreher 2017). Sexual citizenship becomes a marker of a nation's true democratic ideals, upholding human rights in contrast to foreign "others," projected as oppressive and violent. Sexual normativity is essential for the neoliberal citizenship agenda. Single queers, queers with disabilities, and queers of color—unwelcome in America—remain largely unwelcome in fandom's new America. This changes the parameters of political affect from the perspective of oppressed fans who may find themselves excluded.

The importance of nationalism for queer and disabled subjects is particularly evident from a reading of the rare trial fic ending with Barnes' conviction. In DarkCaustic's *Twice* (2017), Barnes suffers an incurable spinal injury after being shot during his escape from Serbia following the events of *Captain America: Civil War* (2016). This injury causes limited mobility, chronic pain and incapacitates him from contributing to the nation-state in capitalistic or militaristic ways. Goodley and Lawthom (2019) suggest that people like Barnes may feel immense pressure to conform to neoliberal-ableist norms that dictate citizens should be "ready and able to work, productively contribute" and be "capable, malleable, and compliant" (235). In addition, Rogers resigns from his role as Captain America to take care of Barnes during his incarceration by the U.S. government. Barnes' debilitating injury and Rogers' romantic support after giving up the Captain America mantle to take care of Barnes do not provide conditions for victory. Barnes is given the death sentence, which he refuses to appeal. The story ends with Barnes' execution, Rogers' refusal to resume his role as Captain America, and his subsequent suicide. The lack of public sympathy despite their queer relationship in the story shows how severe disability negates queer inclusion and the critical role nationalism plays in the inclusion of queer/disabled bodies. In this case, Barnes' critical or "severe" disability (McRuer 2010) is unassimilable in the neoliberal ableist state and society Goodley and Lawthom (2019). Such exclusions in the body politic point to the "uneven biopolitical incorporation" (McRuer 2010, 169) of queer/disabled bodies where nationalism is not performed or achievable. Their deaths result from the exclusionary biopolitics where their disabled bodyminds form part of human assemblages targeted for death rather than life.

The politics of emotions in fandom are linked to performances and practicalities of affective citizenship in the contemporary world. Barnes' acceptance of the execution order, refusal to file an appeal, or escape, coupled with Rogers' uncontested acceptance of that decision and rejection of a nationalist condition to value life, demonstrates their resistance to the hegemonic state-sanctioned ways of living and being. The politics of incarceration and marking certain populations for "slow death" (Berlant 2007) limit what disabled, marginalized subjects can do. Puar argues that slow death is "in some sense a mode of neoliberal and affective capacitation or debilitation as mediated by different technological assemblages" (2017, 31). Denied the potential of affirmative assemblages—for instance, through the governmental confiscation of Barnes' prosthetic—and marked towards debilitation, the very act of choosing death offers a mode of regaining bodily agency. As Puar argues, political disablement is a way for oppressive powers to extract value from maimed subjects. The rejection of such affective citizenship then acts as a form of resistance. Readers of the story replicate this acceptance as evident from the actions of the characters. The "unhappy" trial story is met with satisfied but unhappy fans. A reader, Avaaricious, commented, "This writing has left me with an ache in my chest. This is something they couldn't escape. There were no last-minute reprieves, no magical rewinds, just a little bit of cruel fate…. So powerful" (AO3, September 2017). The attribution of pleasure from unhappiness and the affective forces of negative feelings are useful in reorienting emotional vocabularies. This is particularly true when considering those whose identities and experiences of marginalization are unassimilable in the real world and fandom. The transformation of sentiments and capacities evident in the actions and experiences of (critically) marginalized characters and fans is a powerful political affect.

Politicizing Emotions: Fandom and "Feel Good" Diversity

The works of political assimilation that I discuss in this essay provide a glimpse into how fans feel good in fandom by writing stories where they can imagine the happiness of certain dispossessed or marginalized identities with whom they identify. White queer and disabled minorities embody desirable and assimilable diversity in the fandom public. In her analysis of disability publics in India, Michele Friedner (2017) demonstrates how disability "functions as a form of 'feel good' non-threatening diversity" (350). I argue that something similar is noticeable in fandom. Just as the inspiring representations of disabled people in public spaces in India allow able-bodied citizens to feel good about the imagined "beneficence of the nation" (350), fandom's inclusion of (white) queer/disabled characters allows fans to feel good about their counterpublic and its diversity. Fandom is repeatedly projected as valuable because it represents, most often, queer bodies and desires, and less often, disability and (mental) health. Such theorizations of representation and pleasure conceal the racial and national dimensions of who is allowed to feel good in and through fandom.

Disability, particularly mental health, functions as a kind of "feel good" category instead of race and nationality whose very elicitation ushers in the specter of controversy and hate, or "bad politics." This is particularly evident in the Marvel fandom, where stories on mental health conditions are abundant. From hundreds of stories of Stark dealing with anxiety and PTSD to those exploring Rogers's loneliness and depression, fans are deeply invested in writing their favorites a happy ending that considers mental health questions with empathy and nuance. Disability in Marvel fanfiction is a category that is often represented in ways that allow one to feel good through the integration of marginalized identities, but which privilege whiteness and U.S. supremacy. It is easier to feel good about disability representation in Marvel fandom than racial representation.

In contrast, racial "others" are further marginalized in fandom. This is evident in the exclusionary treatment of Black, Indigenous, and People of Color (BIPOC) fans in many global media fandoms. When BIPOC fans raise racial representation and discomfort issues, they are repeatedly met with accusations of censorship and being an anti-fan, or someone who derails discussions and deliberately criticizes something to spread hate or derive enjoyment. Stitch, a black fan who has spoken extensively about racism in fandom in mainstream media and fan spaces and has over 5600 Twitter followers, is a frequent target of harassment. Recently (June 2021), some *Star Wars* fans accused Stitch of bullying and tried to get her fired from her job as a writer for *TeenVogue*, an American online publication aimed at young women. In doing so, fans deliberately misused the language of social justice in defense of white feminism and queerness. In response to the controversy involving weaponizing womanhood, fan scholar Lucy Baker explained that this is done by presenting fandom as marginalized and prioritizing fans' "feels" (Twitter, June 2021) about their fan object over real life people and social issues. This incident also demonstrates how white feelings are sometimes privileged over the lives of people of color, and particularly Black people. Such incidents indicate how representational strategies and dynamics of media fanworks reflect and reproduce structural issues of racism and white/U.S. supremacy in fandom. This demonstrates how race and nationality destabilize assumptions about fandom's progressive politics despite, and sometimes through, the accommodation of disabled and sexual minorities.

Conclusion

This essay studies the politics of disability representation in the Marvel fandom by focusing on the construction of the queer/disabled subject through the character of Bucky Barnes in the Winter Soldier trial narrative. This narrative highlights the cultural politics of representation in Marvel fandom through a self-conscious political narrative of citizenship. Using the frame of affective citizenship, I analyze fan cultural politics in terms of the larger politics of citizenship and political belonging. I find that the test of citizenship in which Barnes typically emerges triumphant privileges white nationalist queers. By revealing the limits of fandom politics, fans reinstate ideas of Western progress and supremacy that allow and celebrate the assimilation of privileged queer and disabled identities instead of racial and national others. By demonstrating how disability intersects with sexuality, race, and nationalism in ways that affectively align it with hegemonic power structures for citizenship, I hope to contribute to scholarship on disability representation and citizenship. By placing race and nationalism at the center of this disability analysis and privileging the perspectives of people of color fans, the racialized parameters of the political affects engendered in fan engagement are interrogated. The politics of emotions in fandom reveals that disability, particularly in mental health conditions in Marvel fandom, sometimes operates as a "feel good" diversity in opposition to the "bad feelings" associated with race.

REFERENCES

Ahmed, Sara. 2014. *Cultural Politics of Emotion*. Edinburgh, UK: Edinburgh University Press.
Allcott, Hunt, and Matthew Gentzkow. 2017. "Social Media and Fake News in the 2016 Election." *Journal of Economic Perspectives 31* (2): 211–36. doi: 10.1257/jep.31.2.211.
Ayata, Bilgin. 2019. "Affective Citizenship." In *Affective Societies: Key Concepts*, edited by Antje Kahl, 330–340. New York: Routledge.

Berlant, Lauren. 1997. *The Queen of America Goes to Washington City*. Durham, NC: Duke University Press.

Berlant, Lauren. 2007. "Slow Death (Sovereignty, Obesity, Lateral Agency)." *Critical Inquiry 33* (4): 754–780. doi: 10.1086/521568.

Blickstein, Tamar. 2019. "Affects of Racialization." In *Affective Societies: Key Concepts*, edited by Antje Kahl, 152–165. New York: Routledge.

Dandrow, Christine. 2016. "Fandom as a Fortress: The Gendered Safe Spaces of Online Fanfiction Communities." *Media Report to Women 44* (1): 6–23.

DarkCaustic and Elendrien. 2017. *Twice*. Archive of Our Own. https://archiveofourown.org/works/11252988/chapters/25156479.

dreadnought. 2017. *Baghdad Waltz*. Archive of Our Own. https://archiveofourown.org/works/10261136/chapters/22734353.

dropdeaddream and WhatArefears. 2014–2015. *Not Easily Conquered* series. Archive of Our Own. https://archiveofourown.org/series/115516.

Duxbury, Scott, Laura C. Frizzell, and Sade L. Lindsay. 2018. "Mental Illness, the Media, and the Moral Politics of Mass Violence: The Role of Race in Mass Shootings Coverage." *Journal of Research in Crime and Delinquency 55* (6): 766–797. doi: 10.1177/0022427818787225.

fallingvoices and radialarch. 2014. *United States V. Barnes, 617 F. Supp. 2d 143 (D.D.C. 2015)*. Archive of Our Own. https://archiveofourown.org/works/2304905/chapters/5071058.

Fortier, Anne-Marie. 2010. "Proximity by Design? Affective Citizenship and the Management of Unease." *Citizenship Studies 14* (1): 17–30. doi: 10.1080/13621020903466258.

Fortier, Anne-Marie. 2013. "What's the Big Deal? Naturalisation and the Politics of Desire." *Citizenship Studies 17* (6–7): 697–711. doi: 10.1080/13621025.2013.780761.

Fraser, Nancy. 1990. "Rethinking the Public Sphere: A Contribution to the Critique of Actually Existing Democracy." *Social Text* (25/26): 56–80. doi: 10.2307/466240.

Friedner, Michele. 2017. "How the Disabled Body Unites the National Body: Disability as 'Feel Good' Diversity in Urban India." *Contemporary South Asia 25* (4): 347–363. doi: 10.1080/09584935.2017.1374925.

Goodley, Dan. 2019. "Critical Disability Studies, Brexit and Trump: A Time of Neoliberal-Ableism." *Rethinking History, 23* (2): 233–251. doi: 10.1080/13642529.2019.1607476.

Grech, Shaun. 2016. "Disability and Development: Critical Connections, Gaps and Contradictions." In *Disability in the Global South*, edited by Shaun Grech and Karen Soldatic, 3–19. Cham: Springer.

G.V.A. 2019. Home. *Gun Violence Archive*. https://www.gunviolencearchive.org/.

Habermas, Jurgen. 1991. *The Structural Transformation of the Public Sphere: An Inquiry Into a Category of Bourgeois Society*. Cambridge, MA: MIT Press.

Hartman, Saidiya. 2008. *Lose Your Mother: A Journey Along the Atlantic Slave Route*. New York: Macmillan.

Hellekson, Karen, and Kristina Busse. 2009. Fan Privacy and TWC's Editorial Philosophy. *Organization for Transformative Works*.

Hickey-Moody, Anna. 2013. "Affect as Method: Feelings, Aesthetics and Affective Pedagogy." In *Deleuze and Research Methodologies*, edited by Rebecca Coleman and Jessica Ringrose, 79–95. Edinburgh, UK: Edinburgh University Press.

Hickey-Moody, Anna. 2015. "Carbon Fibre Masculinity: Disability and Surfaces of Homosociality." *Angelaki 20* (1): 139–153. doi: 10.1080/0969725X.2015.1017394.

Hill Collins, Patricia. 2004. *Black Sexual Politics: African Americans, Gender, and the New Racism*. New York: Routledge.

Holm, Malin. 2019. "*The Rise of Online Counterpublics: The Limits of Inclusion in a Digital Age.*" PhD diss., Uppsala University.

Johnston, Joe, dir. 2011. *Captain America: The First Avenger*. United States: Marvel Studios.

Kornhaber, Spencer. 2021. "The Superhero Fantasies of Trump's Mob." *The Atlantic*, January 9. https://www.theatlantic.com/culture/archive/2021/01/alternate-reality-trump-capitol-mob/617596/

Mathews, Gordon. 2020. "The Hong Kong Protests in Anthropological Perspective:

National Identity and What It Means." *Critique of Anthropology 40* (2): 264–269. doi: 10.1177/0308275X20908303.

McKinnon, Sara L. 2009. "Citizenship and the Performance of Credibility: Audiencing Gender-Based Asylum Seekers in US Immigration Courts." *Text and Performance Quarterly 29* (3): 205–221. Doi: 10.1080/10462930903017182.

McRuer, Robert. 2006. *Crip Theory: Cultural Signs of Queerness and Disability.* New York: New York University Press.

_____. 2010. "Compulsory Able-Bodiedness and Queer/Disabled Existence." *The Disability Studies Reader 3*: 383–392.

Metzl, Jonathan M., and Kenneth T. MacLeish. 2015. "Mental Illness, Mass Shootings, and the Politics of American Firearms." *American Journal of Public Health 105* (2): 240–249. doi:10.2105/AJPH.2014.302242.

Mitchell, David T., and Sharon L. Snyder. 2015. *The Biopolitics of Disability: Neoliberalism, Ablenationalism, and Peripheral Embodiment.* Ann Arbor: University of Michigan Press.

Mods. 2016. The Winter Soldier trial [Blog Post]. *The Stucky Library.* Tumblr, January 25. https://thestuckylibrary.tumblr.com/tagged/minipost:wstrial.

Puar, Jasbir K. 2007. *Terrorist Assemblages: Homonationalism in Queer Times.* Durham, NC: Duke University Press.

_____. 2017. *The Right to Maim: Debility, Capacity, Disability.* Durham, NC: Duke University Press.

Reisman, A. 2016. "The Story Behind Bucky's Groundbreaking Comic Book Reinvention as the Winter Soldier." *The Vulture.* http://www.vulture.com/2016/05/buckywinter-soldier-history.html.

Rosaldo, Renato. 1994. "Cultural Citizenship and Educational Democracy." *Cultural Anthropology 9* (3): 402–411. doi 10.1525/can.1994.9.3.02a00110.

Russo, Anthony, and Joe Russo, dir. 2014. *Captain America: The Winter Soldier.* United States: Marvel Studios.

_____, dir. 2019. *Avengers: Endgame.* United States: Marvel Studios.

Sedgwick, Eve Kosofsky and Adam Frank. 2003. *Touching Feeling: Affect, Pedagogy, Performativity.* Durham, NC: Duke University Press.

Skogland, Kari, dir. 2021. *The Falcon and the Winter Soldier* [TV series]. United States: Disney+.

Slaby, Jan, and Jonas Bens. 2019. "Political Affect." In *Affective Societies: Key Concepts,* edited by Antje Kahl, 340–351. New York: Routledge.

Speranza. 2014. *4 Minute Window.* Archive of Our Own. https://archiveofourown.org/works/3130037.

Stitch's Media Mix. 2021. "If You Have No Idea What's Going On: I'm Being Harassed for Writing About Racism in Fandom (on My Site, My Still-private Main Account, Now for Teen Vogue) in a Way That Doesn't Cater to Racists or Other POC That Let Themselves Be ACTUALLY Weaponized in Defense of Racism." [Twitter thread], May 29, 2021. https://twitter.com/stitchmediamix/status/1398502820236640257.

Thomas, Elizabeth. 2019. "Trump's Claims and What Experts Say About Mental Illness and Mass Shootings." *ABC News,* August 23. https://abcnews.go.com/Politics/trumps-claims-experts-mental-illness-mass-shootings/story?id=65101823.

Waggoner, Jess. 2016. "Oh Say Can You ___ ": Race and Mental Disability in Performances of Citizenship. *Journal of Literary & Cultural Disability Studies 10* (1): 87–102. muse.jhu.edu/article/611314.

Wei, John. 2014. "Queer Encounters Between Iron Man and Chinese Boys' Love Fandom." *Transformative Works and Cultures (17)*. doi:10.3983/twc.2014.0561.

Enabling New Perspectives
of (Super)Power and Disability
in Jeremy Scott's *The Ables*

ROBIN E. FIELD *and* CHRISTOPHER BOUCHER

In the twenty-first century, young adults encounter an increasing number of characters with disabilities in popular media. On television, the high school dramedy *Glee* features guitarist Artie Abrams using a wheelchair and cheerleader Becky Jackson living with Down syndrome. More mature young people may witness teenager Walter Junior use crutches to walk due to cerebral palsy on *Breaking Bad*, and chuckle as Tyrion Lannister sarcastically addresses prejudiced comments about his small stature on *Game of Thrones*. In addition to realist films such as *Forrest Gump* (1994) or *The Fundamentals of Caring* (2016), the superhero genre offers Daredevil, Batgirl/Oracle, and Professor X combatting limitations traditionally associated with disability. Notably, young adult fiction in the twenty-first century has increasingly portrayed characters with disabilities to challenge negative perceptions and educate young people about how to understand disability within American culture. Indeed, since 2004 the American Library Association has offered the Schneider Family Book Award to "an author or illustrator for a book that embodies an artistic expression of the disability experience for child and adolescent audiences" ("Schneider Family Book Award"). Novels such as *Marcelo in the Real World* (2009), *Five Flavors of Dumb* (2010), *Wonder* (2012), and *Paperboy* (2013) have been scrutinized by academics, taught in middle and high school classrooms, and enjoyed by young and adult readers alike. Another young adult novel, Jeremy Scott's *The Ables* (2015), uniquely brings together both the realistic portrayal of disability and the fantastical depiction of superpowers in its protagonist Phillip Sallinger, a blind twelve-year-old with telekinetic abilities. *The Ables* has been widely read by young people, as indicated by its status as a #1 "Amazon Hot New Release" and a #1 Barnes & Noble best-seller after its release (Cooper 2015). For some young readers, *The Ables* may offer their first sustained engagement with characters with disabilities as central, rather than peripheral, figures.

The Ables offers a fascinating nexus of identity for its young adult readers to explore. Importantly, Scott's novel places readers in Phillip's first-person perspective, a viewpoint that unmasks ableist assumptions and questions the limitations often proscribed to people with disabilities. Scott portrays Phillip and his friends, all of whom have different disabilities, as being better able to fight the villainous Mr. Finch, who is ready to destroy the world to discover the identity of the most powerful superhero. In contrast, superheroes without disabilities doubt these boys' abilities to protect themselves, let alone help the larger community. Scott's novel allows its young readers to identify ableism by depicting discriminatory situations experienced by Phillip and his friends, who are placed in the special education classroom of their school for children with superpowers. Scott uses the idea of "normal" people to challenge what "abnormality" truly is. Such is the case when the superheroes must hide their powers from the wider population to most effectively protect non-superheroes (i.e., "normal" people) from danger. Young readers are even alerted to how the very language they use to communicate with each other perpetuates ableism. Scott's representation of superheroes with disabilities performs the important cultural work of reshaping the worldview of young adult readers. *The Ables* underscores the (super)power of storytelling, as these readers will not be *able* to understand the world in quite the same way after having inhabited Scott's fantastical world where kids with disabilities are the saviors, rather than those who must be saved.

The stereotypes about disability held by young readers are immediately challenged in the opening chapters of *The Ables*, as Scott interrogates commonplace notions of being "able" by introducing twelve-year-old Phillip Sallinger. Phillip just wants to be a "normal" kid, but as a blind person, he reluctantly concedes that he has a disability. After his family moves to the small town of Freepoint, Phillip's father upends his world by informing him that Phillip and his family members are superheroes, as are most people in Freepoint. Phillip is telekinetic, like his father; his mother is a transporter who can move herself and anyone or anything she touches anywhere around the world; and his younger brother Patrick has super-speed. While Phillip's blindness makes his superpower more challenging to control, he can soon move objects with his mind. The existence of superheroes—or custodians, as those in Scott's fictional world are dubbed—complicates the ideas of who is able-bodied (and thus "normal") and disabled (or "not normal"). In this novel, ability now includes superpowers—which means "normal" people do not have these abilities. Custodians, therefore, are "not normal" because of their additional powers. Yet this difference is not inscribed as a deficit or disability, as often occurs with others deemed "not normal" by society. "Normal" people lack superpowers and thus need to be cared for in ways they cannot manage themselves—hence "normal" people are *disabled*. This shift in worldview allows readers to imagine themselves as lacking a desired ability by not having superpowers, therefore opening their minds to learning about and empathizing with people with other types of disabilities.

Scott positions Phillip as simultaneously "able" and "disabled" because of his telekinesis and blindness. Phillip has no time to enjoy his newfound status as part of the (super)empowered minority where custodians fight crime invisibly and anonymously in the larger world to keep "normal" people safe. He discovers that his fellow custodians regard him as having a disability, just as he was treated in the "regular" world. Phillip is placed into a special education classroom at Freepoint High School, about which he thinks, "I had never felt so insulted in my short life. I was blind, not disabled. *There's a difference!*" (Scott 2015, 30). Here Phillip demonstrates how he has internalized the very bias that he wishes to resist. He thinks "kids in wheelchairs" belong in a special education classroom, not a blind person like himself (Scott 2015, 30). Phillip even uses the same pejorative language that denigrates people with disabilities when he calls his younger brother a "spaz." As Chloë Hughes (2017) points out, "*Micro-assaults* are conscious and intentional discriminatory slurs and non-verbal behaviors. Ableist micro-assaults include using discriminatory terms like 'spazz,' 'retard,' [and] 'psycho'" (192). Phillip's father not only chides him for the slur by saying, "It's not a nice word," but also informs him that Patrick's hyperactivity is a precursor to his development of super-speed (Scott 2015, 23). Interestingly, Scott's depiction here not only underscores how commonplace ableist micro-assaults and other negative descriptors of disability are, but also complicates the notion that certain conditions *are* disabilities, as in Patrick's hyperactivity. As Lennard J. Davis (2002) writes, "The body is never a single physical thing so much as a series of attitudes about it" (22). By repositioning hyperactivity as a characteristic of a superpower, Scott reminds readers that disability itself is a social construct, rather than simply a medical condition that distinguishes or excludes some people from the larger society.

The special education classroom illustrates how a medical understanding of disability juxtaposes the abilities of "normal" people with the differing abilities of "disabled" people. The special education students vary greatly in their disabilities and their superpowers. One of Phillip's classmates, Freddie, has severe asthma in addition to the superpower of gigantism. Because of his asthma, Freddie cannot inflate himself to become three stories tall without being unable to breathe as well, so his superpower is rendered nearly useless because of his corresponding disability. Like Patrick's hyperactivity, Freddie's asthma is understood differently because of the corresponding superpower. However, in Freddie's case, asthma that may not be treated as a disability in the "regular" world is seen as a life-threatening condition when paired with gigantism, thus complicating how disability is defined and categorized. At the beginning of the novel another classmate, Donnie, who has Down syndrome, has yet to reveal his superpower because he communicates nonverbally. Donnie "has the mind of a young child in the body of a grown man" despite being fifteen (Scott 2015, 33). His imposing stature and silent, impassive demeanor intimidate kids and adults alike. Donnie's combined disability and unknown superpower ability are, according to another classmate, Henry, "even scarier" because nobody has "any idea what danger you might be facing" from him (Scott 2015, 43). Donnie epitomizes the challenge faced by students in the special education classroom: how to hone one's superpower while facing one's personal limitations and societal prejudices against people with disabilities.

The special education teacher, Mrs. Crouch, models a more inclusive understanding of disability for young readers. Mrs. Crouch acknowledges that her students have "special challenges," but she also argues that having a "unique combination of ability and disability" allows them "special opportunities" (Scott 2015, 31–32). Certainly, this is the case with Phillip and his classmates Henry, James, and Bentley. Henry uses a wheelchair because he was "born crippled," as he bluntly describes himself (Scott 2015, 32). Henry's superpower is reading minds, which is not affected in the least by his limited mobility. James is also blind, and he is a transporter like Phillip's mother, who needs some extra description in order to whisk himself and others to brand-new locations. Bentley, who has cerebral palsy and often uses a cane for assistance with balance, is a "mental" with "elevated brain function," or super-smarts (Scott 2015, 35). While Bentley cannot chase after supervillains using his legs, he can outsmart them or use his friends' abilities to achieve the desired end. Indeed, Phillip and his friends embrace Mrs. Crouch's theory that their "unique combination of ability and disability" brings "special opportunities" because they quickly learn to work together to augment their collective (super) powers and abilities. Their disabilities lead them to think more creatively about problem-solving, and as a group, they form an efficient and highly effective team just as capable as—and perhaps superior to—other teams of able-bodied teenager custodians. Their reliance upon teamwork contrasts with the typical American emphasis upon individual accomplishments and working alone, an attitude that appears in many superhero stories that valorize heroes who work independently. Hence, *The Ables* also expands the possibilities for superhero protagonists—able or disabled—by creating heroes who rely upon others to help them save the world. Scott's message is *not* to go it alone, but to work together and ask for help in order to succeed—a particularly important message for young adult readers.

Scott's novel quickly underscores that the attitudes of the larger world about disability are as limiting as any bodily differences may be. Phillip and his friends improve their superpower abilities through practice and teamwork, and their disabilities become less of a hindrance to their endeavors. However, they soon must prove their competence in safely and effectively using their superpowers for the larger community, rather than only for themselves and their families. Most of Freepoint's high school students will compete in the SuperSim, a city-wide crime-fighting simulation where teams of young custodians apprehend criminals using their superpowers. Phillip is thrilled at the prospect of testing himself, but he and his special education classmates are immediately informed that students with disabilities will not be allowed to participate to guarantee the safety of themselves and the other students. Such exclusion may also be categorized as a micro-assault that "prevent[s] access to individuals with disabilities based on a belief that they are unworthy" (Hughes 2017, 192). Phillip is crushed to be excluded, also because his friends cannot imagine themselves being able to compete against the other students. Not only do his special education classmates use disparaging ableist language by telling Phillip he is "crazy" for suggesting that they can compete in the SuperSim, but they also demonstrate internalized ableism by pointing to their own disabilities as reasons for not even entering in the first place (Scott 2015, 59). Only Phillip can imagine how they could viably compete in the contest and even "win some respect" from the other students in the high school (Scott 2015, 61). Phillip's determination eventually changes his friends' minds, with the super-smart Bentley summarizing their perspective: "Our powers and abilities can complement each other and make up for our disabilities. We're not any more or less able to stop crime. We just have to work twice as hard as anyone else to get ready" (Scott 2015, 64). Bentley's words underscore the additional pressure put upon the "special ed kids" to navigate the everyday challenges of their disabilities and prove to the super-empowered world that they are competent and productive custodians.

As often happens in the real world, advocates must employ legal means to demand equal treatment and opportunity for these children with disabilities. Phillip and his friends file an appeal to the school board to participate in the SuperSim. Bentley believes the matter will be simple to resolve, given that their exclusion violates the Americans with Disabilities Act (ADA). Yet at the hearing, the school board president, Mr. Tucker, tells them that only superhero laws apply to their circumstances, not American laws like the ADA. Instead, the case will be decided based upon what will ensure the safety of all participants, which the school board members clearly believe is impossible if the custodians with disabilities are involved. Such capricious application of the ADA is reminiscent of *Toyota Motor Manufacturing Inc. v. Williams* (2002), where the Supreme Court considered whether carpal tunnel syndrome should be accommodated as a disability (Campbell 2005, 125). According to the school board, the custodian population (who are decidedly "not normal" because of their superpowers) does not fall under the ADA, which puts custodians who are doubly "not normal" at a further disadvantage. Young readers perceive "that age-old problem of shifting the goalposts vis-à-vis the normative body," as Fiona Kumari Campbell (2005) describes (125). Whose bodies are normative, and how to regulate the accommodation of non-normative bodies are pressing issues within Scott's novel. Simultaneously, young people witness how the ADA does not always foster the inclusion it was designed to demand, a phenomenon not limited to the super-empowered world of Freepoint.

Because legal remedies such as the ADA cannot help them, Phillip and his friends prove their resolve to the school board through an ingenious demonstration of relational autonomy. As Harold Braswell (2011) posits, "relationships do not necessarily detract from one's autonomy. Rather, the relational constitution of the self creates the condition of possibility for autonomy." Relational autonomy understands individuals as always interdependent, and "this is a shift in a conception of each other as competitive individuals who block each other's flourishing, to collaborators in each other's self realization" (Braswell 2011, 143). Phillip needs to prove that their team poses no danger to others, and he does so through the principle of relational autonomy. He devises a way to demonstrate to the school board how his team can work together to transcend their limitations—that is, to be as "normal" or able-bodied as possible, according to the perspective of the non-disabled custodians deciding whether they may participate in the SuperSim. As a blind person, Phillip should not use his telekinetic powers to move an object that he has not touched or *seen* before. However, he can send Mr. Tucker's gavel flying across the room and into his own hands because Henry, a mind reader, can not only look into others' thoughts but also send his own thoughts—and his *vision*—into others' heads, specifically Phillip's. Phillip, therefore, can overcome the limitation upon his superpower—his blindness—by receiving images from Henry. Unfortunately, the demonstration goes awry when Phillip tries to send the gavel back across the room into the hands of another board member; instead, the gavel smacks her forehead. This mishap only confirms to the school board that the disabled custodians are indeed a danger to others. But more importantly, it also demonstrates that each boy's disability may be surmounted or at least made into less of a liability by working together. Henry makes a similar argument when Mr. Tucker asks him how he would pursue a criminal when his wheelchair could not take him across terrains such as a gravel road or a beach: "I'll get my friend James to teleport me there" (Scott 2015, 114). Working together means that Henry can move about using James' teleporting ability and Phillip can even see for short periods using Henry's vision. Relational autonomy underscores how interdependence is not a weakness but an important strategy for self-realization and success. The concept highlights how these seemingly permanent "disabilities" may be situationally and even temporally specific, a reconfiguration that underscores the constructed notion of disability within American culture.

Scott further interrogates what is considered a disability and who decides after the school board hearing. The special education teacher, Mrs. Crouch, arrives just as Mr. Tucker and the other board members are ready to deny the boys' appeal. Meticulously she demonstrates the hypocrisy of all those custodians in power. One able-bodied man had seriously injured another with his superpower when they were in high school, and others employ disabled custodians or have relatives with disabilities. The most skeptical of them all, Mr. Tucker, himself has a disability, scoliosis, which impairs his mobility but does not affect his superpower. Mrs. Crouch concludes: "If a disabled hero can serve […] as president of the school board, then how can we justify—as a community—telling these children they can't compete? […] The choice is simple: you either believe in them, that they can become productive members of hero society […] or you're just humoring them" (Scott 2015, 124). Mrs. Crouch's words remind readers of what is considered ability and disability. Mr. Tucker's scoliosis is not considered a disability until it compromises his mobility; hence, he was not considered disabled in his youth. Phillip's struggle to acknowledge his blindness as a disability appears to be less the frustrations of a child than the genuine questioning of how "compromised" his life is because of blindness. Jacob Stratman (2015b) observes a similar interrogation of what disability is in Wendy Mass's *A Mango-Shaped Space*, which depicts a girl with synesthesia who "gets to decide how she feels about her own reality" by deciding whether synesthesia is a medical condition or "a part of what makes her whole" (112). Such questions also shift the onus off people with varying abilities toward opening society as a whole for full participation of people of all abilities in the (superpowered) world. As Davis

(1997a) argues, "the 'problem' is not the person with disabilities; the problem is the way that normalcy is constructed to create the 'problem' of the disabled person" (9). Through the boys' demonstration of relational autonomy and Mrs. Crouch's revelations of the board members' own hypocrisy, young readers may realize that the disabilities that Phillip and his friends live with are far less problematic than the discriminatory attitudes and regulations they face from the able-bodied majority.

The rest of the novel continues to probe what a disability is and who should be considered disabled. Once Phillip and his friends are allowed to participate in the SuperSim, they call their team "the Ables." This name refers to superhero history, as the original "Ables" were the six custodians who defeated the supervillain Elben and his superpowered army, which occurred centuries previously. Elben, "the one who can do all," is the only custodian in history who has possessed every possible superpower simultaneously. However, the six Ables defeated him and his army by working together (Scott 2015, 50). As Phillip and his five friends identify themselves as underdogs in the SuperSim, they choose this moniker to highlight both the long odds of their winning the competition as well as their status as societal and high school outcasts. Pushing back against their identity as the "special ed kids," Phillip and his friends demand to be acknowledged as "able."

This homage to superhero history introduces another important plot development: the appearance of Mr. Finch, an older man inordinately interested in Phillip, during the first SuperSim event. Mr. Finch is a Believer, a member of the custodian cult that promotes the prophecy that "the one who can do all" will return (Scott 2015, 50). According to the prophecy:

> He shall return again, an outcast, one who is not like us, who does not see the world as we do, and he shall have all abilities. Where once he used his gifts for death and destruction, his second life shall see them used for life and protection. This one shall not know of his own true depth of power until he suffers great loss and injury, and he alone stands as the last protector between the world and a great power. Only then shall he truly see. Only then shall he embrace his true purpose [Scott 2015, 50].

Finch believes that Phillip must be the second "one who can do all," given that the boy is blind and, therefore, "an outcast, one who is not like us." Finch thinks that Phillip will only realize his powers if he suffers a significant loss. Hence, the older man puts Phillip's mother into a coma and threatens to kill her unless Phillip manifests these additional superpowers. Phillip knows he does not have any additional powers, but he cannot convince Finch of this. As a result, the old man thinks that the boy's suffering must increase for him to "know his own true depth of power."

Finch kills Phillip's mother, kidnaps his father and most of the other Freepoint custodians, and plants a nuclear bomb in the high school. If Phillip does not conjure the powers to save his family and friends—and indeed, the entire population within the radius of the nuclear bomb—everyone will die. Scott's positioning of Phillip, a disabled child, as the only person who can save so many lives seem to be the ultimate tribute to the real and potential abilities that the boy embodies. For young readers, this focus upon Phillip underscores how a person's potential need not be defined according to normative physical or mental abilities is important.

In a startling plot twist, readers learn that Finch is actually Phillip's grandfather, Thomas Sallinger, who was thought to be dead for years. (For clarity, this character will continue to be called "Finch"). This blood tie explains why the megalomaniac Finch would believe Phillip to be the second hero with all superpowers. Finch's own power is "absorption": He can use the superpowers of other custodians he has been in proximity to during the previous few hours. If Phillip had every superpower, Finch would possess these powers by partnering with his grandson. Finch's ultimate goal is for custodians to rule the world, living openly amongst "normal" people while having complete control over them. Finch even argues that the dichotomy of heroes versus villains (both of whom have superpowers) will disappear, leaving only "empowered people" versus "the rest" (Scott 2015, 259). When Finch asks Phillip which side he will take, Phillip replies he will side with "good." Finch cynically responds that "good" does not actually exist; instead, there is only power—which should belong to the empowered, not "normal" people. Finch here is akin to X-Men's Magneto, whose wish to liberate the mutants means viewing humans as inferior. As Tim Perry (2005) argues, "Both physically and morally, [Magneto] sees himself as superior. [...H]e believes Homo sapiens stand as 'the other' to be mastered and, if necessary, erased" (184). While in the past, Magneto and Finch both tried to fight for the good of all, and they were still persecuted and betrayed by others. Consequently, both want to envision a world where the super-empowered do not have to defer to the weaker majority. Scott's parallels to other superhero stories underscore how any minority—whether superheroes or people with disabilities—are regulated by the powerful majority.

Finch uses this power disparity to tempt Phillip to side with him and his cult. He insinuates that having superpowers will make a disabled person such as Phillip more powerful than most of the world. If custodians ruled the world—and if Phillip were "the one who can do all"—the boy would no longer suffer from the social stigma of disability because of his power(s). Such a depiction of disability is troubling, however, as it insinuates that the desired end is to no longer have the disability. Stratman

(2015b), in working with first-year college students to analyze disabled characters, observes: "The belief that disabilities are bad and that they need to be fixed permeates young adult literature and even the thoughts of many of my students" (110). The young adult readers of *The Ables* may embrace such ideas as well, given how Scott follows this trend by having the super-smart Bentley devise ways for Phillip to see. Such a plot development underscores the idea that disabled people should wish to be "cured" and thus be "normal."

Phillip never has to grapple with the temptation of having all the (super)powers in the world, because he is not "the one who can do all": Donnie is. Until the end of the novel, Donnie appears to be a minor character, for reasons that both do and do not relate to the plot twist of him saving everyone from the nuclear bomb. Because of Phillip's blindness and role as the first-person narrator, readers are not given many descriptions of people beyond how Phillip interacts with them or what he thinks internally about them. Only in a few scenes do readers get physical descriptions of the different characters, once the boys realize that Henry can send his vision into Phillip's mind. Phillip uses Henry's vision to "see" his family members for the first time, and readers also learn that Henry is Black while Phillip describes what sights were unexpected to him. Yet never do readers "see" Donnie beyond a few casual words from Bentley on the first day of school that Donnie is over six feet tall and "bigger than most of the teachers here" (Scott 2015, 43). Because of his Down syndrome, Donnie speaks only a few words during the novel. As most of the time Phillip can only hear the conversations, not see his friends as they talk to each other, he forgets at times that Donnie is even there—and thus so do readers. Such treatment of Donnie indicates how disabled people are treated by society at large: They are invisible until they directly affect other people's lives. However, as Davis (1997b) writes, "how strange is this assumption. […] If the population of people with disabilities is between thirty-five and forty-three million, then this group is the largest physical minority in the United States" (2). Scott's novel thus reminds readers to recognize how commonplace people with disabilities are. Writing about young adult literature, Marilyn Ward (2002) concurs: "literature about disabilities and differences can be a powerful tool to heighten the achievement of all students by broadening attitudes and perceptions of self and others" (x).

Because Donnie is invisible for most of the novel, Phillip and his friends—as well as Finch himself—never consider that Donnie could be "the one who can do all." Donnie fits the prophecy quite aptly, as he is even more of an outcast than Phillip, especially after the second SuperSim contest. At this point, the Ables know that Donnie has super-speed, and Phillip asks Donnie to run across town to rescue a "hostage" from a "criminal."

Traveling at immeasurable speed, Donnie approaches the scene of the "crime" but trips over an unconscious and invisible person lying in the road. He smashes into the "hostage" and "criminal," sending them blocks away. Due to his tremendous momentum, he slides down the road, breaking most of his bones and ending up in the hospital for weeks. This terrible accident confirms the school board's concern that disabled children would hurt themselves and others, and they immediately banned the Ables from competing in the final SuperSim contest. The Freepoint community also views Donnie as "some kind of Frankenstein monster" and talks of sending him to a mental hospital (Scott 2015, 256). Although this accident could happen to any custodian with super-speed, not just one with Down syndrome, Donnie is branded a freak who should be separated from "normal" custodians.

People with disabilities have often been labeled as "freaks" throughout history. As Abbye Meyer and Emily Wender (2015) write, "In Western literature, including young adult literature, the freak is perhaps the most common and consistent representation of a disabled character: marked as non-normative, usually supporting and underdeveloped, and functioning to help other characters develop" (73). Indeed, Meyer and Wender (2015) argue convincingly that these freaks allow others to interrogate their physical characteristics and identities (74). Hence, freaks' representation is less about portraying disabled people and exploring their perspectives, than it is about using disability as an impetus for self-reflection. Scott's portrayal of Donnie fits exactly into this paradigm. After the accident, Phillip visits Donnie in the hospital almost daily as "penance" for telling Donnie to use his super-speed during the competition. He notes that Donnie was always happy to see him when he arrived by his hospital bed but that such happiness only made him feel guiltier: "He usually smiled broadly whenever I walked in. It made me feel so much worse when he did that. The poor guy didn't understand much about the world and might never know how bad a friend I had really been to him" (Scott 2015, 257). Phillip's condescension here can be understood as the solipsism of a twelve-year-old, except for the fact that the rest of Freepoint shares it. Donnie does understand much more about the world than others give him credit for. This is clear at the end of the novel when he saves everyone from the nuclear bomb. Using Phillip's perspective about Donnie to guide the reader's understanding of this character allows for the surprising revelation that Donnie is the second "one who can do all." But it also reveals—and perpetuates—negative understandings of disabilities such as Down syndrome that turn people with these conditions into spectacles and freaks, rather than permit their lived experiences to be understood by other characters in the text and by readers. Many young readers view people with intellectual and developmental disabilities less favorably than those with physical or sensory impairments (Hughes 2017, 190–91). Because Phillip acts this way toward Donnie, his behavior serves as a negative model for interacting with people with intellectual disabilities such as Down syndrome. However, it is probable that young readers will not comprehend Phillip's actions as a negative model without critical analysis guided by teachers or other adults.

Even as Donnie is portrayed as the biggest "freak" of the novel, Scott underscores Donnie as a superlative custodian. At the end of *The Ables*, Donnie saves the day, becoming the ultimate superhero for the custodian world and the regular world on the novel's periphery. Although he is not present during most of the battle of Freepoint, Donnie knows to come when he is needed most. In his quest to provoke Phillip to manifest the additional powers held by "the one who can do all," Finch has murdered dozens of custodians and set off the three-stage bomb. During the first two stages of dynamite and C4, Finch waits for the dead and injured custodians to provoke Phillip before using power to save them all from the final stage: the nuclear bomb. When it is clear that Phillip cannot save them, Finch teleports to safety, leaving his grandson and countless others to die. At that moment, Donnie arrives in a flash of blue light, alternately running and flying to scoop up the injured and move them to safety. Scott allows time to inexplicably slow down for Phillip during this rescue so that he may witness Donnie manifesting the various superpowers needed to save the day. Donnie even pauses to say to Phillip, "Don't worry, Phillip. Donnie fix," words that echo Phillip's promise to his friend when he visited the injured Donnie in the hospital weeks earlier (Scott 2015, 353). Donnie saves everyone from the nuclear bomb by using "the black-hole power," where he turns himself into a black hole that sucks up the expanding mushroom cloud that collapses on itself and disappears, taking Donnie with it. Everyone but Phillip sees the nuclear bomb in one second and then nothing in the next. The second "one who can do all" vanishes as soon as he is revealed as the ultimate hero—invisible once more.

As Phillip, the child who is blind, is the only one to "see" what happened, many custodians are skeptical that Donnie was the one who saved Freepoint. With Finch gone, Phillip should not have been able to see, for he had sight during the first two stages of the bomb only because Finch had allowed him those visions. Phillip "sees" Donnie save the townspeople despite his lack of sight and the impossibly fast time it took for Donnie to accomplish his rescues. Certain townspeople label Phillip's sight as "the hallucinations of a traumatized kid" (Scott 2015, 257). However, most reluctantly acknowledge that Donnie is the only person who could have enacted such a rescue. Phillip notes that "it was just hard for some people to admit that their salvation had come from a kid like Donnie, especially the ones who'd been the most outspoken against him earlier" (Scott 2015, 357). Indeed, the memorials erected in Freepoint hardly acknowledge Donnie's integral role in the town's survival. A small plaque is installed only after Bentley files numerous legal suits demanding its placement. Instead of accepting that Donnie is their savior, the residents of Freepoint focus their approbation upon Phillip and his friends. As Phillip puts it, "We were the disabled kids they found acceptable to call heroes" (Scott 2015, 357). Because they were scorned and underestimated for so many months, Phillip and his friends welcome this change of attitude, even as they recognize that it comes at Donnie's expense. Indeed, Phillip notes that Donnie's role in the battle of Freepoint would probably be deliberately forgotten (Scott 2015, 357). Because the other boys are being treated as "big heroes," they let their absent friend fade from the collective consciousness of Freepoint (Scott 2015, 359). Ultimately, Donnie is too much of a "freak" for even custodians to accept with their wide range of superpowers.

Should this stigmatizing of Donnie be considered a failing of *The Ables*? Given that Scott has made central not just one disabled boy, but six of them—and that the narrator of the novel is disabled—*The Ables* certainly pushes the boundaries of how children with disabilities are depicted in young adult literature and genre-defying canon of superheroes. However, the erasure of Donnie is not the only problematic aspect of this text. At times Scott is unable to adhere to the rules of his own fictional universe. Scott often has trouble portraying what Phillip should and should not see as a blind person. One important moment where this slippage occurs is when Finch kills Phillip's mother. Phillip is visiting Donnie in the hospital, and he tells us how Donnie "usually smiled broadly whenever I walked in" (Scott 2015, 257). As Phillip can see only when Henry is with him projecting his own sight into Phillip's head, Phillip should not know that Donnie smiles at him when he arrives unless someone else informs him of this fact, which does not occur in the text. During this visit, Finch appears while Donnie is sleeping to ask Phillip to join the Believers. Finch does not give Phillip sight in this scene, which is emphasized by the boy narrating details about other sensory information, such as how he feels a breeze whenever Finch gesticulates (Scott 2015, 260). When Phillip refuses to join Finch and the Believers, the older man kills Phillip's mother, who is down the hall in the hospital. It is here that Scott slips most significantly. Phillip realizes what is happening first through sound: the frantic beeping of the life-support machines and medical staff rushing toward her room. But Scott also writes that there were "white blurs speeding past me pushing various carts and barking out orders" (Scott 2015, 263). One of these details should be beyond Phillip's capability to register. Even though he can hear the carts rolling by and people speaking, he should not be able to see "white blurs." As Jen Scott Curwood (2013) convincingly contends, "young adult literature should [...] provide accurate portrayals of individuals with disabilities" (18). While Scott's lapse may demonstrate the challenges of utilizing a blind narrator, his project demands such details be consistent to fully depict the experiences of a blind child.

In addition to Scott's uneven portrayal of his protagonist, he limits his depiction of Freepoint to a white, male, heteronormative world. Henry is the only character of color mentioned in the book. Scott spends only two short paragraphs having Phillip discover that Henry is Black through Henry's projection of his vision into Phillip's brain. Phillip says of this revelation: "Some things just never occur to you when you're blind"; he then breezily notes that Henry's race made no difference to him: "it's easy to be color-blind when you're also regular-blind" (Scott 2015, 128). Scott's depiction of race as merely skin color downplays the social reality of race and racism, which even superpowered individuals should understand and engage with. Additionally, Scott focuses almost exclusively on male characters. Despite naming two girls in the special education classroom, Scott never makes Penelope and Delilah an active part of the plot. Phillip only becomes friends with his male classmates, which may be explained in part by the social tendencies of heterosexual adolescent boys. However, the entire novel has a surprising dearth of significant female characters. Mrs. Crouch, the special education teacher, changes the outcome of the school board hearing but then fades out of the action. Phillip's mother is put into a coma by the villain Mr. Finch halfway through the novel and remains unconscious until her death near the end. Scott's creation of a largely male world perpetuates discrimination against women and girls, both in the real world and the superhero universe. José Alaniz (2014) also comments upon this androcentric depiction in his argument in *Death, Disability, and the Superhero*: "the superhero serves as an entry point for interrogating the social construction of the (male) body, disability, death, illness, and 'normality' in postwar American popular culture" (5). Scott perpetuates this "normality" of Freepoint further by populating the town with heterosexual married couples with children—no single parents or gay couples appear. Such limited representation is ironic given the important themes of inclusion and open-mindedness otherwise promoted within the novel.

Not only do accuracy and representation matter in representing disability, but so does the seeming minutiae of short phrases and individual words. Indeed, in describing the strategies used by the authors in his edited collection, *Lessons in Disability: Essays on Teaching with Young Adult Literature*, Stratman (2015a) writes, "any book about disability is really a book about language" (6). Scott himself references the importance of deliberately and carefully using language when he portrays the "blind humor" that Phillip and James employ. Every so often, one of their friends will say something like, "Did you see that?" Phillip and James reply, not surprisingly, "No" (Scott 2015, 82). While both boys find such moments hilarious, these moments underscore how even everyday phrases perpetuate ableist assumptions. This "blind humor," as Phillip and James call their deadpan reactions, demands an acknowledgment from their friends about their use of ableist language, which then leads to changes in their understanding and interactions with one another. These "blind humor" moments may lead to greater introspection about the language young readers use daily. But despite Scott's laudable emphasis upon identifying ableist language, he stumbles in his language when he portrays Phillip using the word "see" in its metaphorical, rather than literal, sense. While narrating how Finch teleports him and his friends to Cleveland to teach them a lesson, Phillip says, "I'd been to a lot of places in my young life. Between our moves and vacations, I'd seen over a dozen states already. But I'd never been to Cleveland" (Scott 2015, 149). To avoid repetition of the verb "been," Scott uses "seen." Given Phillip's humorous response to the word "see" in previous instances, it is unlikely that the boy would casually invoke "seeing places" rather than saying "visiting places" or even repeating "been places." While these errors may seem innocuous, it is important to expect verisimilitude in portraying a blind character and narrator like Phillip. Telling new stories and representing those previously relegated to the background—or omitted from stories entirely—is always a laudable endeavor. However, it is crucial to do justice to these characters with disabilities because there are so few other representations to rely upon.

Meyer and Wender (2015), in discussing *Wonder* and *Marcelo in the Real World*, underscore the importance of guiding young people through the fraught depictions of disability in these texts, lest these readers come away with their reactions about disability confirmed—such as feeling sorry for the characters with disabilities or believing they could "get better" if they tried to be "normal" (92). The same may be said of *The Ables*. While this novel pushes back against certain negative depictions of (dis)ability, it also perpetuates other misrepresentations, thus undermining some of its positive characteristics. This is not to say that young adults should not read *The Ables*. Indeed, these readers are already enthusiastically embracing this book and its sequel, *Strings* (2019). Ideally, teachers or adult readers would read this novel together to challenge young readers to acknowledge the text's flaws and think more carefully about disability in their everyday lives. As Sandra Q. Williams, Christine D. Inkster, and Joan K. Blaska (2005) argue, "Reading books about characters with disabilities and chronic illnesses opens the door for children to ask questions and facilitates discussion about these types of likenesses and differences. This helps to build a foundation for acceptance of people who may look or act differently" (71). Jeremy Scott's novel allows young adult readers to contemplate differences inscribed upon bodies that may be brand new.

Furthermore, such contemplations may change how these young people interact with disabled persons in their own lives. Janine J. Darragh (2015) points out that "in attempts to be polite, students will just ignore the disability altogether, not realizing that they are dismissing the person as well. Students need to learn that it is natural and even appropriate to 'see' a difference" (141). In addition to "seeing a difference" and recognizing our various personhoods, young people also look to books such as *The Ables* to "see" themselves. One fan asked Scott in a subreddit discussion to consider including in the sequel a character with a learning disability such as their own auditory processing disorder (Scott 2016). Novels such as *The Ables* allow readers to understand themselves in new ways. When first being able to see by receiving Henry's vision, Phillip says, "Some things just never occur to you when you're blind" (Scott 2015, 128). The same may be said of readers without disabilities: some things never occur to you when you do not have a disability. *The Ables*, and other novels portraying characters with disabilities, allow readers of all abilities to comprehend the world anew. After doing so, young adult readers may demand more inclusive understandings of the world from their peers and American society.

References

Alaniz, José. 2014. *Death, Disability, and the Superhero: The Silver Age and Beyond*. Jackson: University Press of Mississippi.

Braswell, Harold. 2011. "Can There Be a Disability Studies Theory of 'End-of-Life Autonomy'?" *Disability Studies Quarterly* 31 (4). doi: 10.18061/dsq.v31i4.1704.

Campbell, Fiona Kumari. 2005. "Legislating Disability: Negative Ontologies and the Government of Legal Identities." In *Foucault and the Government of Disability*, edited by Shelley Tremain, 108–132. Ann Arbor: University of Michigan Press.

Cooper, Tillman. 2015. "Interview with Jeremy Scott," *Target Audience Magazine*, http://tamagazine.com/interview-with-jeremy-scott/.

Curwood, Jen Scott. 2013. "Redefining Normal: A Critical Analysis of (Dis)ability in Young Adult Literature." *Children's Literature in Education* 44: 15–28. doi: 10.1007/s10583–012–9177–0.

Darragh, Janine J. 2015. "Using YA Literature That Portrays Disabilities as Canonical Companions." In *Lessons in Disability: Essays on Teaching with Young Adult Literature*, edited by Jacob Stratman, 123–148. Jefferson, NC: McFarland.

Davis, Lennard J. 1997a. "Constructing Normalcy: The Bell Curve, the Novel, and the Intervention of the Disabled Body in the Nineteenth Century." In *The Disability Studies Reader*, edited by Lennard J. Davis, 9–28. New York: Routledge.

_____. 1997b. "Introduction." In *The Disability Studies Reader*, edited by Lennard J. Davis, 1–6. New York: Routledge.

_____. 2002. *Bending Over Backwards: Disability, Dismodernism, and Other Difficult Positions*. New York: New York University Press.

Hughes, Chloë. 2017. "The 'Words Inside': 'Disabled' Voices in Contemporary Literature for Young People." *Journal of Literary & Cultural Disability Studies* 11 (2). doi: 10.3828/jlcds.2017.14.

Meyer, Abbye, and Emily Wender. 2015. "Teaching and Reading *Wonder* and *Marcelo in the Real World* with Critical Eyes." In *Lessons in Disability: Essays on Teaching with Young Adult Literature*, edited by Jacob Stratman, 72–99. Jefferson, NC: McFarland.

Perry, Tim. 2005. "Mutants That Are All Too Human: The X-Men, Magneto, and Original Sin." In *The Gospel According to Superheroes: Religion and Popular Culture*, edited by B. J. Oropeza, 171–187. New York: Peter Lang Publishers, Inc.

Scott, Jeremy. 2015. *The Ables*. Franklin, TN: Clovercroft Publishing.

_____. 2016. Comment on "Howdy. I'm Jeremy Scott, Author of the Ables & Occasional YouTube-type Person, and You Can AMA," *Reddit*, February 29. https://www.reddit.com/r/books/comments/48bzzt/howdy_im_jeremy_scott_author_of_the_able/.

"Schneider Family Book Award," *American Library Association*, http://www.ala.org/awardsgrants/schneider-family-book-award.

Stratman, Jacob. 2015a. "Exploring Disability Through Young Adult Literature." In *Lessons in Disability: Essays on Teaching with Young Adult Literature*, edited by Jacob Stratman, 1–7. Jefferson, NC: McFarland.

_____. 2015b. "(Re)Defining Disability Through Young Adult Literature." In *Lessons in Disability: Essays on Teaching with Young Adult Literature*, edited by Jacob Stratman, 100–122. Jefferson, NC: McFarland.

Ward, Marilyn. 2002. *Voices from the Margins: An Annotated Bibliography of Fiction on Disabilities and Differences for Young People*. Westport, CT: Greenwood Press.

Williams, Sandra Q., Christine D. Inkster, and Joan K. Blaska. 2005. "The Joan K. Blaska Collective of Children's Literature Featuring Characters with Disabilities or Chronic Illnesses." *Journal of Children's Literature* 31(1): 71–78.

"It is I, Super Grover, Here to Challenge Ableism!"

DAISY L. BRENEMAN

> "Presenting the further adventures of everybody's favorite hero, the monster who's faster than lightning, stronger than steel, smarter than a speeding bullet, it's Super Grover! (And I am cute, too!) And now, on to our story…"

With this introduction, the lovable, furry superhero, Super Grover, crashes onto the television screen. Created by Jim Henson and performed originally by Frank Oz, Super Grover, of the beloved children's television show, *Sesame Street*, occupies the liminal space of a superhero without any apparent superpowers. Super Grover gives audiences insights for resisting ableism through exploring the social and rhetorical construction of disability identity to imagine more just arrangements that foster dignity. Jim Henson's Muppets, and *Sesame Street*, have roots in social justice and offer liberatory potential, as explored in a body of critical work (Garlen and Graham 2009; Liebert 1976; Mandel 2006; Kraidy 2002; Serlin 1998). The show, as *Sesame Street* writer and chronicler Louise Gikow (2009) notes, "was all about inclusion, in the most natural way imaginable" (180). One of the show's founders, Joan Ganz Cooney, helped launch *Sesame Street* through the Children's Television Workshop (CTW) in 1968, with the belief that the show could be a social justice intervention to address the achievement gap between disadvantaged and middle-class children (Davis 2008, 67–68). The show aimed to "lead by example" with an integrated cast that addressed each other "with kindness, respect, and tolerance" (Davis 2008, 142). *Sesame Street's* wide range of characters and actors have fostered diversity and inclusion to cultivate a deep sense of community. Through its careful attention to social identity constructions, the show respects diversity without creating power hierarchies. Media scholar Ute Sartorius Kraidy (2002) argues that with its diverse human and puppet cast, or "collage of individuals" (23), *Sesame Street* resists giving one cultural identity more priority than another (17).

Over the years, *Sesame Street* has been on the cutting edge of disability representation and has played a meaningful role in disability inclusion efforts. Media educator Edward Palmer (1988), a Children's Television Workshop founder, noted that CTW positively represented disability by "simply show(ing) everybody relating to everybody else, on everyday matters, in warm and simple human terms" (95). *Sesame Street* writer Emily Perl Kingsley, who helped discover Deaf cast member Linda Bove through the Little Theater of the Deaf, focused on disability inclusion early on in her work (Davis 2008, 232). That focus intensified in 1974, when her son, Jason, was born; Kingsley (1996) writes that "overnight, my academic interest in disability issues became intensely personal" (75). Jason, who co-authored the book *Count Us In: Growing up with Down Syndrome* (1994), became a regular actor in the show when he was fifteen months old. Emily Kingsley recalls that "it became vitally important to me to let people know that kids like Jason had the potential to learn and that they need not be invisible" (qtd in Davis 2008, 233). Since the early days, the show has featured a range of actors and characters with disabilities. As Emily Kingsley helped ensure, they modeled "a world in which all children are understood, accepted, cherished, and respected" (77).

Over the past half-century, the show has impacted children and the communities they create as adults. As children's literature scholar Carol Billman noted in 1982, "*Sesame Street* has become a staple in our cultural heritage" (15). Sesame Street offered a safe haven during an unsettled childhood and created characters to be loved and feel loved by kids like me. One loveable character, Grover, who is "complex and flawed, multifaceted and compelling" evolved during the show's early seasons (Johnston 2008, 18). His superhero manifestation, Super Grover, debuted in Season 5 (1973–1974). Super Grover's character vaguely echoes that of Superman; using a phone booth, he changes into a cape and helmet. His non-super-hero persona is Grover Kent, a mild-mannered Acme doorknob salesman. Frequently crash landing, getting his cape caught, and getting himself into other situations, Super Grover, while well-meaning, does not quite match the traditional expectations for a superhero.

The relationship between superheroes and ableism is complex, as a growing body of work reveals (Alaniz and Henderson 2014; Ratto 2017; Germaine 2016; Cocca 2014). Superheroes reinforce the myth of bodily perfection (Stone 1995) and represent a distinct break from socially defined norms ripe for critical interrogation. As disability studies scholar Lyndsey Row-Heyveld (2015) notes, discussing superpowers "provides a rich, wide-ranging context for the study of nonstandard bodies" and "examining the spectrum of physical variation reveals the many forces that shape those constructions, as well as how superpowers and disability wield genuine power in our world despite the artificiality of those categories" (520–21).

Representations of superheroes have an impact on how individuals view themselves as educational leadership scholar, Genie Bingham Linn (2011) writes, superheroes like Super Grover exhibit "loyalty and courage" and a "willingness to take risks while working for a cause greater than self" (176). While Super Grover has a certain type of courage, and a definite desire to help, he does not have superpowers. A superhero without apparent superpowers, Super Grover creates a rich opportunity for challenging ableism and offers a more inclusive, ethically just way of ordering the physical and social world. *Sesame Street* is inherently about experimentation and forging new possibilities as its creators "made an excellent start at formulating questions that had never before been asked" (Tierney 1971, 296). A "great experiment" (Liebert 1976, 165) from the beginning, *Sesame Street* was about a dream for something better, part of Jim Henson's greater vision. As Muppet scholar Elizabeth Hyde Stevens (2014) notes, "We love the Muppets because they gave us a worldview—a profoundly idealistic, yet profoundly realistic worldview—that many of us carry into our adulthoods." This worldview is one in which equity, social justice, dignity and care make strong, diverse communities possible. The Muppets and *Sesame Street* urge us to imagine greater possibilities.

Imagination helps bring a complexly embodied Super Grover to life. As disability studies scholar Rosemarie Garland-Thomson (2016) writes, the Muppets are fruitful for interrogating disability because they "all departed from fully human characteristics in quirky, oddly endearing ways. They were human-animal hybrids or engaging freak show figures" (xi). Grover is blue and furry but displays human qualities such as an intense desire to help and a tendency to make mistakes. The human/Muppet relationship is complex and fluid, as are many relationships. On Sesame Street, humans and Muppets live, sing, dance, learn and love together. Muppets, including Grover, are written, voiced, performed, envisioned, and crafted by humans. Materially, Grover is sticks and cloth, an object performed by a human being, the multi-talented Frank Oz. But Grover is more, just as humans are more than biological cells and fluid—more than our containers. Muppets take on a new identity, connected to but more than either the performer or the physical puppet. This synergy between Muppet and performer transcends the human/Muppet binary to teach us about what it means to exist (as human or otherwise). Ben Underwood (2009) argues that the Muppets are popular because they "Muppetize" their audience: "When you watch the Muppets, you become a Muppet," thus blurring and challenging the human and Muppet boundaries further and reminding us how much we can learn from each other.

Muppet scholar Gideon Haberkorn (2009) notes, "Muppets are especially useful when it comes to thinking about self and identity [...] and a prism through which we reflect on and gain a deeper understanding of our selves" (25). Muppets are not humans, but humans are intrinsically and necessarily connected to their being, further challenging the binary and providing learning opportunities. Even their creator, Jim Henson, acknowledged, "Muppets have always had a life of their own, and we who do the Muppets serve that life and the audience" (Jones 2013, 168). As a member of that audience since my earliest memories, I recognize that the character with the helmet and cape we call Super Grover is a relational figure, called into existence—as we all are, by those who love him.

Super Grover assists us in reconciling the tension between ethics of care and dignity, which is fundamental in disability studies and justice studies. Super Grover establishes dignity for his fellow Muppets—and, by extension, the human audience witnessing this happen—through his care. Through a nuanced display of interdependence, Super Grover yields exciting possibilities for constructing communities of care that also respect agency. This sense of care was a feature of the Muppets and Sesame Street, which Jim Henson helped establish.

In addition to caring, Jim Henson embodied another essential quality: a sense of fun. As Super Grover's performer, Frank Oz, says, the legacy of the Muppets "is really Jim—having fun and doing work" (qtd in Setoodeh 2017). Super Grover accomplishes his work by being adorable, laughing, and using humor to cope with challenging situations and frustration at his foibles. Women's studies scholar Michelle Ann Abate (2009), notes that "unpacking the subversive nature of the ostensibly harmless fun" of the Muppets can make nonsense meaningful (591). Both subversiveness and fun undergird the methodology and approach of this essay. Analyzing ten episodes of Super Grover that first aired between 1973 and 1990, I focus on classic *Sesame Street* for many reasons. One, it is the Sesame Street I grew up on. By 1990, a new generation of kids was watching, and Gen X'ers, the target audience for the *Sesame Street* Ganz Cooney and colleagues created, were no longer the show's focus. In addition, the show and Super Grover experienced major transitions during the late 1980s, as many in the original cast began leaving the show or at least turning over major characters as part of the transition process. Indeed, Frank Oz began the handover of Grover to Eric Jacobsen during this time.

Each episode of classic Super Grover shares a familiar plot: Super Grover sees someone in distress or need, whether over a haircut, a stack of boxes to be moved, groceries to be carried, a fight over an apple, catching the bus, or any number of scenarios that may cause a young person distress. Often the character is crying and afraid. Super Grover crash-lands into the scene (while he can kind of fly, he never mastered landing). As Super Grover attempts to find a solution to the problem, the character in distress is typically the one who actually solves the problem. Meanwhile, Super Grover often needs help; getting his head out of a fence, recovering from a crash, or getting a cat off his cape. Most episodes end with a positive outcome, and leave the audience laughing. *Sesame Street* in the Jim Henson era and beyond was about fun, community, and caring. Through humor, fun, and the embrace of possibility, Super Grover gives scholars and viewers alike a fruitful space for both resisting ableism, and exploring the social construction of identity, questioning our definitions of failure, and building more just communities through a relational, connected sense of care.

Like most forms of oppression and discrimination, ableism is so pervasive and manifests itself in so many ways that disrupting it requires multiple innovative tools and approaches (Loja et al. 2013). Super Grover challenges ableism and the ableist construction of able-bodied/disabled binaries through his very existence, a superhero without superpowers (or, at least, minimal ones). Super Grover refers to his superpowers in every episode: a super mind, muscles, and everything else. His lack of self-consciousness is empowering and mirrors that of Muppet creator Henson, who, as Joan Ganz Cooney notes, "could talk about wanting a world of peace and love without a trace of irony or self-consciousness" (Gikow 2009, 41). While Super Grover is concerned with the category of "superhero," he has not internalized an external definition of it. For Super Grover, putting on the helmet and cape and knowing he is Super Grover is enough. His embodiment of a superhero leads one to question the very definition of power—and the power of definitions. What is a superhero? Who sets these categories, and why, how, when, and for whom? These are all questions disability studies ask about the social, rhetorical, and political construction of disability (Linton 1998, 142–146). When one is "super," as when disabled, there must be a "normal" for comparison. And, in Super Grover's Metro City, Sesame Street and the world, there is no "normal" to be found. During the first episode, Gordon says, "Everything happens here. You're gonna love it" (Borgenicht 1988, 17). Everything (and nothing) is normalized: a green grouch in a trashcan, an imaginary friend Snuffleupagus, a giant yellow bird, and twiddlebugs all (co)exist on this street. The very nature of Muppets calls "normal" into question—a word that, for disability scholars like Simi Linton (1998) and *Sesame Street* writer Kingsley (1996) alike, "still catches in my throat" (75).

In addition to challenging categories, Super Grover also offers opportunities to interrogate the fraught concepts of failure, resilience, and courage. Super Grover highlights, for example, the link between the constructed definitions of success and failure, and the interpretation of outcomes. This has powerful implications for how humans view their own bodies and their operation, and how changing socially constructed definitions can liberate—especially concerning questions of efficacy. Often, it is Super Grover's false expectations that result in something not working. For example, in the episode "Dial S for Super Grover," Super Grover believes that yelling out Shirley's window will help Bobby, who lives blocks away, understand that his friend cannot play as they had planned; it, of course, does not. In another instance, Super Grover believes hopping up and down while saying, "wubba, wubba" will turn on a computer; again, it does not. His expectations for a successful outcome are faulty. But, because Shirley remembers that she can call Bobby on the telephone to tell him she cannot play because she has to work on a paper, she accomplishes what needs to be done, as does the Muppet child who discovers the computer's "on" button. The audience, of course, recognizes the mismatch between the expectation and the outcome; we are in on the joke, and we understand that, of course, what Super Grover was trying would not work. Being cognizant of the disconnect, and fully aware of the inevitability of failure, gives the audience useful knowledge and perspective. Failure is so expected that it is not scary or disappointing. But, Super Grover's obliviousness to failure also signals that he does not subscribe to external definitions of failure.

Shedding the social expectations (mythologies) of perfection, of things always working, goes a long way toward shattering shame and disappointment; if it is known that things sometimes do not work, one may be more prepared for that eventuality. The lived experience of bodies failing to do as "expected" by ableist ideologies is one of many strengths of people with disabilities, and disability culture; this is one of many contributions disability makes to conversations about the human experience. Journalist and memoirist John Hockington (1995) notes that "the belief that around the next corner there was going to be some obstacles fit well into my own sense of the world acquired from a wheelchair [...] Disabled people expect things not to work" (263). Georgina Kleege (2006) poignantly highlights this deep and valuable knowledge of failure in *Blind Rage: Letters to Helen Keller,* writing "Making do is not such a foreign concept to me. For the Normals, making do is dreadful even to contemplate. What would life be without a leg, without eyesight, without hearing, they worry. Life would be life, you and I say. Flawed, limited in some ways, rich and varied in others" (182). Super Grover's defiance toward accepting how things "should" go emphasizes a practical way to address realities, and a powerful antidote to able-centric thinking about outcomes.

Solutions and outcomes are often insignificant in Super Grover's world. Super Grover often remains blissfully unaware that he never actually solves the problems he encounters. He exalts the "good idea" of moving groceries to an empty box in the "Broken Grocery Bag" episode, without noting whose idea it was (not his). In the "Barbershop" episode, he exclaims "I have made a great discovery. Haircuts do not hurt," even though it took extraordinary effort on the part of the barber to illustrate this fact to Super Grover. His demonstrations have the power to define how we interpret outcomes—and Super Grover almost always interprets himself as the hero. He flips the scenario, not reading his failure but rather the very practical result of solving a problem. These episodes also remind the audience that people can accomplish things in several ways, and trying is where the learning occurs. By ridding cultures of externally-imposed definitions of success and failure, audiences participate in shattering ableism. Super Grover models that people can find joy in various outcomes, regardless of whether or not they align with external definitions of success or failure. In most cases, he understands a situation is resolved, perhaps in an unexpected way, and that is all that matters. Thus, even though by some standards he "fails," he does not internalize shame or even accept the definition. This offers productive potential for resisting the stigma and shame attached to "failure" inherent in ableism.

Since he is not overly concerned with external judgments about his powers while wholeheartedly embracing being a superhero, he models agency and self-definition for the audience. Such self-confidence, or "comfort with one's identity and internal loci of approval" is a crucial feature of social justice allyship—one potential tool for working toward more just arrangements (Broido 2000). When Super Grover does choose to accept input from others, it is from only those he loves, and who validate him. For example, in the "Barbershop" episode, he notes, "Oh, Mommy would be so proud. Once again, Super Grover has done something." He finds courage and power in the judgments of those he loves, and ignores the rest. Because his moxie is authentic, it does not come across as hubris. What is more, while he rarely recognizes limitations, he fully understands how adorable he is—hence, "And I am cute, too!" Even when he has fallen on his face, literally, he maintains a positive self-image. For the audience, this resistance to outside definitions of adorableness can be powerful. While "cute" can be a problematic concept, it can also carry some liberatory potential, as noted by scholars such as Elaine M. Laforteza (2014). Like other problematic qualities or labels, adorable can be (re)claimed for empowerment. The key here is self-definition, a foundational task of resistance. Linton (1998) identifies "control, self-determination, and self-definition" as essential elements of the work of disability studies. As Eli Clare (2001) argues,

"The goal isn't to make irrevocable difference disappear. [...] What has changed is how I perceive my irrevocable difference, how I frame it, what context I place it into" (363). Gaining control of the framing and definition of one's self, body, and mind, especially for those who have been classified as "other," is empowering and can foster self-advocacy and social justice.

Also empowering is Super Grover's emphasis on process, which resists traditional success/failure and acceptability notions. Each episode spends the bulk of its time letting the protagonist work through a problem. The audience witnesses the dilemma in detail, such as "my mommy told me to take a bus home and I don't know where to get a bus," or "my mother said I have to move these three heavy boxes off the steps onto the porch, but I am not strong enough"; "my computer isn't working. Something's wrong. Nothing's happening." Each episode spells out the problem, then allows the viewer to watch as the characters work through it, often after several attempts that do not solve the problem. Eventually the solution is discovered near the end, but the audience remains focused on the problem-solving process for most of the episode. Super Grover often goes through a messy, chaotic, and funny, process of trial and error. Whether trying to scream out a window to a distant friend, using glue to carry home groceries, bending fence bars rather than finding an exit to leave the playground, or saying "wubba, wubba," Grover shows that sometimes it takes all kinds of paths before we find something that works. And, sometimes we never find what works, and that is okay, too. Through Super Grover, audiences witness the "let me think" moments and the attempts that fail. It is not about the traditional superhero tropes of the savior and the victory, but rather about the collaborative effort one can put into solving complex problems, even those that generate tears and despair.

This move from product, performance, and hierarchy to a collaborative process reflects a notable impulse in disability studies. Robert McRuer (2004), for example, identifies the normative forces at work in traditional composition, which focuses on the "fetishized final product" (57). McRuer (2004) argues crip theory keeps our attention "on disruptive, inappropriate, composting bodies" and highlights process as an important project of resisting "compulsory able-bodiedness" (57). Chris Foss (2015) echoes this emphasis on process as vital to universally designed educational settings (484).

Process also helps Super Grover develop resilience. After crash landing into most episodes, Super Grover never wavers in his determination to help someone in crisis. Then, at the end of each episode, Super Grover, often in his own new pain or crisis, looks toward his next adventure. At the end of the "Apple Battle" episode, he claims to be "off to save the world and other good stuff." Despite being thwarted by a cat standing on his cape, at the end of "Bus Stop," Super Grover wants to travel "onward and upward to do brave deeds." Right before crashing into a tree in the "Boxes" episode, Super Grover notes he "must go to help other people." No matter what adversity he confronts, he persists. As Katherine Runswick-Cole and Dan Goodley (2013) note, "resilience" as a socially constructed concept has traditionally reinforced the "discrimination and marginalization" of people with disabilities (67). However, we can rescue and reconstruct the concept of resilience through a more holistic approach that acknowledges resources, community, power, and social justice. Super Grover's resilience is internally cultivated but relies on an environment and community that empower him to keep trying. He is in the loving context of Sesame Street, which nurtures inclusion and full participation rather than constructing barriers. Super Grover cultivates resilience through connection to others and his insatiable desire to make the world better.

Courage is another of Super Grover's (re)claimed qualities. In the "Barbershop" episode, Super Grover erroneously tells the scared Willy Nilly that the haircut will hurt as feared, "but you must be brave. You must smile through your tears. You must endure the agony, bear the pain, ignore the ouchness." This is a complicated utterance. Unfortunately, it echoes the "buck up, kid" message that many people with disabilities endure, a message that reinforces the medical model of disability and places the burden on the individual. Kleege (2006) critiques such narratives, arguing that "disability has very little to do with the nobler emotions—courage, fortitude, pluck—and more to do with the practical matter of finding a way to live in a world not designed for them" (177). The ableist ascription of courage to people with disabilities can reinforce the dangerous individualism and rejection of collective responsibility for eliminating ableism and barriers to access; the concept of an individual "overcoming" barriers is used to deny society's responsibility to eradicate them (Linton 1998). Courage can be weaponized against those who exhibit it. On the other hand, it can also serve as a tool of resistance and a necessary quality when remaking the world in equitable ways. The Barbershop episode troubles the definition of bravery by having Super Grover extol the necessity of courage in connection with a haircut; the absurdity throws off our expectations. Because, as the audience well understands, there is no need to fear haircuts—as proven in the episode, haircuts do NOT hurt—the message rings as an amusing testament to endurance and resilience. Super Grover's courage is one-of-a-kind, because his very existence defies conventional definition.

Super Grover proves brave and resilient without reinforcing the "inspiration" trope applied to superheroes and people with disabilities alike. He can be a superhero without reinforcing some of the damaging supercrip typologies, such as that which Sami Schalk (2016) identifies as the "superpowered supercrip narrative" that tends to present unexamined and uncomplicated versions of extraordinary powers (81). Super Grover gives us an alternative representation of heroness that is marvelously nuanced and funny. After all, the "meh" reaction of people who realize it's not a bird or a plane but "just" Super Grover in most episodes clues the audience in that others have not quite bought into his superheroness. Or, if they have, they accept him as the superhero he actually is, not some idealized version. Even Super Grover needs some reminders, as in the "Bus Stop" episode; once the child whose mom wanted him to take the bus discovers how to catch it, he says, "I think my problem is solved." With his "super mind," Super Grover's response of "It is? How did I do it?" shows his own confusion about his superpowers and the very slippery nature of the social constructs about the body and identity. Ability is not as straightforward or "normal," as hegemonic ableism would have us believe.

In all of these ways, Super Grover challenges ableism and offers possibilities for reconstructing the world—based not on power hierarchies but on equitable, relational structures that, through caring, better support the dignity of all individuals. Though he lacks superpowers, Super Grover teaches us about the powers that matter. He serves as an ally for individuals and supports them in achieving dignity and agency. Often, his very presence matters, as it gives the character in distress the confidence to find a solution. This respectful approach to support that honors autonomy echoes what Nancy J. Evans, Jennifer L. Assadi, and Todd K. Herriott (2005) argue is the main feature of disability allyship: being "encouraging and helpful in their interactions" while also "respecting the autonomy of individuals" (74). Sometimes being present—and caring—is the central way to empower and support others.

By caring enough to want to help, Super Grover helps. To love is the greatest superpower, one that defies all rules and invites us into the unknown, into vulnerability, into true interconnectedness. When we enter into relation with others, there will be pain, sacrifice, need, and intensity. To love, we must also embrace our vulnerability, something Super Grover certainly does. While he is impervious to external judgment, he acknowledges that "superheroes bruise easily" ("Barbershop"); this highlights pain as a universal. Sharon Dale Stone (1995) argues that because "bodily suffering and discomfort are a part of the human experience," embracing disability "does not mean acknowledging our own helplessness, it means acknowledging our humanness" (422). Super Grover is more than willing to admit his own pain, and he stays open to it; his pain allows him to connect with others.

Empathy is another of Super Grover's endearing qualities. Quite touching in the Barbershop episode is the deep respect with which Super

Grover listens to Willy Nilly, who fears the haircut. While Willy's mother and barber dismiss his fear of a haircut as silly, Super Grover tends to the boy with empathy and care to discover the root of his problem. Because he feels pain, Super Grover connects with others who feel pain and shows he understands what it means to be in need. Nancy Mairs (1986) identifies this as a major gift of disability: "It has opened and enriched my life enormously, this sense that my frailty and need much be mirrored in others, that in searching for and shaping a stable core in a life wrenched by change and loss, change and loss, I must recognize the same process, under individual conditions, in the lives around me" (48).

Super Grover's efforts to help are rooted in caring and connection. The ethics of care contribute a great deal to the project of accounting for justice for people with disabilities, especially since disability was long excluded from conversations about justice, including by theorists such as John Rawls (Hartley 2011, 120). Critical theorists raise critical questions about human interdependence and agency. At root in this tension are our very notions of what it means to be human. For so long, thinkers (ensconced in ableism and other forms of oppression) conceptualized humans as needing independence, which is not a realistic or even desirable goal for many. As feminist disability studies scholar Eva Feder Kittay (2001) argues, "to stigmatize dependency, ignore its frequency, and valorize only a particular segment of human possibility is to shirk our collective responsibility to take care of one another and to ensure that we are well taken care of by someone for whom our well-being matters deeply" (575). Suppose we instead shape our thinking about how humans interact, cooperate, live, love, *together,* bound by reciprocity and mutuality. In that case, we move away from hegemonic notions of what it means to contribute to a community. By moving contribution into new territory and noting that we contribute through the essence of our existence with others, we better account for all humans' full participation and dignity.

A sticking point remains the issue of being cared for, creating a power imbalance and reinforcing dichotomies and hierarchies. The question of how we conceive of "help" must be addressed with nuance and care. Disability scholar Joseph W. Schneider (1988) suggests that assuming that "people with disabilities need and want others' help and care [...] obscures the fact that we all—able bodied and disabled alike—sometimes want and need such help" (66). This is not to flatten out the very real differences in access needs created by ableist design; Schneider (1988) acknowledges that for people with disabilities "such 'normal' dependence may come at an extraordinary cost" (74). Inequities in access and the reality that people with disabilities must navigate the physical and social barriers arising from ableism and ableist design mean that, until we correct such inequities, there will be differences in the perception of, access to, and reliance upon help. In addition, as Schalk (2016) notes, "the appeal to a sentimental universal humanity" is a mechanism of problematic supercrip narratives (84).

That said, affirming that people are interconnected, and deeply rely on each other in many ways, can advance social justice efforts. Many scholars, such as Schneider (1988) and Stone (1995), argue that needing help is inherently human and should be recognized as what connects us. Super Grover challenges the helper/helped binary by highlighting that we all need help, emphasizing the value of needing help, and the learning and growth that occur when we open up to need (ours and others). Interdependence is imperative for acquiring an account of justice that includes disability. Super Grover participates in the solution that Jenny Morris (2001) suggests reconciling the tension between care approaches and human dignity approaches to justice: "the recognition of our difference (including our dependence), because of our impairments, can thus become a passport to the recognition of our common humanity" (15). Needing help makes us human, a monster—created, built, written about, and performed by a human—teaches us that. While there is a danger in erasing diversity and difference and denying power imbalances, there is also power in pointing out that need is universal. Mairs (1986) identifies help and humor as sources of strength: "I may find it easier than other cripples to amuse myself because I live propped up by the acceptance and the assistance and, sometimes, the amusement of those around me" (44). Acknowledging help (especially help given inclusively and equitably) as strength can disrupt traditional and oppressive notions of help as weakness.

Kleege (2006) acknowledges the power and trickiness of providing help: "I don't enjoy feeling like we exist to offer illuminating insights to the Normals. But in my more generous moments (few and far between as they are), I feel it's something worth doing. They need a lot of help" (182). Marginalized groups, including people with disabilities, should never be forced into either needing or giving help; but, destigmatizing help, and recognizing the power of reciprocity, can be a tool of resistance to ableism. A recurring theme in Super Grover is his switching roles from helper to needing help as he attempts to provide it. For example, in "Fence Exit," he gets his head stuck in the bars of a fence while attempting to help a child get out of the playground; the child then finds his way out by finding the "Exit" sign. Or, in the "Bus Stop" episode, the boy Grover was trying to help ends up teaching Grover that "b-u-s" spells bus. They mutually learn and help together. Kraidy (2002) argues that *Sesame Street* pedagogy challenges the "authority/subordinate dichotomy" and "encourages self-esteem by demonstrating that teaching and learning are an inherent part in everybody's interaction" (21).

This highlights the fluidity of the relationship—one can be teacher and learner, helper and helped simultaneously, in cycles, or in different and new ways. Helping is a dynamic concept, and often it completely depends on our perspective. Super Grover is empowered by the belief that he has helped, and in his presence, the "helpee," the character in distress, finds a resolution to the problem. In some sense, both parties both help and are helped, just in varying degrees and ways. Thus, it is possible to have the impulse to help—to want to make someone's life better—without the power baggage that this can entail. We can help others while acknowledging them as equitable, deserving of respect, kindness, care, and dignity. Such a stance—avoiding interacting with people in a patronizing and condescending manner and instead "treating them as equals deserving of respect—is a crucial quality of disability allyship" (Evans, Assadi, and Herriott 2005, 75). Interactions with each other should consider power dynamics, and resist hierarchy and categorization, especially when offering help.

This fully inclusive view of service also addresses one of the rights that is often removed from people with disabilities because of ableism: the right to make contributions, and to have those contributions recognized. As justice scholar Terry Beitzel (2014) notes in his exploration of the therapeutic community Gould Farm, serving others when you are also in need of help moves away from paternalism and instead creates a "reciprocity effect" that helps all, and bestows "worth" and value to individuals (148). It is therapeutic to help others; it provides dignity to participate in bearing one another's burdens. We can always accomplish more when we work together, and create space for the contributions of all—as Super Grover illustrates. Though problems are often solved individually, the solving happens in the presence of others. We can conquer our fear of haircuts, move heavy boxes one by one, ride the bus, turn on the computer, share apples, and make a phone call, especially when we have the support of a well-intentioned superhero, or any other friend. Especially during troubled times, cooperation is a superpower.

The beautiful interplay of individual empowerment and reciprocity is apparent in Super Grover. The Muppet kids in each episode learn to address a challenge, and work toward a solution; their problem-solving is a victory, one that happened in the meaningful and caring presence of Super Grover. They are caring *with* and *through* each other (Dolmage 2015). While each episode depicts distress—the sort of distress young children feel—it also depicts a collaborative effort to reduce barriers and remove distress through empowerment. The child who was supposed to be "saved" by Super Grover to the rescue, is rescued through their clever solution—in the presence of Super Grover, and because Super Grover cared.

We are all saved by our cared-for selves, emphasizing an integrated self/ other relationship.

Except for the (troublesome) "Phone Booth" episode, in which Super Grover carries the Muppet child in the phone booth above the child's protests, most episodes depict Super Grover (intentionally or otherwise) respecting bodily autonomy and choice. He oversteps boundaries in the "Phone Booth" episode, and his paternalism and denial of agency make him a less-than-ideal ally in this case. Though, as Keith E. Edwards (2006) argues, "fear of making mistakes and not being the 'ideal ally'" is dangerous, and prevents people from becoming active allies (54). At least he tries, and at least we can learn from his mistakes. Still, even in this episode, the lost child in distress had already figured out she could call her mother for help. Feeling empowered to solve problems independently, they gain valuable skills—in part because they are in a setting surrounded by loving others that encourages them to do so. The characters in distress do not reinforce the dangerous and ableist trope of passivity noted by Linton (1998, 25). Rather, they become active agents who work toward solutions in a supportive community. Super Grover allows us to accept a definition of justice and the construction of a world that accounts for autonomy and choice, as well as dependence and need.

By their own account, scholars such as Foss (2015) and Kittay (2001) arrive at their accounts of justice through parenting children with disabilities. Family is vital to Super Grover's discoveries, and his definitions of self. We know Super Grover shares a close bond with his mother and invokes her often by saying she would be proud of him. In the "Apple Battle," Super Grover attempts to break up two brothers fighting over an apple by using his "Super Talking"—asking, "Did I ever tell you what my mommy says about fighting?" and after an interlude—and after the boys have stopped fighting—ends up sharing her wise words: "Don't do it." During the interlude, Super Grover waxes poetic about his mother: "Did I ever tell you about my Mommy? What a sweet mommy she is. Her name is Super Mommy." He details her pretty fur, and that she is so nice to him, interjecting, "Oh, I love my mommy. I remember when I was just a little ball of fur, she would sing to me." Super Grover begins to sing the song she sang to him, "Rock-a-bye Super Baby." As he sings, the boys pause and realize the better way is to share the apple instead of fighting. They recall what their own mother has told them. Once they begin to share, Super Grover is satisfied, knowing Mommy will be proud of him.

Through Super Grover recounting his mother's love the boys remember the value of sharing, and it strengthens their bond as brothers and resolves the conflict through the inherently caring act of sharing food. Sharing is presented as a much "better way" to approach the problem

("Apple Battle"). There is much emphasis on collaboration, and caring; through friends, family, and community we find answers. In Super Grover, relationships are valued, ethics become relational, and positive outcomes through a positive process are achieved through family and community bonds. Love and relationships are tools of empowerment.

Just as Super Grover invokes his mother, other characters pose their dilemmas, and solutions, in terms of the needs of others, especially family. For example, the girl in "Dial S for Super Grover" is quite concerned about her connection to her friend. She rejects Super Grover's suggestion that she not tell the friend she cannot make their playdate because she does not want to hurt the relationship. Characters worry about not knowing how to take a bus home ("Bus Stop"), or being at dinner on time ("Fence Exit"), or getting a haircut ("Barber Shop"), or being able to move boxes ("Boxes") because these are things their mothers wanted them to do. Whether they are worried about mom being mad or the missed chance to share a meal with family, the primacy of relationship and connection is clear. Such relationships are reciprocal; each community member is respected and valued for what they can do and contribute. And the most prominent contribution is just being there. While Super Grover believes he has superpowers—he frequently references his super thinking, super arms, super thinking, super talking—time and again, it is not the exercise of superpowers but rather the sheer force of his presence that makes the difference. In teaching Super Grover, characters offer as well as receive.

Super Grover refuses to be thanked for his efforts, which helps address power imbalances in the helper/helped relationship. According to the old pity/charity models of disability, a person with a disability, when receiving "assistance," should be passive, grateful, and meek. However, Super Grover proactively rejects perceived expressions of gratitude (though, often, the character being "helped" had no intention of thanking him). In the "Computer" episode, Super Grover notes, "Do not bother to thank me—I must be off to save other little boys and girls in distress." In the "Boxes" episode, he says, "No, do not try to thank me, I live to serve, now I must go to help other people." He again tells the little girl in "Dial S" that there is "no need to thank me, little girl, it is just another job well done by Super Grover." While he is a little less humble there, he expresses no need for gratitude; right after that, he crashes into the door trying to save the next person in need. Even while in pain, he offers advice: "If you ever become a superhero, little girl, always remember to open the door before you fly away." So, he is considering others, wanting to spare them the pain of the crash by offering wise advice. His service orientation is genuine, regardless of the expression of gratitude. The refusal of thanks disrupts traditional charity models that demand it, thus disempowering individuals.

Super Grover pushes us toward a complex model of gratitude that is reciprocal, even when what is offered is flawed and imperfect. Each character gets and gives respect and gratitude, not compulsory, but born from mutuality, membership in a community, and love. After all, we get a lot by giving, particularly when that happens in an equitable community that actively strives to reduce power imbalances—and Sesame Street is that very kind of community. Super Grover emphasizes that gratitude is not the reason for service; we serve because we are all an important part of our communities, and service is just what we should be doing. Of course, it helps that it feels good to serve. And, in the "Fence Exit" episode, he reveals what he gets from helping: "Please do not thank me—helping people is my joy and pleasure." He says later, "I am here but to serve[....] That makes me feel so good." That he says this while his head is stuck between two fence bars further demonstrates that life is not perfect, and he feels great pleasure serving others.

This joy in service theme is echoed in "Broken Grocery Bags," when Super Grover tells Judy Finstermacher—who solved her problem by realizing she could use an empty box to carry them—"Thank you for being such a good little girl and allowing me to help you." The audience knows that she solved the problem herself, thus questioning the notion that being "good" means allowing people to help. But, it also does something else; it shows that gratitude runs both ways. Many of us want to feel like we can make a difference for other people, contribute to a community, and bear another's burdens, regardless of how much social power we have. And sometimes all we need to do to accomplish these goals and harness this power is to *be* with others. Super Grover captures something very poignant about the nature of helping and being helped—with an emphasis on connection. He helps move us away from individualistic notions of independence. Though he empowers the characters he helps to solve problems independently, they are not alone—they are in his presence. Sesame Street is a place that nurtures community and rejects the idea of the individual, even as it nurtures individuals; this synergy is powerful. We are at our best when we are empowered, autonomous individuals working together in a community.

On Sesame Street, individuals do not all need to be the same to be worthy of dignity and respect; diversity enhances our worth. This is the very point of the last episode of Super Grover that aired within Jim Henson's lifetime—"Super Grover and Elmo." In this episode, Elmo claims that because he and Super Grover both enjoy being pals, they are the same. Super Grover repeatedly tries to explain the concept of "different." When Elmo asks why they are different, Super Grover attempts to explain that Super Grover is big and Elmo is little; an additional explanation is "because I am Super Grover," and "because of all the things I can do that you cannot do." What follows is a fun game of imitation, with Elmo repeating "Wubba, wubba" and all kinds of other silliness. After Elmo's insistence that they are the same, Super Grover concedes, "Okay, okay, how about if we just say we are the same in some ways, okay, but we are different in other ways, at the same time, how about that? Okay, Okey Dokey?" Elmo replied "okey, dokey, Elmo like that," and they end the episode with a fun game of imitation. They agree on both common ground and acceptance of difference and agree to be good friends through it all. We are all the same, and we are all different.

Rhetorician Jim Corder (1986) argues that while "we have not learned how to let competing normalities live together in the same time and space," with time and attention, listening and love, we can learn to "speak a commodious language, creating a world full of space and time that will hold our diversity" (31). Super Grover and *Sesame Street* as a whole create this space and time. Difference and similarity can co-exist. Love unites. Diversity is represented as a positive—for example, Super Grover is blue, and the Muppets depicted in each episode represent a wide array of colors, shapes, and sizes; all are valued and respected. Unruliness is also a rule on Sesame Street and Super Grover—anything goes on this street. For instance, Oscar can be Grouchy, Snuffy can be real or imagined, and Super Grover can put on a cape and become a superhero out of his deep impulse to serve or just because they feel like doing it. This helps model for kids that we can love each other across difference, work together in a community, and dream for something better.

Caring *for* and *with* is a meaningful path to justice; it ensures that we build communities that provide meaningful inclusion, access, equity, and dignity to all members. The expression of care in Super Grover is touching. Super Grover does not like to see people in distress, and responds immediately, even though it typically involves a painful crash, and a series of events that challenge him and involve risk to himself. His biggest accomplishment is showing that he cares through his presence and by listening and *trying*. In each episode, he genuinely seeks to understand what others need, without passing judgment. Now, sometimes Super Grover misunderstands the situation or disregards intention. Like humans, he has not necessarily mastered finding ways to respect agency and choice— but he tries. He reveals that we are all fallible, and need to practice vigilance when recognizing what others need and want to live lives of dignity. But we can honor the ways Super Grover connects deeply with other characters, and shows love just by showing up. He offers the loving gesture of caring, and caring enough just to try something. The outcome does not matter. Because, as Super Grover knows, there is always another episode, the next time to be tested. It just takes time and patience, trying and reconfiguring. That is how we remake the world to be more just and inclusive, through caring and trying, and trying again.

And, even in painful processes, we can still embrace fun. One of the best parts of *Sesame Street* scholarship is getting to, always, play. To remember the joy and possibility of sitting down to visit my favorite Street, where we can all find a place of caring, acceptance, and love. To leave behind the despair of the now to remember the lessons of *Sesame Street*—including that it is possible to build a beloved community of love and respect and fun (Mandel 2006, 9). *Sesame Street* is about possibilities and hopes for the future. Of all the things that Super Grover gives, one of the most valuable is that he makes children laugh as they learn. Viewers can find a superheroness in the very ordinariness, and in relationship with others.

Muppets, in their very existence, are about connection—piles of felt brought to life by the genius of their performers and a company of people of multiple backgrounds, talents, abilities, and perspectives, as well as the bountiful imagination of their audience. A young Jim Henson saw his mother's discarded felt coat and dreamt Kermit into existence, an act of vision and love that profoundly affected generations (Jones 2013, 47). Muppets defy boundaries and embrace the impossible, the absurd, the amazing, monsters who at the core are (literally) human, crafted and written and performed by humans for humans. Muppet structure, words, and movement are connected to the human inside and become more than that human; they become something wholly new, especially as they interact with their Muppet and human brethren. This unique way of existence, their impossible embodiedness, also captures the essence of disability studies: asking questions about socially-constructed categories; existing in new forms of interdependence that respect bodily and personal autonomy as it acknowledges human connectedness and mutual need; living and giving in the community; caring for and with one another; existing for the very reason of making another's life better; and creating, together, a street built on hope, love, and possibility. The generation(s) raised on Sesame Street must continue to value and enact those lessons.

Super Grover is love, hope, generosity, and kindness, with just enough zaniness to rescue him from being boringly maudlin. Super Grover lacks superpowers, except that he captures imaginations and hearts. Super Grover offers spaces to critique ableism and new, accessible pathways to more just arrangements through caring. With his reassuring and adorable presence, he empowers us to be our better selves and live our better lives. With this, Super Grover is once again "off to save the world, and other good stuff." He reminds us that together we can dream of and create something more, something better. Up, up, and away we go. If our capes get stuck, if we crash into things, if we misread a situation or over/under estimate our abilities and our impact on others, we just keep caring and loving and serving and trying and working toward liberation. We are all Super Grover, loving and goofy and vulnerable and broken and just doing our best, and never, never giving up the desire to make the world better and always finding the courage to persist. And we are cute, too.

References

Abate, Michelle Ann. 2009. "Taking Silliness Seriously: Jim Henson's *The Muppet Show, the Anglo American Tradition of Nonsense, and Cultural Critique.*" *The Journal of Popular Culture 42* (4): 589–613. doi: 10.1111/j.1540–5931.2009.00698.x.

Alaniz, José, and Peter D. Halverson. 2014. *Death, Disability, and the Superhero: The Silver Age and Beyond.* Jackson: University Press of Mississippi.

Beitzel, Terry. 2014. "The Content and Context of Justice." In *One Hundred Years of Service Through Community: A Gould Farm Reader,* edited by Steven K. Smith and Terry Beitzel, 137–149. Lanham, MD: University Press of America.

Billman, Carol. 1982. "Sesame Street Lives!" *Children's Literature Association Quarterly 7* (2) (Spring): 15–18. doi: 10.1353/chq.0.0565.

Borgenicht, David. 1988. *Sesame Street Unpaved: Scripts, Stories, Secrets, and Songs.* New York: Hyperion.

Broido, Ellen M. 2000. "The Development of Social Justice Allies During College: A Phenomenological Investigation." *Journal of College Student Development 41* (1): 3–18. https://eric.ed.gov/?id=EJ614298.

Clare, Eli. 2001. "Stolen Bodies, Reclaimed Bodies: Disability and Queerness." *Public Culture 13* (3): 359–365. https://www.muse.jhu.edu/article/26252.

Cocca, Carolyn. 2014. "Re-Booting Barbara Gordon: Oracle, Batgirl, and Feminist Disability Theories." *ImageTexT: Interdisciplinary Comics Studies 7* (4). http://imagetext.english.ufl.edu/archives/v7_4/cocca/.

Corder, Jim. 1986. "Argument as Emergence, Rhetoric as Love." *Rhetoric Review 4* (1): 16–32. JSTOR https://www.jstor.org/stable/465760.

Davis, Michael. 2008. *Street Gang: The Complete History of Sesame Street.* New York: Penguin.

Dolmage, Jay. 2015. "An Afterword: Thinking Through Care." *Pedagogy: Critical Approaches to Teaching Literature, Language, Composition, and Culture 15* (3): 559–567. doi: 10.1215/15314200–2917185.

Edwards, Keith E. (2006). "Aspiring Social Justice Ally Identity Development: A Conceptual Model." *NASPA Journal 43* (4): 39–60. doi: 10.2202/1949–6605.1722.

Evans, Nancy J., Jennifer L. Assadi, and Todd K. Herriott. 2005. "Encouraging the Development of Disability Allies." *New Directions for Student Services 110*: 67–79. doi: 10.1002/ss.166.

Foss, Chris. 2015. "Individual Redemption Through Universal Design; Or, How IEP Meetings Have Infused My Pedagogy with an Ethic of Care(taking)." *Pedagogy: Critical Approaches To Teaching Literature, Language, Composition, and Culture 15* (3): 477–491. doi: 10.1215/15314200–2917057.

Garland-Thomson, Rosemarie. 2016. "Foreword." *Disability in Comic Books and Graphic Narratives,* edited by Chris Foss, Jonathan Gray, and Zach Whalen, x-xii. New York: Palgrave Macmillan.

Garlen, Jennifer C., and Anissa M. Graham. 2009. *Kermit Culture: Critical Perspectives on Jim Henson's Muppets.* Jefferson, NC: McFarland.

Germaine, Alison Elizabeth. 2016. "Disability and Depression in Thor Comic Books." *Disability Studies Quarterly 36* (3). doi: 10.18061/dsq.v36i3.5015.

Gikow, Louise. 2009. *Sesame Street: A Celebration of 40 Years of Life on the Street*. New York: Black Dog & Leventhal.

Haberkorn, Gideon. 2009. "The Muppets as a Metaphor for the *Self*." In *Kermit Culture: Critical Perspectives on Jim Henson's Muppets*, edited by Jennifer Garlen and Anissa Graham, 25–39. Jefferson, NC: McFarland.

Hartley, Christie. 2011. "Disability and Justice." *Philosophy Compass* 6 (2): 120–132. doi: 10.1111/j.1747–9991.2010.00375.x.

Johnston, Bret Anthony. 2008. "What Furry Old Grover Can Teach Us About Plot." *Writer* 121 (12): 18–19. https://www.glimmertrain.com/bulletins/essays/b60johnston.php.

Jones, Brian Jay. 2013. *Jim Henson: The Biography*. New York: Ballantine.

Kingsley, Emily Perl. 1996. "Sesame Street: Modeling a World That Respects Every Child." *Exceptional Parent* 26 (6): 74–77.

Kingsley, Jason, and Mitchell Levitz. 1994. *Count Us In: Growing Up with Down Syndrome*. New York: Harcourt Brace.

Kittay, Eva Feder. 2001. "When Caring Is Just and Justice Is Caring." *Public Culture* 13 (3): 557–579. https://muse.jhu.edu/article/26257/pdf.

Kleege, Georgina. 2006. *Blind Rage: Letters to Helen Keller*. Washington, D.C.: Gallaudet UP.

Kraidy, Ute Sartorius. 2002. "Sunny Days on *Sesame Street*?: Multiculturalism and Resistance Postmodernism." *Journal of Communication Inquiry* 26 (1): 9–25. doi: 10.1177/0196859902026001002.

Laforteza, Elaine M. 2014. "Cute-ifying Disability: Lil Bub, the Celebrity Cat" *M/C: A Journal of Media and Culture* 17 (2). doi: 10.5204/mcj.784.

Liebert, Robert M. 1976. "Evaluating the Evaluators." *Journal of Communication* 26 (2): 165–171.

Linn, Genie Bingham. 2011. "A (Super) Heroic Vision of Leader Self." *Journal Of Leadership Education* 10 (2):172–179. doi: 10.12806/V10/I2/AB1.

Linton, Simi. 1998. *Claiming Disability: Knowledge and Identity*. New York: New York UP.

Loja, Ema, Maria Emília Costa, Bill Hughes, and Isabel Menezes. 2013. "Disability, Embodiment and Ableism: Stories of Resistance." *Disability & Society* 28 (2): 190–203. doi: 10.1080/09687599.2012.705057.

Mairs, Nancy. 1986. "On Being a Cripple." *The Kaleidoscope* 13: 42–48. https://www.wheelersburg.net/Downloads/Mairs.pdf.

Mandel, Jennifer. 2006. "The Production of a Beloved Community: *Sesame Street's* Answer to America's Inequalities." *The Journal of American Culture* 29 (1): 3–13. doi: 10.1111/j.1542–734X.2006.00270.x.

McRuer, Robert. 2004. "Composing Bodies; Or, De-Composition: Queer Theory, Disability Studies, and Alternative Corporealities." *JAC* 24 (1): 47–78. https://www.jstor.org/stable/20866612.

Morris, Jenny. 2001. "Impairment and Disability: Constructing an Ethics of Care That Promotes Human Rights." *Hypatia* 16(4): 1–16. https://www.jstor.org/stable/i290897.

Palmer, Edward L. 1988. *Television and America's Children: A Crisis of Neglect*. New York, NY: Oxford UP.

Ratto, Casey M. 2017. "Not Superhero Accessible: The Temporal Stickiness of Disability in Superhero Comics." *Disability Studies Quarterly* 37 (2). https://dsq-sds.org/article/view/5396/4649.

Row-Heyveld, Lindsey. 2015. "Reading *Batman*, Writing *X-Men*: Superpowers and Disabilities in the First-Year Seminar." *Pedagogy* 15 (3): 519–526. Doi: 10.1215/15314200–2917105.

Runswick-Cole, Katherine, and Dan Goodley. 2013. "Resilience: A Disability Studies and Community Psychology Approach." *Social and Personality Psychology Compass* 7 (2): 67–78. doi: 10.1111/spc3.12012.

Schalk, Sami. 2016. "Reevaluating the Supercrip." *Journal of Literary and Cultural Disability Studies* 10 (1): 71–86. doi: 10.3828/jlcds.2016.5.

Schneidre, Joseph W. 1988. "Disability as Moral Experience: Epilepsy and Self in Routine Relationships." *Journal of Social Issues* 44 (1): 63–78. doi: 10.1111/j.1540-4560.1988.tb02049.x.

Serlin, David. 1998. "From *Sesame Street* To *Schoolhouse Rock*: Urban Pedagogy and Soul Iconography in the 1970s." In *Soul: Black Power, Politics, and Pleasure*, edited by Monique Guillory and Richard C. Green, 105–120. New York: New York UP.

Sesame Street. 1974."Super Grover Helps with Boxes." Season 5, episode 0588. January 30. PBS.

_____. 1974. "The Telephone Booth." Season 5, episode 0674. April 23. PBS.

_____. 1975. "Super Grover at the Bus Stop." Season 6, episode 0708. January 1. PBS.

_____. 1975. "Super Grover at the Barbershop." Season 6, episode 0717. January 14. PBS.

_____. 1975. "Super Grover and the Fence Exit." Season 6, episode 0746. February 24. PBS.

_____. 1975. "Super Grover and the Apple Battle." Season 6, episode 0786. April 21. PBS.

_____. 1979. "Super Grover and the Broken Grocery Bag." Season 10, episode 1289. April 19. PBS.

_____. 1984. "Super Grover and the Computer." Season 16, episode 1971. November 26. PBS.

_____. 1987. "Super Grover and Elmo." Season 20, episode 2343. April 29. PBS.

_____. 1990. "Dial S for Super Grover." Season 21, episode 2745. May 11. PBS.

Setoodeh, Ramin. 2017. "Frank Oz on the Legacy of Jim Henson's Muppets." *Variety,* March 12. https://variety.com/2017/film/news/frank-oz-muppets-jim-henson-1202007251/

Stone, Sharon Dale. 1995. "The Myth of Bodily Perfection." *Disability & Society 10* (4): 413–424. doi: 10.1080/09687599550023426.

Stevens, Elizabeth Hyde. 2014. "Millennials Just Don't Get It: How the Muppets Created Generation X." *Salon.* April 5. https://www.salon.com/2014/04/06/millennials_just_dont_get_it_how_the_muppets_created_generation_x/.

Tierney, Joan D. 1971. "The Miracle on Sesame Street." *Phi Delta Kappan* 52(5) (January): 296–298. JSTOR.

Underwood, Ben. 2009. "How to Become a Muppet; Or, the Great Muppet Paper." In *Kermit Culture: Critical Perspectives on Jim Henson's Muppets*, edited by Jennifer Garlen and Anissa M. Graham, 9–24. Jefferson, NC: McFarland.

The Joker

Disrupting Perceptions of (Dis)ability in Batman Comic Books

Sean Thomas Milligan

Disability studies have been an emerging lens of literary criticism, especially in the last half-century. Comic studies have similarly been gaining recent popularity (Kukkonen 2013, 125). It is unsurprising that these two fields intersect in profound ways. As these fields of study grow and intersect, graphic narratives will incorporate more disability-related themes and people with disabilities. Graphic narratives are rich for communicating about ability and ableism. There are several nonfiction graphic memoirs about illness, disease, and disability. Graphic novels like *Mom's Cancer* (2006) by Brian Fies or *My Degeneration: A Journey Through Parkinson's* (2015) by Peter Dunlap-Shohl are two that address disability issues seriously. Sometimes the bright colors, occasional campiness, and "POW" and "KABOOM" of superhero comics can overshadow the seriousness of its themes. Superhero comic stories, on the other hand, go into great depth regarding illness and disability in the real world. As this essay's analysis shows, superhero comics provide vital insights into deconstructing the ableist standards that shape popular understandings of disability. This is in contrast to the belief that comic books are historically and now inferior intellectual mediums. Audiences should not dismiss the medium or the superheroes with disabilities as inferior.

This analysis focuses on the Joker from the *Batman* series, who is perceived as having a mental health condition that makes him "crazy" and "insane" and shuns him from so-called "normal" treatment. The Joker is undoubtedly not a social justice warrior for disability related issues; he is an evil, murderous criminal who commits acts of violence, including but not limited to mass poisoning and sexual assault. However, he is undeniably interesting and can serve as a portal into a meaningful and productive discussion of ableism. His perceived status of having a disability can help audiences investigate mental health categories and representations in disability studies. For this analysis, the Joker's facial disfigurement is considered a disability due to the discrimination that such a condition can warrant in the real world. It is a fact that psychological studies have proven that people experience fear-avoidance when they encounter someone with facial disfigurement (Bennington-Castro 2012). Moreover, while he exists as an exaggeratedly mentally disturbed villain, the Joker also destabilizes these categories. The Joker does not intend to fight injustices, but he is a disruptive force, an agent of chaos, and as such, disrupts the social conditions that encourage categorization, labeling, and ableist "othering" of disability. The Joker offers empowering and disempowering perspectives on disability due to his complex nature as a disrupter of social norms. His actions accentuate the absurdity of ableism while mocking disability and using non-normative bodies for comedic gesturing. To understand the various effects the Joker has on conversations about ableism, laughter theory is used to demonstrate how the Joker's performance of disability is destructive yet simultaneously constructive for people with disabilities and disability studies.

This analysis begins by exploring some of the signature traits and characteristics of the Joker. One of the Joker's signature crimes is applying a toxin that forces the victim's facial features to mimic the Joker's. In *Batman: The Man Who Laughs* (2003), a reporter stands outside the infamous Arkham Asylum speaking into a microphone in front of news station cameras. She begins to cough, her skin is bleached white, and her hair turns blonde to green. Her eyes are tinged with this same green color, and then her lips pull away from her gums into a gruesome grin. Suddenly she begins to laugh, "Heh … heh … heh … heh--," and then she topples over sideways, dead. The Joker steps out of the shadows behind her to take his place before the cameras, looking strikingly similar to the dead reporter who, moments before, was alive. This demonstrates the Joker's proficiency with chemicals that produce a striking and immediate effect on his victims. The Joker remains loyal to his essence as a jester on center stage when in front of a camera. He is always performing for an audience and commits his crimes, including murders, with over-the-top theatrical flourishes. He pushes his face on his victims, blurring the borders between them and him; society and the other. Because the Joker's rejection of normalcy permeates this liminal region, categorical barriers are dissolved as his victims acquire his likeness.

A similar moment of transference is seen in *The Killing Joke* (1988). The Joker is in the process of acquiring a run-down, derelict amusement park to serve as the setting and headquarters for one of his elaborate schemes.

One panel depicts a small needle concealed in the palm of the Joker's hand as he speaks to the park owner. The Joker pats the man on the back and soon begins walking away. The man looks strikingly similar to the Joker, even more so than the reporter from *The Man Who Laughs*. Now with white skin and wide, staring eyes, the park owner grins hideously, with blood oozing from the corner of his mouth. The man is dead. Again, we see the Joker's victims adopting his likeness against their will. This time, the Joker has no immediate audience but leaves the corpse behind for a future audience when the crime scene is inevitably discovered. The Joker rarely attempts to hide evidence of his crimes because he always performs; he wants them to be found. Otherwise, he would have no audience, no one to persuade, influence, or introduce to his way of perceiving the world.

The Joker engages in a disruptive projection of his corporeal likeness and personality. Laughter is a performative action and is infectious because his victims mimic it. It involves the ability to effect change in those who laugh, witness laughter, or are laughed at. As Benjamin Kaiser (2016) says, "Laughter is an event of alteration" (608). Kaiser (2016) claims that "laughing has the possibility to change everything which is in its environment" (609). Jester characters like the Joker utilize the transformative power of laughter through telling jokes and engaging weapons such as the toxin that forces laughter and smiles to challenge conceptions of normalcy. The altering effect of laughter can be harmful or empowering, depending on the situation. As Mio Bryce and Hanae Katayama (2009) explain, laughter "is a universal human urge to laugh at others' mistakes, misfortunes, or inferiority because doing so imparts to us a sense of superiority and triumph" (125). Indeed, Henri Bergson proposes that laughter is a social activity that can exclude "the ones laughed about" (Kaiser 2016, 611). In this way, laughter is a form of punishment.

The Joker is guilty of punishing his victims through humor while performing deadly pranks. Bergson's (2016) theory of laughter as social punishment helps explain how the Joker uses his humor to effect some social change. However, this change is not always punishing in nature. Thus, the social aspects of Bergson's theory are best merged with the corporeal aspects of Helmuth Plessner's theory of laughter to understand the Joker. As explained by Kaiser, "Plessner's main interest lies on the conflict happening within the person" (2016, 612). Laughter is an uncontrolled force "that involuntarily bursts out of someone" (Kaiser 2016, 612). When experiencing laughter, "man [sic] is experiencing the other to his controlled behavior, the outbreak of laughter overcomes usual boundaries" (Kaiser 2016, 612). However, for the Joker, laughter is not always an uncontrolled and involuntary force. He laughs deliberately to change events or the people around him.

Plessner (2016) argues that laughter can also stem from an internal crisis within the individual. Characters like the Joker channel this internal, supposedly uncontrollable phenomenon into a social tool. The Joker's humor is both a social and corporeal force that effects both his internal self and external personality. In terms of self-direction and agency, laughter can originate from internal or external stimuli and may be an uncontrollable reaction that robs people of the ability to control their laughter. This lack of agency is reminiscent of certain mental health conditions which can also cause, through biological means, a disruption in one's experience or behavior. Laughter and mental health conditions can both act as unwanted intrusions into one's psyche.

When humor is used as a social tool, it has the propensity to challenge normativity, subvert ableism, and denounce limited binary classifications of "abled" and "disabled." For instance, "crip humor" is quite popular among disability circles to share jokes about non-normative bodies and minds. By reappropriating the term "crip" and its associated humor, this type of joking has become an empowering tool (Hamscha 2014). As Hamscha states, "The appeal of the term *crip* lies in its potential to rattle people and provoke them to reflect on their understanding of bodies, minds, normalcy, deviance, health, and sickness" (2014, 356). It makes sense to examine characters like clowns, jesters, and fools, because these are individuals whose profession is based on laughter and often non-normative figures. Jesters, like the Joker, engage in crip humor, making non-normativity a part of their act. As previously mentioned, this occurs when the Joker's likeness and mannerisms project on others and when he makes jokes about being "crazy" or "insane."

In literature, various royal courts would employ "fools" or "court jesters" as playthings that also possessed subtle but profound wisdom, not necessarily immediately evident to others. Interestingly, fools in literature from medieval texts to modern comic books are often exhibited as having some physical trait that makes them abnormal or subnormal, with a non-normative appearance or a variation of bodily ability. Furthermore, fools are often depicted in media as manifesting mental or physical disability, if not both. This correlates with how once upon a time in Rome, kings and the wealthy kept people with physical or mental disabilities as "fools," which they abused for self-amusement (MNGCDD 2021). Thus, in fiction and non-fiction, those fools with disabilities are perceived as monstrous, evil, and dangerous. Cynthia Barounis (2016) explains this apprehension, acknowledging that "the Joker's criminal behavior, coupled with his facial disfigurement, may initially seem to place him in a long line of disabled villains" (305). The Joker's facial disfigurements serve as a visual marker of disability or otherness. However, in addition to the physical traits that make up the Joker and his disfigurement -his scars, bleached skin, and dyed green hair—like other fools, he possesses madness as part of his act. Jan Kott's (1964) characterization of the fool as a disruptive agent is useful. However, he claims that "The Fool does not follow any ideology" but then describes an ideology that the fool does follow. The fool's ideology is that he rejects but also disrupts "law, justice, [and] moral order." It is not that the fool does not follow an ideology, but that he has a specific ideology based on disrupting and rejecting social norms. The Joker embraces this ideology. This disruption of social power is central to the goals of fools like the Joker. When inhabiting the role of court jester, fools can share critical insight about the king. They might even mock them in ways that other characters could not without fear of incurring the king's wrath. Clowning around affords the jester a certain degree of safety and places the jester in the king's confidence.

The Joker's "madness" is an equally, if not more visible, aspect of his apparent disability. The Joker is a supposedly "mad" villain who appears to align himself with psychopathological illnesses. His portrayal of mental illness, however, does not accurately represent how real-world people experience and exhibit mental health conditions. It is easy to understand why the Joker draws very little sympathy from his critics as he engages in wanton destruction and bloodshed. As for the characters in the fiction, why should they want to give any benefit of the doubt to someone who makes them live in fear? For disability studies critics, the Joker represents a potentially problematic portrayal of disability because he suggests mental health conditions make people dangerous. Similarly to how the public, elected officials, and media representatives wish to blame mass shootings in the twenty-first century on mental health issues, the Joker perpetuates this image of disability that is violent and menacing (ADAPT 2021).

Despite this, there may be ways in which *Batman* comics and graphic novels make available a more nuanced reading of the Joker. The Joker is a performer, putting on an act of mental health conditions, and his audience consists of both characters in the story and the reader. Indeed, the Joker is tremendously creative, weaving his madness into his jokes and performances. The Joker often makes puns about insanity, moves in unnatural yet theatrical ways, and dances and sings while performing his crimes. The Joker, in many ways, channels his madness into creativity, using it as the crux of his jokes and performances. While nothing washes away the fact that the Joker commits atrocities, the way he performs as a jester or clown for his audience results in a shift in social power dynamics. At his core, the Joker is an agent of chaos, reveling in disruption and challenging norms. In utilizing his version of disability humor or crip humor, the Joker insists on laughing at society. Still, the concerns of disability studies scholars who see the Joker as a negative, damaging portrayal of illness are valid. As previously mentioned, the Joker's actions are inexcusably evil and violent, and he certainly does not represent mental illness with much accuracy. However, Joker is a jester, performing for an audience, which cannot be ignored. And yes, critics can take issue with his performance if they view it as harmful. But what is undeniable is the Joker's disruptive nature and his tendency to sow chaos wherever he goes and whatever he does. The Joker is aligned opposite traditional norms and expectations and thus can be seen as an unwilling ally of disability studies.

Each author and artist offers their own take on the Joker, resulting in many different iterations of the same character. The Joker made his earliest appearance in the first issue of *Batman* in 1940 (Eason 2008). From the outset, the Joker exhibited many of the characteristics he is known for today, including his iconic bleached skin and green hair and seeming to take pleasure in chaotic murders (Eason 2008). A 1954 book titled *Seduction of the Innocent: The Influence of Comic Books on Today's Youth*, written by psychiatrist Frederic Wertham, resulted in a public outcry against comic books (Eason 2008). Wertham believed comic books influenced criminal behavior and possessed sexual imagery (Eason 2008). This backlash had the effect of making the Joker less threatening as he focused more on jokes and theft rather than murder (Eason 2008). This is not the Joker generally known today, as films like Christopher Nolan's *The Dark Knight* (2008) and comic storylines like those seen in Scott Snyder's *Batman: Death of the Family* (2014) presents a much darker, more violent character.

The Joker's relationship with Batman is that of a jester to his king. It is the Joker who more overtly insists on this categorization of their relationship. For example, in *Batman: Death of the Family* (2014), the Joker calls himself "[Batman's] faithful court jester." The Joker explains his role as court jester, stating, "It's the jester's job to entertain, but he often has another job, too. A deeper job. And that's to deliver bad news to the king." The Joker portrays himself as a servant to the king trying to assist the king in a beneficial role. This seems to mirror other instances of literary fools enjoying a privileged position in which they can communicate candidly with their king without fear of facing the repercussions that other characters might be subject to. Later in this same comic, the Joker demands Batman take his "rightful place" on a throne (Snyder 2014). The Joker makes it clear that he is serving Batman as a fool to a king.

The Joker's past is never truly revealed. In Alan Moore's *Batman: The Killing Joke* (1988), ten of the forty-eight story pages are spent detailing the Joker's past as a failed comedian who gets involved with crime to provide for his family, eventually falling into a vat of chemicals while evading the police and Batman. These chemicals bleach the Joker's skin and dye his hair and act as the final catalyst that drives him to madness, as seen in the final panel of the origin story scenes in which the Joker is clutching his head while laughing (Moore 1988). Despite spending so many pages of a relatively short piece telling this origin story, the Joker later states, "If I'm going to have a past, I prefer it to be multiple choice!" (Moore 1988). Hinting that the story is likely inaccurate, the Joker leaves his past mysterious. This destabilization of the Joker's origin story has the effect of facilitating his otherness. When met with a force as unknowable and unpredictable as the Joker, other characters and the comic reader seek an origin that explains a character's current behavior. Indeed, Barounis (2016) states that "disability must be explained by placing disabled subjects in the continual position of having to supply non-disabled people with a reason for their non-normative embodiments" (317). When left without an explanatory origin story, those around the Joker resort to labeling him as simply a "freak" to explain away his behavior. The Joker is easier to perceive as different and abnormal if left without an origin and thus easier to ostracize.

Fools act as one half of the equation in a struggle of social hierarchies. These stories exhibit clashes between normative and non-normative, rich and poor, known and unknown. Batman is, of course, the superhero alter ego of multi-billionaire Bruce Wayne. Even if the Joker's past is not the one shown to us in *The Killing Joke* (1988), where he is poor and struggling, this is still the image of the Joker given and juxtaposed to the upper-class upbringing of Bruce Wayne in the story. There is a tension between these social classes represented by Wayne and the Joker. And while Batman counts himself among the wealthy and kingly, he also views himself as superior to the Joker in other ways. Batman and other characters are constantly calling the Joker "freak" or similar terms. The public perceives him to be a freak. A reporter evidences this in *Batman: The Man Who Laughs* when he asks Police Commissioner Jim Gordon, "Is it true police have dubbed this *freak* the Joker?" (Brubaker 2003; emphasis mine). In addition to the freak label, the eagerness of the press and the police to name him the Joker shows an acceptance of the Joker's lack of identity. The public is eager to accept that this man is a complete unknown without a real name because it further solidifies him as other, separating the Joker from the crowd. This is more than a simple acceptance of his differentness but an active participation in differentiating the Joker from their perception of normalcy. Creating a media narrative that the Joker is different from "normal" facilitates labeling him as a freak.

In *Batman: Death of the Family*, Batman proclaims that the Joker is "nothing—but degenerate filth" (Snyder 2014)! Similarly, in *Batman: Arkham Asylum*, Batman calls the Joker a "Filthy degenerate" (Morrison

1989). Terms like freak and degenerate have a long and ugly history of acting as pejoratives to both people with non-normative bodies and LGBTQIA community members. Barounis acknowledges this, explaining that "the word *freak* carries with it a particularly painful history regarding the exploitation of people with non-normative bodies" (312). Nicholas Edsall writes that around the time when the original Batman was created, "The open discussion and spread of liberal views on sexuality and sexual deviance provoked a reaction that ultimately became linked with other social concerns, many of them couched in the vocabulary of degeneration and decline" (2006, 137–38). Indeed, the *Batman* texts give plenty of reason to suspect that Batman exhibits increased aggression towards the Joker because of the Joker's exaggerated performance of homosexuality. On countless occasions, the Joker refers to Batman with terms of endearment like "honey" or "sweetheart." In *Arkham Asylum* (1989), the Joker speaks in front of Batman to a hostage, saying, "Kiss me, Charlie! Ravish me!" (Morrison). *Arkham Asylum* (1989) is full of sexual references, both implicit and explicit. Another incident of particular interest involves the Joker showing an inkblot test to Batman and asking what he sees (Morrison). Batman responds that he does not see anything, but the Joker is dubious, stating, "Not even a cute little long-legged boy in swimming trunks?" (Morrison 1989). This is a reference to Batman's sidekick, Robin, who is usually seen wearing clothes that expose his legs and who dies at the Joker's hands (much has been written about Batman and Robin's relationship; for more, see Goldstein 2014; Medhurst 2013; Shyminski 2011, et al.).

With dialogue like this, it is hard not to read innuendo into some of the Joker's other comments, such as when he says to Batman, "I like a man who can take the pressure" (Morrison). An instance in this same story when the Joker elicits a "degenerate" retort from Batman is when the Joker tells Batman to "loosen up" as the Joker slaps Batman's posterior (Morrison). It becomes more likely that there is a link between Batman's use of the terms "freak" and "degenerate" and hostility towards LGBTQIA individuals as he uses these terms in response to the Joker's sexual humor. Having no qualms about calling the Joker a freak or degenerate, Batman and others establish him firmly as part of a class that is distinctly subnormal in an injurious way not dissimilar from the disparaging tone historically seen used towards people with disabilities, LGBTQIA community members, and minorities. The Joker challenges Batman's sexuality, causing a subtle disruption of Batman's view of the Joker as a degenerate, as Batman must consider his own sexuality.

The Joker's ambiguous origins, disabilities, and physical appearance make him other. If Batman is his king, the Joker comes from significantly less prestigious beginnings. The reader never finds out with certainty where the Joker is from and what he has been through. But while Batman is usually written with a detailed and well-established origin, with the deaths of his parents and the following events, the Joker is a man without a known past. If the story the reader is given in *Batman: The Killing Joke* happens to be accurate, then the differences between the histories of the Joker and Batman are distinctly different. The Joker struggled with poverty while Batman was born into wealth. However, even if the Joker's story is not true, it shows the need for the fool of the Batman universe to have a story of poverty, as opposed to the riches of his king. The fact that the reader is even presented with such a story, whether it is true or simply one possible origin of the Joker, demonstrates that poverty and riches are associated with the fool and king and disability and ability respectively. This distinction between the characters' origins demonstrates how the Joker and Batman exist on opposite ends of a social power dynamic. Batman comes from, and Bruce Wayne represents, all the wealth, prestige, means, and opportunity his station entails. Meanwhile, the Joker lacks everything from wealth to opportunity and even a definitive identity. Batman's wealth and status in society represent an ideal that the Joker can never obtain, except through crime. Thus, the Joker and Batman are opposed in terms of ability versus disability and class from a socioeconomic viewpoint. This further cements the Joker as a representative of the underprivileged and marginalized.

Interestingly, Robin was not only killed by the Joker but also by the reader. The original issues of the *A Death in the Family* storyline included a page at the end of one issue where Robin's fate after an explosion was unknown (Starlin 1988, 97). This page asked the readers to call one phone number if they wanted Robin to survive the blast, and another phone number if they wanted the character to die (Starlin 1988, 97). Ultimately, the readers called in and voted to kill Robin. Batman finds the boy's body and the reader is given a full-page panel of Batman carrying Robin's bloody and broken corpse in a subsequent comic issue (Starlin 1988, 108). This is one way the medium of comics, with a storyline divided into issues that end with cliffhangers, invites readers to participate in the story. Readers always play an active role in comics, because comics require our brains to do some of the work. Comic panels contain static, unmoving images, and yet between these static images action takes place. Events, people, and objects are in motion. The reader must do the work in their mind's eye and imagination to make the action flow, visualize movement, and process the passage of time between still shots. Readers played an even more active role than usual in this specific comic, perhaps more than the Joker himself, in killing Robin. In this way the readers engage in destroying the person possibly closest and most important to Batman. The readers are on the Joker's side, even if only subconsciously, working to disrupt the upper stratum of hierarchy in which Batman and his friends reside. Importantly, once again, the Joker is not a champion for social justice but rather a disrupting and challenging entity. The Joker disrupts even the readers' expectations by drawing them in on his plans and effectively making the reader his accomplice. Also disrupted are the expectations of a typical campy superhero story in which the hero always wins the day.

The Joker challenges the idea that madness is impairing. In Moore's *Batman: The Killing Joke*, the Joker states that "Faced with the inescapable fact that human existence is mad, random, and pointless, one in eight of them [average people ...] crack up and go stark slavering buggo! Who can blame them? In a world as psychotic as this ... any other response would be crazy." The Joker makes the point that rationality is nonsensical in an irrational world. He advocates for the acceptance of madness as the only appropriate response to life in a mad world. Indeed, the Joker explains his situation by saying "When I saw what a black, awful joke the world was, I went crazy as a coot" (Moore). In *Batman: Arkham Asylum*, a doctor theorizes that with the Joker "we may actually be looking at some kind of super-sanity [...] A brilliant new modification of human perception. More suited to urban life at the end of the twentieth century" (Morrison). Again, the Joker and some medical doctors in stories like *Arkham Asylum* recognize madness as a possible advantage for life in a chaotic world. In any case, the Joker challenges conceptions of ability and disability as binary categories while also attacking the concept of disability as stigmatized. Rather, like madness in response to a mad world, it can be empowering.

The Joker's skill in poison-making is particularly interesting in a discussion about humor, because the poison generally turns the victim's skin white, causes uncontrollable laughter, and contorts their faces into a grin, mimicking the Joker's own demeanor and appearance. This uncontrollability of laughter recalls Plessner's theory of laughter as an internal force that exists as the other to an individual's sense of control over their bodies (Kaiser 2016). This laughter, caused by the Joker's toxins, is uncontrollable for the victim but is intentionally caused by the Joker. Laughter in this instance does not exist as a purely internal force but as something caused by an outside party. In this sense, the Joker's poisoning recalls Bergson's theory of laughter as a social force that excludes or punishes the one laughed about. But the laughter induced by the toxins is not exclusionary, at least in the way outlined by Bergson. Rather, the Joker is bringing a portion of his experience of disability into the immediate lives of others, making his experience of disability inclusive. The Joker's victims experience disability as the Joker experiences it—as a social construct. This is a situation that feels so immediately ridiculous that it causes this uncontrollable laughter. The victim, previously perceiving themselves as "normal" and "abled," experiences the other to this belief. This serves as the stimulus to their laughter, for they can do nothing else. Yes, the Joker is punishing people by poisoning them. But the victim is the one laughing in situations involving the Joker's toxin. To better understand the Joker, we require a theory of laughter that borrows elements of both Plessner and Bergson's theories. The victim's dilemma is socially-induced, both in the sense that it is caused immediately by the Joker's toxin, as by experiencing the other to their socially-constructed conception of normalcy. This socially-induced dilemma manifests corporeally as laughter and a change in facial features, such as the signature grin.

The Joker acts as a source of carnival humor in the Batman universe. This concept of the carnivalesque has been historically significant, with many events appearing in the Middle Ages that employed carnivalesque elements. Bakhtin (1984) describes the importance of carnival humor in events such as the Feast of Fools and other feasts and fairs (5). As Bakhtin writes, "All these forms of protocol and ritual based on laughter and conse-crated by tradition existed in all the countries of medieval Europe" (1984, 5). As demonstrated by its pervasive nature, humor played an important role in medieval society. The carnival atmosphere features a "suspension of all hierarchical precedence" (Bakhtin 1984, 10). This temporary disrup-tion of social rank affords "a special type of communication impossible in everyday life" (Bakhtin 1984, 10). People from varying castes were able to mingle during carnival time in an atypical way. This temporary shift in communication and interaction was vital as it provided for "liberation from norms of etiquette and decency imposed at other times" (Bakhtin 1984, 10). The carnival is a time of renewal in which people are free of the typical constraints of rationality.

One of the effects of the carnival atmosphere is that it disrupts the social hierarchy. As Bakhtin notes, "clowns and fools [...] mimicked seri-ous rituals" (1984, 5). In doing so, the clown or fool, usually the focal point of laughter, instead shifts the subject of laughter to the serious rituals and the individuals involved. In *A Death in the Family*, the Joker mimics the seriousness of a United Nations assembly meeting after being appointed Iran's ambassador (Starlin 1988, 120–139). In front of the General Assem-bly of the U.N., he jokes "[Iran's] current leaders and I have a lot in com-mon. Insanity and a great love of fish" (Starlin 1988, 134). The Joker then fills the room with his deadly laughing gas through a device he had hid-den under his clothes (Starlin 1988, 135). The Joker seems drawn to serious events like this, as the solemn, stately setting provides a stark contrast to his jokes and his administration of laughing gas. Like real-world and fic-tional fools before him, the Joker brings elements of the carnivalesque to serious environments. Laughter works as a disruptive force in these settings where it is not expected.

The carnivalesque is seen in events like the medieval Feast of Fools, in which the carnival atmosphere affords a suspension of rank. Bakhtin describes the imagery of feasts, writing that "No meal can be sad. Sadness and food are incompatible" (1984, 283). This seems odd with feast imagery when the Joker organizes the feast in question. In *Batman: Arkham Asylum*, a two-page spread features the Joker proclaiming, "Let the Feast of Fools begin," while a dinner table in the background features a man laying upon it with inmates of the asylum wielding weapons around him (Morrison). Furthermore, in *Batman: Death of the Family*, the Joker organizes a "feast" where Batman and his companions are seated around a table lined with cloche covers. These covers are presumed to contain the faces of Batman's friends (Snyder 2014). This seems incompatible with Bakhtin's claim that sadness and food do not belong together. But Bakhtin does state that "death and food are perfectly compatible" (1984, 283). In short, Bakhtin proposes a distinction between sadness and death. Certainly, the Joker organizes Feasts of Fools in which death imagery is omnipresent. This association of violence with the sustaining substance of food is part of the Joker's act.

The Joker makes it clear that he is performing an act when he commits his crimes. This is not to say he is not committing crimes, or they are in some way faked, but that he is committing his crimes for the benefit of an audience. This audience might be whoever discovers the crime scene, the police, reporters, Batman, and, once reported, the general public. In *Batman: Death of the Family*, the Joker begins an important announcement by exclaiming "let's cue the music and the lights" (Snyder). Indeed, the climax of his scheme in this comic is very theatrical. The Joker manages to capture and tie up Batman and his associates like Robin and Nightwing, positioning them around a dinner table (Snyder 2014). Batman's friends are wearing bloodied bandages around their faces and the table is lined with cloche covers that are lifted to reveal their faces (Snyder 2014). In this comic, the Joker's face has been removed and he has fashioned it into a mask so he can wear it again. In removing the faces of his victims, the Joker is making them suffer the same thing that he suffered. It is later revealed that the Joker's victims were drugged and their faces were unharmed, as the faces under the dish covers must have been model replicas. The Joker has not harmed Batman's companions (at least physically; these events could certainly be mentally harmful). The Joker could have easily harmed or killed them while he had them unconscious, in his power, but chooses instead to simply make them think they had their facial skin removed. This demonstrates that the Joker values the performance of his crime over the actual violence, at least in this case. Indeed, in other comics the Joker has the option to harm but instead takes the opportunity to make a joke, as seen in *Batman: The Killing Joke* in a scene in which the Joker pulls a gun on Batman and fires, but it is a prank gun that reveals a flag that reads "CLICK CLICK CLICK" (Moore 1988). Although the Joker does not remove the faces of Batman's companions in *Batman: Death of the Family*, he does rig the dinner area with explosives so that when Batman stands from his chair the place is engulfed in flame (Snyder 2014).

Indeed, Barounis (2016) explains that the Joker engages in exaggerated "camp performances [which] can be read as a bridge between queer and crip critiques of the social, demolishing the very categories upon which traditional narratives of pathology, disorder, and inspirational overcoming rely" (319). The Joker merges sexuality and ability into a performance to deconstruct the categorizations of pathology that plague society as a limiting force. These categorical labels are a limiting force because they work to predetermine what type of person someone is if they fall into a particular category. Categorical labels influence how people think of the individuals in these categories and tell people how they should be and act. The Joker seeks to disrupt this system, and a major part of how he does this is through performance and laughter.

This theatrical use is vital to the Joker's delivery of humor to obtain his goals because it highlights the fact that he is a clown. But the Joker's audiences, both in his fictional world and the audience of the comic book readership, may not necessarily find the humor in the jokes the Joker tells. To remedy this, the Joker has ways of projecting laughter onto those around him. Most important to the Joker is his signature poison. The effects of this toxin are seen in many comics featuring the Joker, including *Batman: The Man Who Laughs* (2003) which, as mentioned earlier, features a warehouse which contains many of the Joker's victims displaying the signature white skin and forced smiles. Another exemplary instance of this toxin's effects is seen in Moore's *Batman: The Killing Joke* during a scene in which the Joker purchases a decrepit, run-down amusement park and injects the seller with poison during a handshake via a concealed pin on his glove. The man's appearance, within seconds, becomes nearly identical to that of the Joker. This toxin enables the Joker to project society's perception of him as a cackling, facially-disfigured man onto those around him with more normative bodies.

The Joker has other ways of assigning his own non-normative qualities to Others. In several instances, the Joker either bribes or threatens others into wearing makeup and hair dye to mimic his appearance. This is seen at the beginning of *Batman: The Killing Joke* in a scene in which Batman confronts the Joker in a jail cell but discovers the character to be another inmate wearing makeup (Moore). The Joker has persuaded another inmate to stand in for him so that the Joker can escape the prison without his absence being noticed. This method mimics the Joker's appearance but usually does not account for his personality and laughter unless combined with a dose of poison. However, the Joker is able on certain occasions to make others laugh without even utilizing his toxin. In the final pages of *Batman: The Killing Joke*, the Joker tells a joke and the story ends with both the Joker and Batman laughing together. These panels are interesting because their laughter merges on the page in a series of "HAHAHAs." The lettering has a slight erratic slant to it that usually indicates the Joker's laughter, but with both men laughing the lettering of their laughter is indistinguishable from one another on the page. Through telling a genuine joke, the Joker causes Batman to mimic his laughter and come to understand his worldview a little bit more.

The Joker destroys the categorical labels of normal and abnormal by projecting non-normativity onto others, crossing the boundaries created by these labels. When the Joker is around, the distinction between normal and abnormal is blurred. The Joker exhibits distaste for the categorization of normalcy. In *Batman: The Killing Joke*, the general conflict revolves around the Joker's kidnapping of Commissioner James Gordon in an attempt to drive him mad (Moore). The Joker, speaking in front of his minions, displays Gordon in a cage and says "Ladies and gentlemen [...] I give you … the average man! Physically unremarkable, it has instead a deformed set of values" (Moore 1988). The Joker positions the average as something to be placed inside a cage and stared at by a crowd. This reverses society's typically imposed roles in which the non-normative body would be objectified as an oddity. This is perhaps the strongest instance in comic books of the Joker directly challenging perceptions of normalcy and destabilizing categorization and labeling of roles. The Joker questions why it is the non-normative rather than the normative body kept figuratively caged and ogled.

The Joker wants those around him to laugh at Gordon for embodying normalcy. Laughter is a powerful tool, and there exist many jokes that target disabilities. Tom Shakespeare observes that "People with visible impairments are among the key comic stereotypes of western culture" (qtd. in Barounis 306). And as Barounis explains, comedy focusing on disabilities can be "double-edged [...] constituting [people with disabilities] as laughable spectacles in some circumstances and as empowered agents of humor in others" (306). The Joker is closer to an "empowered agent of humor" because of the way he causes a shift in the focus of laughter. The Joker urges a redirection of laughter toward the normative and society's insistence on categorization. As Beth Haller explains, "As disabled people move from being laughed at, to laughing at themselves, to laughing at their situation and at nondisabled people, they simultaneously challenge the prejudice within our culture, and demand the acceptance of disability as an acceptable and respectable dimension of social diversity" (qtd. in Barounis 307). In using his toxins and jokes, the Joker shifts the focus of laughter to nondisabled people as they adopt the Joker's appearance and mannerisms. But it is not a matter of laughing at the disfigurement itself that comes with the Joker's poison. The laughter is directed at the breakdown of categorical barriers as non-normative qualities are projected onto otherwise non-disabled bodies. The subject of the Joker's poison becomes a parody of disability that encourages an empowering brand of disability humor. The Joker uses comedy as a deconstructive force in disrupting categorization, but it is also a constructive force fostering an empowered environment for non-normativity.

Laughter's healing and constructive power is evident in the common phrase "laughter is the best medicine." Indeed, this phrase is the focus of wordplay in Nolan's film *The Dark Knight* (2008), in which the Joker operates a truck with lettering on the side which reads "LAUGHTER IS THE BEST MEDICINE." The Joker has painted a red letter "S" in front of this phrase so that it reads "SLAUGHTER IS THE BEST MEDICINE." Indeed, the Joker uses laughter as a medicinal force for coping with the harsh realities of life. But he also employs violence. The wordplay on the truck displays the Joker's capacity to combine militant violence with therapeutic laughter into a unique force. The violent aspect of the Joker's nature underscores his desire for a destructive breakdown of perceptions of normalcy. The violence inherent in the Joker's crimes cannot be ignored. Indeed, his aggressive, destructive way of challenging socially-accepted normativity can be seen as violent. However, the Joker's violence also mirrors the violent nature of categorization and labeling in society. When names like "freak" and even simply "disabled" are applied to individuals, this is a violent occurrence in that it is socially harmful. The individuals are demeaned and made to be lesser. Victims of dehumanizing labels are at risk for actual physical violence as well. The Joker uses violent methods to attack a violent institution. Again, none of this is to say that the Joker is a "good guy" or in any way excuse his murders and other crimes. Instead, it is to underscore how the Joker is a valuable character for study under the lens of disability studies.

One question that has been considered to some extent in this paper is whether the Joker is truly mentally ill or not. To state it more clearly, Joker is not impaired in the usual sense. However, since disability is a socially constructed concept, the Joker can be said to be disabled. But he does not truly suffer any real-world illness. His "madness" is an act. The Joker is a fool performing the role of court jester to Batman, his perceived king. And in his performances, the Joker takes control of the codes of disability used to force categorization on disabled persons. The Joker redefines madness as a logical response to an illogical world and forces this version of madness on others through poisoning. The Joker does not suffer from any real-world illness, meaning, as previously stated, that his condition is not an accurate real-life depiction. Rather, he is a larger-than-life character putting on an elaborate act. Taken as an exaggerated performer and an agent of chaos, the Joker's nefarious doings do not necessarily harm the work of disability studies. Rather than acting as an example of the disabled criminal, the Joker mocks the social construction of disability. In a way, the Joker acts not only as a disabled figure but as a representation of social labeling forces themselves. As society violently forces categories of ability and disability on individuals, so too does the Joker, in his way. The Joker's poisoning forces an image of disability (laughing, "crazy," and disfigured) on others. The Joker's victims reflect his visual image of disability. This is why the Joker is such an interesting and useful figure for disability criticism. He is a disabled figure who also, like society, forces disability on others. The Joker represents this social power as he re-enacts the violent labeling system that he, himself, is victimized.

The Joker's use of poison and jokes evokes humor in those around him. The Joker embodies disability, and by extension, disfigurement as an exaggerated performance that facilitates his comedic act. In performing his act and causing his audience to laugh, whether genuinely or through the force of his toxin, the Joker represents a force for an empowering disruption of social hierarchies in which categorical and binary labels of disabled and non-disabled, normative non-normative are challenged and destroyed. For these reasons, the Joker offers a unique and exciting possibility as a character who is a force for effecting social change and fostering an increased understanding of ability as something that exists on a broad spectrum rather than a narrow and idealized set of binaries.

The Joker shows potential to be quite valuable to disability, queer, and non-normative studies. In the Joker, audiences find an unlikely partnership with a character so often maligned by those who encounter him. In examining a long line of non-normative and disabled villains in fiction, we find that the Joker is a nuanced and complex character who defies easy categorization. I would urge critics not to cast him aside as a harmful depiction of illness but to find in him a character ripe for exploration as an agent of societal change, and in fact, a character who demands such change. The Joker is indeed violent, and he is indeed destructive. However, suppose we can acknowledge his criminality without allowing it to become a barrier to his study. In that case, we find a character who, like many disability studies critics, attacks and resists binary categorization and societal expectations of normalcy. We should treasure such a character study.

REFERENCES

ADAPT. 2021. "ADAPT Denounces Blaming of Mass Shootings on Mental Health." https://adapt.org/adapt-denounces-blaming-of-mass-shootings-on-mental-health/.

Bakhtin, Mikhail. 1984. *Rabelais and His World*. Bloomington: Indiana UP.

Barounis, Cynthia. 2013. "'Why So Serious?' Cripping Camp Performance in Christopher Nolan's *The Dark Knight*." *Journal of Literary & Cultural Disability Studies 7* (3): 305–19. doi: 10.3828/JLCDS.2013.26.

Bennington-Castro, Joseph. 2012. "Facial Disfigurement: Revulsion People Feel Tied to Fear of Contagion." *HuffPost Science*, July 25. https://www.huffpost.com/impact/science.

Brubaker, Ed. 2003. *Batman: The Man Who Laughs*. New York: DC Comics.

Bryce, Mio, and Hanae Katayama. 2009. "Performativity of Japanese Laughter." *The International Journal of the Humanities 6* (9): 125. doi: 10.18848/1447-9508/CGP/v06i09/42538.

Dunlap-Shohl, Peter. 2015. *My Degeneration: A Journey Through Parkinson's*. University Park: The Pennsylvania State University Press.

Eason, Brian K. 2008. "Dark Knight Flashback: Joker, Part I." *Comic Book Resources*, July 16. https://www.cbr.com/dark-knight-flashback-the-joker-pt-ii/.

Edsall, Nicholas C. 2006. *Toward Stonewall: Homosexuality & Society in the Modern Western World*. Charlottesville: U of Virginia P.

Fies, Brian. 2006. *Mom's Cancer*. New York: Abrams Image.

Goldstein, Rich. 2014. "Holy Homophobia, Batman! A Queer Reading of the Dark Knight." *The Daily Beast*, April 14. https://www.thedailybeast.com/holy-homophobia-batman-a-queer-reading-of-the-dark-knight.

Hamscha, Susanne. 2014. "Crip Humor." In *Gender: Laughter*, edited by Bettina Papenburg, 349–362. New York: Macmillan Interdisciplinary Handbook.

Kaiser, Benjamin. 2016. "Laughing and Alterities. on the Movement of Alterity in the Philosophies of Laughter." *Filozofia 71* (7): 608–12. https://www.researchgate.net/publication/316256870_Laughing_and_alterities_on_the_movement_of_alterity_in_the_philosophies_of_laughter.

Kott, Jan. 1964. *Shakespeare, Our Contemporary*. Garden City, NJ: Doubleday & Company, Inc.

Kukkonen, Karin. 2013. *Studying Comics and Graphic Novels*. Chichester, MA: John Wiley & Sons.

Medhurst, Andy. 2013. "Batman, Deviance and Camp." In *The Superhero Reader*, edited by Charles Hatfield, Jeet Heer, and Ken Worcester, 237–251. Jackson: University of Mississippi Press.

Minnesota Governor's Council on Developmental Disabilities. 2021. Objects of humor. https://mn.gov/mnddc/parallels/one/4.html.

Moore, Alan. 1988. *Batman: The Killing Joke*. New York: DC Comics.

Morrison, Grant. 1989. *Batman: Arkham Asylum*. New York: DC Comics.

Shyminsky, Neil. 2011. "'Gay' Sidekicks: Queer Anxiety and the Narrative Straightening of the Superhero." *Men and Masculinities 14* (3): 288–308. doi: 10.1177/1097184X10368787.

Snyder, Scott. 2014. *Batman: Death of the Family*. New York: DC Comics.

Starlin, Jim. 1988. *Batman: A Death in the Family*. New York: DC Comics.

About the Contributors

Christopher **Boucher** studies professional writing and creative writing at King's College in Pennsylvania. He was awarded a grant from the King's College McGowan Center for Ethics and Social Responsibility to investigate ethics and disability in young adult literature. He leads the Comic Book and Media Club and hopes to write young adult fiction that both inspires and educates.

Daisy L. **Breneman** has a joint appointment with University Advising and Justice Studies at James Madison University. She also serves as co-coordinator of the interdisciplinary disability studies minor, and teaches a course on disability and justice. Her teaching, service, and scholarly interests include disability studies, popular culture, social justice, storytelling, digital humanities, and ethical reasoning. Her co-authored essay appeared in *Negotiating Disability: Disclosure and Higher Education* (University of Michigan Press, 2017).

Robin E. **Field** holds a Ph.D. and is a professor of English and the director of the Center for Excellence in Learning and Teaching at King's College, in Pennsylvania. Her research and teaching focuses upon intersectional identity in contemporary literature. She has published essays on Jhumpa Lahiri, Alice Walker, Sandra Cisneros, and others in journals and essay collections. She is the author of *Writing the Survivor: The Rape Novel in Contemporary American Literature.*

Divya **Garg** is an assistant professor at Lloyd Law College, Greater Noida, India. She completed her MA in English from Jawaharlal Nehru University, and BA (Honors) in English from Lady Shri Ram College for Women, University of Delhi. Her essay "(Un)Sanctioned Bodies: The State-Sexuality-Disability Nexus in *Captain America* Slash Fan Fiction" was published in *The Darker Side of Slash Fan Fiction: Essays on Power, Consent and the Body* (McFarland, 2018).

Amber E. **George** holds a Ph.D. and is associate professor in social philosophy at Galen College. She has presented her work at several disability studies and media studies conferences, is a member of the Eco-ability Collective, the Conference Awards Chair of the Central New York Peace Studies Consortium, and the director of Finance for the Institute for Critical Animal Studies (ICAS). She has edited several books involving media and disability studies and is the managing editor of the *Journal for Critical Animal Studies* (JCAS).

Kelly A. **Kane** holds a Ph.D. and is an assistant professor of psychology at Glenville State College, where she researches the impact of fictional narratives on related real-world attitudes and behaviors. Her past presentations include "The Pathologizing of Lewis Carrol in Contemporary Interpretations of Alice" (2014) and "How Many Fingers Am I Holding Up: Marvel's Disappearing Disabilities" (2018). She teaches classes on the psychology of media stereotyping and on the limitations of psychological measurements such as standardized tests.

Grace **McCarthy** holds a Ph.D. from Wilfrid Laurier University with an interest in disability in film and literature. She earned her MA in 2015 from the University of Alaska Fairbanks. Her research integrates disability studies, sociological theory, and adaptation theory to develop the filmic stare. Her dissertation uses the filmic stare specifically to explore representations of disability in film adaptations of early modern drama.

Sean Thomas **Milligan** has a BA in psychology and an MA in English literature. He has taught English courses at SUNY Oswego and Cayuga Community College. He studies the intersection of narrative and illness, and is particularly interested in the way that comics and graphic novels incorporate visual elements to represent non-normative bodies and minds. He examines the many autobiographical comics focusing on illness and disability and also studies superheroes and their place on the spectrum of normativity.

Tatiana **Prorokova-Konrad** is a postdoctoral researcher at the Department of English and American Studies, University of Vienna, Austria. She holds a Ph.D. in American studies from the University of Marburg, Germany. Her research interests include war studies, ecocriticism, gender studies, and race studies. She is a coeditor of *Cultures of War in Graphic Novels: Violence, Trauma, and Memory* (Rutgers University Press, 2018).

Sue **Scheibler** is an associate professor in film, TV and media studies in the School of Film and Television at LMU. She holds graduate degrees in Biblical studies and philosophy of religion and a Ph.D. in critical studies from the University of Southern California. She has published in *The Bloomsbury Research Handbook of Chinese Philosophy and Gender; Theorizing Documentary; The Alternative Media Handbook; War: Interdisciplinary Investigations, Signs,* and assorted journals.

Shanti **Srinivas** holds an Ed.D. and is the associate chair of the Arts & Sciences Department at Galen College of Nursing. She is also assistant professor of sociology at Galen and serves as the co-chair of the college's Diversity, Equity, and Inclusion Council. She is passionate about championing social justice causes for all species, specifically relating to the natural environment. Her daily routine revolves around self-care practices and topics on social and environmental awareness.

Courtney **Stanton** holds a Ph.D. and is assistant teaching professor for the Writing Program at Rutgers University–Newark. She teaches a variety of first-year and honors writing courses, along with advanced courses in public speaking and writing for social change. She completed her doctoral work in composition and rhetoric at Temple University in Philadelphia. She presents regularly at conferences, and her work has appeared in *Double Helix, Powerlines,* and *The Journal of Pedagogic Development.*

Index

www.ingramcontent.com/pod-product-compliance
Lightning Source LLC
Chambersburg PA
CBHW031136270326
41929CB00011B/1642